# Privatisation in Ireland

# Privatisation in Ireland

## Lessons from a European Economy

Dónal Palcic

and

Eoin Reeves

First published 2011 by
PALGRAVE MACMILLAN

Palgrave Macmillan in the UK is an imprint of Macmillan Publishers Limited, registered in England, company number 785998, of Houndmills, Basingstoke, Hampshire RG21 6XS.

Palgrave Macmillan in the US is a division of St Martin's Press LLC, 175 Fifth Avenue, New York, NY 10010.

Palgrave Macmillan is the global academic imprint of the above companies and has companies and representatives throughout the world.

Palgrave® and Macmillan® are registered trademarks in the United States, the United Kingdom, Europe and other countries

ISBN 978-0-230-24892-2        hardback

This book is printed on paper suitable for recycling and made from fully managed and sustained forest sources. Logging, pulping and manufacturing processes are expected to conform to the environmental regulations of the country of origin.

A catalogue record for this book is available from the British Library.

A catalogue record for this book is available from the Library of Congress.

10   9   8   7   6   5   4   3   2   1
20   19   18   17   16   15   14   13   12   11

Printed and bound in Great Britain by
CPI Antony Rowe, Chippenham and Eastbourne

*To Julie*
D.P.

*To Deirdre*
E.R.

# Contents

# List of Figures

# List of Tables

# List of Abbreviations

| | |
|---|---|
| AIB | Allied Irish Banks |
| ACC | Agricultural Credit Corporation |
| APE | Agence des Participations de l'Etat |
| APSS | Approved Profit Sharing Scheme |
| BCM | Babcock and Brown Capital Limited |
| BoI | Bank of Ireland |
| BT | British Telecom |
| CBFSAI | Central Bank & Financial Services Authority of Ireland |
| CEO | Chief Executive Officer |
| CGBS | County and Group Broadband Scheme |
| CIE | Córas Iompair Éireann |
| CMO | Common Market Organisation |
| ComReg | Commission for Communications Regulation |
| CPI | Consumer Price Index |
| CSO | Central Statistics Office |
| CWU | Communication Workers Union |
| DIRT | Deposit Interest Retention Tax |
| DSL | Digital Subscriber Line |
| EBITDA | Earnings before Interest, Tax, Depreciation and Amortisation |
| EBR | Exchequer Borrowing Requirement |
| EBS | Educational Building Society |
| EC | European Commission |
| ECTA | European Competitive Telecommunications Association |
| EEC | European Economic Community |
| EMU | European Monetary Union |
| EU | European Union |
| ESB | Electricity Supply Board |
| ESOP | Employee Share Ownership Plans |
| ESOT | Employee Share Ownership Trust |
| ESPS | Employee Share Participation Scheme |
| FTTB | Fibre-to-the-Building |
| FTTH | Fibre-to-the-Home |
| GBP | Great Britain Pound |
| GDP | Gross Domestic Product |
| GFCF | Gross Fixed Capital Formation |

| GNP | Gross National Product |
|---|---|
| HSDPA | High Speed DownLink Packet Access |
| ICC | Industrial Credit Corporation |
| ICG | Irish Continental Group |
| ICT | Information and Communication Technologies |
| ICTU | Irish Congress of Trade Unions |
| IDA | Industrial Development Authority |
| IEFF | Income Efficiency |
| IL&P | Irish Life & Permanent |
| IMF | International Monetary Fund |
| INBS | Irish Nationwide Building Society |
| INPC | Irish National Petroleum Corporation |
| IPO | Initial Public Offering |
| IRP | Ireland Punt (Pound) |
| ISEQ | Irish Stock Exchange Quotient |
| JOCSSB | Joint Oireachtas Committee on State-Sponsored Bodies |
| LBO | Leveraged Buyout |
| LLU | Local Loop Unbundling |
| MAN | Metropolitan Area Network |
| NBS | National Broadband Scheme |
| NCC | National Competitiveness Council |
| NDP | National Development Plan |
| NESC | National Economic and Social Council |
| NGB | Next Generation Broadband |
| NGN | Next Generation Network |
| NORA | National Oil Reserves Agency |
| NPRF | National Pensions Reserve Fund |
| NRA | National Roads Authority |
| ODTR | Office of the Director of Telecommunications Regulation |
| OECD | Organisation for Economic Co-operation and Development |
| PBITE | Profit Before Interest Tax and Exceptional Items |
| PDs | Progressive Democrats |
| PESP | Programme for Economic and Social Progress |
| PNR | Programme for National Recovery |
| PO | Public Offering |
| PS | Private Sale |
| PSBR | Public Sector Borrowing Requirement |
| ROA | Return on Assets |
| ROCE | Return on Capital Employed |
| ROE | Return on Equity |
| ROI | Return on Investment |

| | |
|---|---|
| ROS | Return on Sales |
| SEFF | Sales Efficiency |
| SME | Small and Medium Enterprises |
| SOE | State-Owned Enterprise |
| STT | Singapore Technologies Telemedia |
| TFP | Total Factor Productivity |
| TSB | Trustee Savings Bank |
| USD | United States Dollar |
| VAE | Value-Added per Employee |

# Acknowledgements

This book could not have been written without the help and support of family, friends, and colleagues.

We are particularly grateful to the following for casting a critical eye over different chapters and providing helpful comments: Eamonn Casey, John Cullinan, Gerard Downes, John Garvey, Dermot McCarthy, Fergal O'Brien, Gerald O'Nolan, James Ryan and Tom Turner.

Our editor, Elaine Vaughan, provided a lending hand just when it was needed and we are very grateful for her help in correcting and editing the manuscript. We take full responsibility for any errors that remain.

We thank Gemma Papageorgiou, Taiba Batool, and all the staff at Palgrave Macmillan for their help in bringing this book to publication.

We wish to acknowledge our friends and colleagues at the University of Limerick who have provided support and encouragement over the years.

We are also grateful to the editors and publishers of *Administration* for granting permission to utilise material from the following article: Palcic, D. and Reeves, E. (2010a) 'Costly Business: Privatisation and Exchequer Finances in Ireland', *Administration*, Vol. 58(1), 29–53.

Finally we wish to express our debt of gratitude to our families: Julie, Deirdre, Shane, Ally and Jenna and our parents, Michael, Úna, Pat and Maureen.

*July 2010*

# Introduction

Of the many initiatives adopted to meet the challenge of improving public service delivery around the world, few have been as prevalent and controversial as privatisation. For some, privatisation is seen as sinister and synonymous with the neo-liberal version of globalisation that provokes high profile demonstrations at events such as G-8 summits and meetings of the World Trade Organisation. For others, privatisation is seen more benignly, as offering a means of rolling back the frontiers of the state and tapping into superior private sector enterprise and ideas. Regardless of one's standpoint, there is little doubt that privatisation has captured the imagination of politicians and scholars since it first became popular in the late 1970s.

In this book, we focus on one type of privatisation, the transfer of state-owned enterprises (SOEs) to private ownership. In countries around the world, governments have increasingly withdrawn from the provision of goods and services which, for a variety of reasons, had traditionally been provided by the public sector. However, the international pattern of privatisation has been uneven, and different countries have implemented privatisation policies at different speeds in different sectors. Each country has its own story in terms of the factors that have driven privatisation policy, the rationales presented for the sale of individual SOEs, the methods employed to dispose of assets, and the eventual outcomes.

Here we focus on a single country experience. It is now 20 years since Ireland embarked on a programme of privatisation. Since the first disposal, that of the Irish Sugar Company in 1991, a number of further sales have been executed, bringing about significant change in the composition and activities of the Irish SOE sector. It is therefore opportune to evaluate the outcomes of privatisation policies in Ireland and to address the lessons learned in the course of the privatisation experience.

1

Although the transfer of public enterprise to private ownership can be traced as far back as Fascist Italy in the 1920s, it has only attracted attention since the privatisation programme in the United Kingdom (UK) commenced in the early 1980s. Since then, a considerable literature has emerged dealing with many of the questions that arise as a result of such policies.

From an economic perspective, the impact of privatisation on the efficiency of service delivery has commanded most of this attention in terms of theoretical and empirical analysis. Initially, the theoretical analysis of privatisation struggled to keep pace with real world developments, as the adoption of privatisation policies was to a large degree unexpected. Indeed, the sale of SOEs was not an explicitly described component of economic policy as articulated in the British Conservative Party election manifesto prior to the 1979 General Election. As the UK privatisation programme gathered momentum, and similar policies gained popularity in other countries (for example, New Zealand and France), there were significant developments in the economic theory of privatisation. Principal-agent theory, especially when employed in tandem with arguments from property rights and public choice perspectives, provides a theoretical rationale for privatisation to improve economic efficiency. However, the power of this rationale arguably depends on the efficiency of capital markets and the degree to which they constrain managerial (agent) behaviour (Parker, 2003).

Theoretical contributions on privatisation continue to develop with new perspectives, such as those on incomplete contracting, increasing the sophistication of analysis. Yet the conclusions from the theoretical literature remain equivocal. It does appear that ownership matters, but whether public or private ownership is superior depends on a number of factors, not least the degree of competition faced by the firm. The lack of definitive theoretical conclusions points to the importance of empirical studies of privatisation and this strand of the literature also continues to develop. Whereas some statistical studies covering large samples of enterprises from different countries are supportive of the case for privatisation (for example, Megginson *et al.*, 1994), in-depth country-based studies are not as clear-cut (for example, Martin and Parker, 1997). The importance of issues in relation to governance and competition cannot be ignored. Overall, the net benefits of privatisation, in theoretical and empirical terms, are unclear.

The wider economic effects of privatisation concern its distributional impacts and how different stakeholders are affected by the sale of SOEs. The welfare of stakeholders such as taxpayers, shareholders, employees and consumers has also commanded focus in the privatisation literature, albeit to a lesser degree than questions in relation to enterprise performance. This is partly explained by the methodological challenges involved in measuring overall social welfare effects, but this is an aspect of privatisation that should be of critical concern for policymakers.

The early analysis of privatisation was mainly derived from the UK experience. Different strands emerged in the literature as privatisation policies were adopted by countries in Eastern Europe and the former Soviet Union, as well as developing countries in Latin America, South East Asia and, to lesser degree, Africa. Moreover, the move towards increased economic integration in the European Union (EU) was a key factor in increasing the popularity of privatisation programmes from the early 1990s. The fact that Europe accounts for the majority of global sales in terms of revenues accrued by governments is, to a large degree, explained by the number of privatisations in utility sectors, namely transport, water, energy and telecommunications. Many of these enterprises have transformed into major multinational enterprises and this development is commanding increasing attention from scholars and policymakers in recent years.

The privatisation of utilities has been complicated by the fact that they generally hold considerable market power in their domestic markets. As a consequence, governments have had to develop privatisation policies in tandem with the establishment and maintenance of regulatory frameworks, as well as effective competition policy regimes. These developments have also raised theoretical and practical issues that have commanded the attention of the research community and the literature on competition and regulation intersects with much of the work on privatisation.

Despite the extent of privatisation activity over the last 30 years, and the development of a significant body of academic literature on the topic, there is a dearth of in-depth country-based studies of privatisation, particularly in Western Europe where the literature is dominated by the case of the UK. This is to be expected given the pioneering approach to privatisation adopted by policymakers in the UK, but there are limits to the relevance of the UK experience for countries with different economic characteristics and histories.

The history and impact of privatisation in most EU countries differ considerably from the experience in the UK in terms of the timing and rationale for privatisation policies, as well as factors that have shaped the post-privatisation performance of relevant enterprises (for example, regulatory frameworks). Moreover, the implications of privatisation policies can vary depending on the nature and characteristics of the economy (for example, small open economy versus large closed economy). This significant gap in the literature provided the original impetus for the research presented here, which uses the experience of Ireland as the basis for a wider discussion of the complex assortment of factors that impact on a country's experience of privatisation.

In relative terms, Ireland was slow to adopt privatisation policies. France, Spain, New Zealand and Australia were among the countries that had disposed of shares in SOEs before the first sale was executed in Ireland in 1991. Since then, roughly half of Ireland's commercial public enterprises have been sold and the state has withdrawn from activities such as telecommunications, aviation and the production of steel and sugar. These changes constitute a considerable restructuring of the Irish economy and, to a large degree, represent a break with the past. As a post-colonial economy, Ireland had relied heavily on SOEs to develop sectors which would produce essential goods and services for the fledgling Irish economy. As a result, public enterprise has played a hugely important role in the economic development of the Irish state since independence in 1922. The establishment of a number of SOEs was initially necessary to develop basic industries such as electricity, particularly in the absence of a strong private sector. By the 1970s, public enterprises were active across a range of sectors including energy, transport, and natural resource-based industries such as sugar and peat production.

A number of international events occurred in the early 1970s that led to a marked reappraisal of the role and activities of SOEs. The breakdown of the Keynesian consensus following the oil crisis of 1973–74 and the advent of stagflation altered the discourse on state involvement in modern economies. The justification for state ownership was questioned due to disenchantment with the commercial performance of SOEs and the quality of services delivery.

Ireland was not immune to such developments, but while other countries pursued radical change in the form of divestiture, the initial approach in the Irish case was to strengthen the commercial remit of public enterprise. This involved strategies based on commercialisation, which included cost-cutting measures such as labour shedding and the closure of commercially unviable enterprises. The drive to privatise SOEs that was apparent in other countries was not necessarily evident in the Irish case. This was attributable to a host of factors, but to some extent it reflected the fact that these enterprises exhibited what public enterprise scholar Ian Thynne describes as 'publicness' (1994). SOEs operated in sectors that were strategically important in economic terms, such as basic infrastructure industries. They also provided services that were critical for the achievement of non-financial objectives, for example, regional development and the delivery of services that add to social cohesion.

Some degree of privatisation was, however, inevitable, particularly in industries that could be described as competitive or contestable. Moreover, Ireland's membership of the EU gave impetus to privatisation policies in the sense that increased liberalisation and the development of competition rules emanating from the EU restricted government support for financially troubled companies, thereby providing justification for divestitures. Ireland's privatisation programme has, in the main, been gradual and pragmatic, although it is true to say that in some instances decisions in relation to divestitures have had ideological underpinnings. Despite the considerable changes brought about by privatisation, it has not been accompanied by any degree of detailed analysis. Therefore, our principal objective is to provide a comprehensive, objective economic analysis of Ireland's privatisation programme since 1991. The analysis is conducted with a view to highlighting key lessons that can provide guidance for policymakers faced with decisions about the future of public enterprise.

We begin with an outline of the historical development of public enterprise and the reasons for the rise in popularity of privatisation as a means of public enterprise reform. Chapter 1 provides an up-to-date review of privatisation activity in Europe over the past 30 years, with a particular emphasis on the last decade demonstrating the continuing popularity of privatisation policies. In Chapter 2, we turn to the theoretical and empirical literature on privatisation. Our particular focus is on how privatisation impacts on enterprise performance, but we do seek to emphasise the wider effect of privatisation in terms of distributional outcomes. The focus on the case of Ireland begins in Chapter 3. This chapter traces the development of Ireland's privatisation programme and provides details on the rationale for each divestiture to date. Events are interpreted in terms of different theories that have been advanced in order to interpret the course of privatisation policies, including the Chicagoan and Virginian schools of public choice, as well as other explanations such as the logic of European integration.

In Chapter 4 we conduct a case-by-case analysis of the impact of privatisation on enterprise performance. The analysis adopts different performance indicators that are suitable for the sectors analysed, and draws attention to determinants of performance beyond changes in ownership. There is little doubt that policymakers are attracted to privatisation on the basis that the sale of assets generates significant revenues for the exchequer. In Chapter 5, we explore how the objective of maximising these revenues is rarely achieved as governments incur a number of costs as part of the privatisation process. Such costs arise due to the necessarily competing objectives of privatisation. For example, the goal of attracting citizens to participate in the privatisation process by purchasing shares generally requires setting prices at a discount. This inevitably conflicts with the objective of maximising exchequer proceeds.

A unique feature of the Irish privatisation process has been the granting of sizeable shareholdings to employees through the establishment of Employee Share Ownership Plans (ESOPs). The allocation of 14.9 per cent of ordinary shares to employees is now the norm when Irish SOEs are privatised. As far as we are aware, the size of this allocation is unmatched in international terms. In Chapter 6, we examine the rationale for such ESOPs and examine the impact of individual ESOPs in terms of the financial gains accrued by employees and the governance implications of large employee shareholdings. Chapter 7 focuses on Ireland's largest privatisation to date. The sale of the state-owned telecommunications company (now Eircom) has proved to be one of the most controversial episodes in Irish business history. The chapter focuses on the post-privatisation period, and details how underinvestment in the telecommunications sector, and broadband technology in particular, has had a detrimental impact of the competitiveness of Ireland's regional economy. The chapter provides a number of lessons arising from the Eircom privatisation that should prove useful to policymakers in Ireland and abroad in the context of future divestiture decisions.

The global financial crisis of autumn 2008 has had far reaching implications for SOE sectors around the world. Governments have been forced to respond to the crisis with a range of strategies that include taking significant ownerships stakes in banks and other private enterprises. The partial or full nationalisation of banks has been commonplace, raising the suggestion that the global economy has embarked on a period of 'state capitalism'. Ireland's economic and banking crisis is one of the most severe in global terms. The downturn in the country's inflated property market triggered a near-collapse of the private banking sector. Unprecedented government intervention has been required to address the problems, including the full and partial nationalisation of a number of financial institutions. Chapter 8 traces the origins of Ireland's banking crisis and details the nature of the government response to date.

To conclude, Chapter 9 takes stock of the lessons from previous chapters. It provides an overview of the extent and nature of public enterprise in the global economy at the beginning of the twenty-first century. It highlights how SOEs continued to play an important role in key industries prior to the global crisis and discusses recent developments, such as the increased international reach of SOEs and the growth of sovereign wealth funds. It concludes by returning to the case of Ireland and considers the future of the SOE sector in the light of lessons from privatisation, international trends in relation to SOEs, and the current global financial crisis.

# 1
# Privatisation in Europe

## 1.0   Introduction

Public provision of essential public services such as transport, water and electricity was the norm across Europe for much of the twentieth century. The last 30 years or so, however, have witnessed a radical break with this tradition, as a number of economic and political factors have led to a reconsideration of the precise role of the state in public service delivery. High on the agenda of many governments has been the reform of State-Owned Enterprises (SOEs). Measures adopted to address perceived problems in the SOE sector include those designed to increase the degree of competition faced by SOEs (through deregulation and liberalisation, for example), alter the nature of regulation (for example, price and access regulation), and change ownership structures through privatisation. Of these changes, the privatisation of SOEs has been the most high profile and often the most controversial. It has brought about enormous industrial restructuring, with whole industries transferred to the private sector, and the role of the state often transformed from that of monopolistic service provider to that of regulator. Privatisation has also had significant redistributional effects in terms of impacting on the availability and prices of public services, as well as transferring non-trivial amounts of benefits to certain categories of stakeholders.

This chapter provides context for the analysis in later chapters by considering the development of privatisation in Europe. Although the focus of this book is on the privatisation experience in Ireland, one of Europe's smaller regional economies, many aspects of economic and social policy in Ireland have been shaped by its membership of the European Union (EU), which dates back to 1973. These aspects include measures of liberalisation and privatisation, some of

8

which have been adopted over time in response to different directives issued by the EU. This chapter traces the origins of privatisation in Europe and reviews the extent of privatisation activity since such policies became widespread. It draws attention to the different factors that have driven privatisation policies in the UK versus the rest of Europe, and reviews the extent of privatisation activity up to the present day. It concludes by noting the surge in SOE sales from 2004–08 and how the recent global financial crisis is impacting on privatisation activity, as well as the role of government in modern economies.

## 1.1 The meaning of 'privatisation'

Although the term 'privatisation' was originally used to describe some of the economic policies of the National Socialist (Nazi) Party in Germany during the 1930s (Bel, 2006), it only gained popular international currency in the late 1970s and early 1980s when countries such as Great Britain, Chile and New Zealand commenced programmes of divestiture of formerly nationalised enterprises. However, global privatisation activity has not been confined to the sale of SOEs, and the term has often been loosely applied to a variety of other public sector reforms, including liberalisation, deregulation and the contracting out of public services. This wide application of the term 'privatisation' highlights the need for clarity about its precise meaning and scope.

Starr (1988) provides a useful working definition of privatisation as any shift in the production of goods and services from public to private. According to Starr (1988: 16–17), this more focused definition of privatisation includes the following sub-categories:

1) The cessation of public programmes and disengagement of government from specific kinds of responsibilities. At a less drastic level, this may involve the restriction of publicly produced services in volume, availability, or quality which may lead to a shift by consumers toward privately produced and purchased substitutes (called 'privatisation by attrition' when a government lets public services run down);
2) The transfer of public assets to private ownership, through the sale or lease of public land, infrastructure and SOEs;
3) The withdrawal of government from the production, but not the financing, of services, for example, through contracting-out or vouchers; and

4) The deregulation of entry into activities previously treated as public monopolies.

This book concentrates on one single variant of Starr's (1988) typology, namely the transfer of SOEs to the private sector (see 2 above), and the use of the term 'privatisation' hereafter refers only to their sale. In this context, it is also relevant to acknowledge that there is no standard definition of SOEs. Here, they are understood to be commercial public enterprises that earn the majority of their income from the sale of goods and services.

## 1.2   Development of state-owned enterprises

In order to place privatisation policies in perspective, it is first necessary to understand the original rationale for the creation of public enterprises in Europe. Megginson and Netter (2001) describe how, throughout history, ownership of the means of production and trade moved back and forth from the public to the private sector. In the early part of the twentieth century, most European governments had little involvement in the economy and there were few SOEs. This situation changed, however, during and after World War One. During the war, governments in some countries took control of strategic war-related industries and maintained control of them after the war ended. These industries were run with relative efficiency and there was a general call for greater nationalisation of private industries (Moore, 1986). Economists in countries such as the UK argued at the time that there were many theoretical benefits to nationalisation, including:

1) The quality of service will tend to advance and the price charged will tend to fall;
2) The industry itself will be more efficient and economically conducted;
3) The board (of the nationalised industry) and its officers must regard themselves as the high custodians of the public interest (Morrison, 1933, cited in Moore, 1986).

After the Great Depression and World War Two, many governments took a more active role in the economy throughout most of the world, taking command of the operation of many companies that provided vital goods and services. During the 1930s, there were a number of major nationalisations, particularly in countries where the Depression hit hardest. The objective of these nationalisations was to rescue companies from collapse and counter the Depression and industrial decline (Clifton *et al.*, 2003). The post-World War Two period was characterised by greater state intervention, with various strategic industries such as telecommunications, electricity, gas and transport brought under the control of governments and given protection from competition, thus enjoying a monopoly status.

In the late 1940s and 1950s, public enterprises in Austria, France and Italy were established in order to rebuild their devastated economies. Many industries that had collaborated with the Germans during the war were taken over by the state, for example, Renault in France and many of Austria's largest enterprises (Parker, 1998). SOEs played a major role in the reconstruction and modernisation of industry, and the success of French and Italian state capitalism during that era served as a model for the UK's Labour party, who embarked on a policy of nationalisation of industry after World War Two (Hager, 1982). Political ideology played a large part in UK industrial policy at the time; depending on whether the Labour party or Conservative party was in power, ownership of a number of firms was transferred over and back from the public to the private sector and there were a number of nationalisations and reprivatisations. For example, British Steel was nationalised in 1949, largely privatised in 1953, renationalised in 1967 and reprivatised in 1988 (Kay, 1993).

A number of writers have analysed the origins and evolution of SOEs in twentieth century Western Europe. Their analyses highlight a number of common factors that apply across different countries. One attempt at generalising the experience across countries is provided by Parris *et al.* (1987: 14–21) who attribute the growth of public enterprise to, *inter alia*:

1) Post-war industrial reconstruction;
2) The political ideology of socialism and its attachment to nationalisation and public ownership;
3) The creation of state-owned fiscal monopolies to finance government expenditure (for example, Sweden and Austria);
4) The rationalisation of important sectors previously characterised by duplication and lack of coordination (for example, electricity and gas sectors in the UK);
5) Regional development (for example, Istituto per la Ricostruzione Industriale (IRI), the state-owned holding company in Southern Italy); and

6)   The development of national wealth in the absence of private sector initiative.

While many of the factors above apply to different countries at various points in history, it is generally recognised that a number of internal factors assist in explaining the precise rationale for the difference in the extent of SOE development in European countries. These factors include the country's institutional framework, its level of industrial development, the political economy of interventionism, as well as other ideological and social reasons (Clifton *et al.*, 2003: 15).

By the 1980s, the size and importance of the SOE sector in many European countries was considerable, with public enterprises making significant contributions to employment, value added and gross fixed capital formation (see Table 1.1). Support for the nationalisation of private industries was eroded over time by a significant deterioration in SOE performance in some countries during the 1970s and 1980s, along with increasing fiscal pressures experienced in most countries from the 1970s onwards. The increased demands on public expenditure and public sector borrowing requirements generally raised the opportunity cost of public finance. Consequently, SOE budgets and investment programmes were constrained in many economies and governments introduced policies of SOE reform or privatisation (Yarrow, 1999). The following section examines the factors underpinning privatisation programmes in European countries.

## 1.3   Origins of privatisation

While the first major programme of privatisation is generally associated with the Thatcher era in the UK, there were some examples of minor privatisation programmes prior to this. Megginson and Netter (2001) claim that the first large-scale ideologically-motivated privatisation programme was implemented by Konrad Adenauer's government in the Federal Republic of Germany during the late 1950s and early 1960s. Other authors, such as Burk (1988), claim that the denationalisation of the UK steel industry in 1953 was the first case of privatisation.

However, recent research by Bel (2009a) shows that the earliest large-scale privatisation programme in a capitalist economy was in fact carried out by Italy's Fascist government between 1922 and 1925. Among the divestitures carried out by Mussolini's government were the privatisation of the state monopoly on match sales, the sale of most of the

Table 1.1  Impact of European Public Enterprises on Employment, Value Added and GFCF in 1991

| | Share of employment (%) (1) | Share of value added (%) (2) | Share of GFCF (%) (3) | Average impact of public sector (1+2+3) | Average impact of public sector 1988 | Average impact of public sector 1985 | Average impact of public sector 1982 |
|---|---|---|---|---|---|---|---|
| Belgium | 9.8 | 7.5 | 8.4 | 8.6 | 10.3 | 11.1 | 12.1 |
| Denmark | 8.2 | 8.7 | 17.6 | 11.5 | 11.9 | 11.4 | 12.0 |
| France | 13.4 | 15.1 | 24.2 | 17.6 | 18.3 | 24.0 | 22.8 |
| Germany | 8.3 | 10.0 | 14.9 | 11.1 | 11.6 | 12.4 | 14.0 |
| Greece | 14.7 | 17.0 | 30.0 | 20.6 | 20.8 | 23.2 | 22.3 |
| Ireland | 8.7 | 11.5 | 16.9 | 12.4 | 14.4 | 15.3 | 15.1 |
| Italy | 13.5 | 20.0 | 23.5 | 19.0 | 19.6 | 20.3 | 20.0 |
| Luxembourg | 3.2 | 5.2 | 4.6 | 4.4 | 4.9 | 4.5 | 5.0 |
| Netherlands | 5.1 | 8.0 | 9.2 | 7.5 | 9.6 | 9.0 | 9.0 |
| Portugal | 10.6 | 21.5 | 30.0 | 20.7 | 24.0 | 22.7 | 23.9 |
| Spain | 6.0 | 8.0 | 12.8 | 9.0 | 10.0 | 12.0 | 12.0 |
| UK | 4.3 | 4.0 | 5.0 | 4.5 | 7.4 | 12.7 | 16.2 |
| EU Average | 8.9 | 10.9 | 15.6 | 11.8 | 13.3 | 15.3 | 16.4 |

*Source*: CEEP (1994). Notes: (1) GFCF = Gross Fixed Capital Formation; (2) Percentage shares above are calculated in relation to *non-agricultural* employment, value added and GFCF; (3) Data for Germany relates to Federal Republic of Germany (West) only.

state-owned telephone networks and services to private firms, and the elimination of the state monopoly on life insurance. The rationale underpinning the programme was mainly political, with the sales used to attract support from industrialists and to raise revenue for the exchequer (Bel, 2009a).

Further evidence of large-scale privatisation programmes in the early twentieth century is provided by Bel (2009b) who documents the privatisation policy pursued by the Nazi party in Germany during the mid-1930s. The Nazi government sold a number of SOEs in different sectors such as steel, mining and banking between 1934 and 1937. Similar to the rationale underpinning the privatisation policy pursued by Mussolini in the 1920s, the sales of German SOEs were used as a tool for building political support among industrialists and the business sector, and to generate much needed revenue for Germany's armament programme (Bel, 2009b).

Bel (2009c) identifies another extensive privatisation programme that has also been ignored in contemporary economic studies of privatisation, that of Puerto Rico in the late 1940s, which the author identifies as the first privatisation policy implemented in a democratic regime. Within two years of the first democratic government elections in 1948, the newly-elected government had privatised every state-owned manufacturing firm in Puerto Rico. In contrast to the political motivations that underpinned earlier privatisation policies in Italy and Germany, pragmatic economic concerns about the performance of the state-owned manufacturing sector, and a desire to attract private investment to foster industrialisation in the country, appear to have been the main drivers of the programme (Bel, 2009c: 30).

Apart from Puerto Rico, in the post-World War Two period, no other government introduced a policy of privatisation until 1959 when Konrad Adenauer's Federal Government implemented a programme of partial privatisations. Shares in the German mining company, Preussag, were offered to lower- and middle-income citizens, with some 80 per cent of the company privatised in total. In 1961, a majority stake in Volkswagen was sold, with low-income buyers granted special rebates. Four years later a 25 per cent stake in the electricity, mining, petroleum and chemical company, VEBA, was sold with shares in the company offered only to low-income groups with incomes below a certain threshold. The sale of shares in VEBA significantly increased the number of shareholders in Germany from approximately half a million to almost three million (Megginson *et al.*, 1994).[1] The rationale behind the German privatisation programme was to foster wider ownership of private property, particularly among lower- and middle-income groups. A similar objective of widening share ownership underpinned many of the privatisations carried out in the UK in the 1980s.

While the privatisation programmes outlined above were undoubtedly important, the most significant programme of privatisation implemented in Europe during the twentieth century was that of the UK which began in the late 1970s and early 1980s.[2] Given the scale and importance of the programme, the following section describes its development in detail.

## 1.4   Privatisation in the United Kingdom

The UK was very much the pioneer of privatisation policies in the 1980s and 1990s. The election of a new Conservative Party government in 1979 came at a time of economic decline and widespread industrial strife. The new government led by Margaret Thatcher was elected on the basis of pro-market policies and the stated intention of tackling public sector inefficiency. The pervasive party view was that the economy had suffered because public enterprises had 'pre-empted resources that would otherwise have been allocated more effectively by the market, and were then protected from the pressures of the market by their monopoly powers' (Young, 1986: 235). Moore (1986: 81) states that British nationalised industries' total return on capital employed had been consistently below that of the private sector since the mid-1960s, and that 'since the early 1970s, the industries' aggregate returns on capital have been around zero'.

The Conservative Party believed that by reducing the role of public enterprises in the economy, the pressure of market forces would promote increased competition and efficiency. In addition, privatisation was offered as a means of reducing the power of public sector trade unions, which was viewed as a key source of public sector inefficiency. Moore (1986) states that public sector trade unions had sustained success in exploiting their monopoly bargaining position and obtaining wage increases without corresponding increases in productivity. In addition, Miller (1997: 399) claims that the government disliked the unions who, in their view, 'often made excessive demands on management and government, weakening the financial positions of SOEs'.[3]

Shortly after the new government assumed power, a working group on nationalised industries was established under the chairmanship of Adam Ridley.[4] This group considered a number of options in relation to nationalised industries, including the possibility of de-nationalising industries that competed in their relevant product markets. It recommended the disposal of shares in private companies held by the state holding company, the National Enterprise Board. Shareholdings in 13 companies were disposed of in 1979–80 raising GBP£120 million. Government-held shares in British Petroleum were sold at different stages over the period 1979–83. Following the disposal of its majority shareholding in British Aerospace in 1981, the government executed a catalogue of transfers to the private sector. Among the other companies sold over the period 1981–84 were Cable and Wireless, Associated British Ports, Enterprise Oil and Jaguar.

This significant level of disposals was somewhat unexpected as privatisation was scarcely mentioned in the Conservative Party's 1979 election manifesto. At the time, these sales were not necessarily considered radical and indeed the Labour Party had executed some minor sales prior to leaving government. These divestitures did however prove popular with the new government and the UK Treasury as they raised useful revenues for the exchequer. Moreover, they chimed with the thrust of the Conservative Party's neo-liberal policies that promoted private enterprise and the reach of the market in the UK economy.

As the first sale of a state-owned utility, the privatisation of the national telecommunications operator British Telecom (BT) in 1984 was the pivotal divestiture in the history of British privatisation. In the early 1980s, BT was planning a large-scale investment programme to upgrade its network. The manner in which the government would be able to support the investment without affecting the public sector borrowing requirement (PSBR) was discussed widely at the time, with no solution reached. To circumvent the problem, the radical decision to privatise BT was taken and 50.2 per cent of the shares of BT were floated on the stock market. The offer was the single biggest share issue in history at that time and met with huge demand. The flotation was three times oversubscribed and enormously successful. Gross proceeds of over GBP£3.86 billion were raised, with the flotation attracting some 2.15 million investors (Parker, 2009).

The success of the BT privatisation cleared the way for the sales of other major utilities. In 1986, British Gas was privatised, followed by the divestiture of SOEs operating in water (1989), electricity (1990–91) and the railways (1995–97). When Margaret Thatcher came to power in 1979, SOEs accounted for approximately 9 per cent of GDP. By 1997, when the Conservative party lost power, that figure had been reduced to less than 2 per cent (Parker, 1998).

A recognised feature of the UK privatisation programme was that it was initiated in the absence of a well defined, coherent set of objectives. In an early contribution to the privatisation debate, Kay and Thompson (1986) described how selling SOEs served a multiplicity of objectives, including the improvement of enterprise efficiency, the raising of exchequer revenues, and the widening of share ownership. They contended that

> At different times each one of these objectives has been sacrificed for others [...] the reality behind the apparent multiplicity of objectives is not that the policy has a rather sophisticated rationale, but rather that it is lacking any clear analysis of purpose or effects; and hence any objective which seems achievable is seized as justification (1986: 19).

While recognising the validity of Kay and Thompson's argument, it is reasonable to conclude that although the objectives attributed to privatisation in the UK evolved in tandem with the expansion of the programme, such objectives are largely consistent with those subsequently offered to justify privatisation programmes as they were adopted around the world. These objectives are summarised by Vickers and Yarrow (1988: 157) as follows:

1) Improvement in enterprise efficiency;
2) Reduction of the PSBR;
3) Reduction of government involvement in enterprise decision-making;
4) Easing problems of public sector pay determination;
5) Widening share ownership and encouraging employee share ownership; and
6) Gaining political advantage.

The widely-regarded success of the privatisation programme in the UK persuaded many other European countries to adopt privatisation programmes of their own. The next section provides a brief overview of the factors underpinning the development of privatisation programmes in Europe.

## 1.5   Privatisation in the rest of Europe[5]

In comparison to the UK, privatisation activity in the rest of Western Europe during the 1980s was on a much smaller scale, with France and, to a lesser degree, Spain, among the few countries to pursue policies of divestiture. During the 1990s, however, there was a surge in privatisation activity in Europe, with countries such as Italy, Sweden and Portugal embracing privatisation with much greater enthusiasm than in the 1980s. Whereas the UK privatisation programme was largely prompted by disenchantment with the performance of nationalised industries, the motivations for selling state assets in Europe owed more to the forces of European integration and monetary union in particular.

Lavdas (1996) examined privatisation programmes in Southern Europe[6] and found that the programmes adopted in these countries were not associated with alleged government failure and the assumed greater efficiency of private enterprises, which had been important factors in the rolling back of state involvement in Western Europe, North America, New Zealand and Australia. The author argued that Southern European privatisations owed 'less to neo-liberal ideas or party platforms and more to the need to tackle deficits and public indebtedness' (Lavdas, 1996: 235). A further reason for the advancement of privatisation programmes in these countries, as well as their fellow European states, was the need to meet the convergence criteria for inclusion in the Economic and Monetary Union (EMU). In some countries privatisation moved from being an instrument of restructuring to an instrument of EMU convergence.

These factors are recognised in a number of studies. Mahboobi (2001: 43) argued that the privatisation drive in the 1990s was prompted by the need to 'reduce budgetary deficits, attract investment, improve corporate efficiency and [liberalise] markets in sectors such as energy and telecommunications'. Mahboobi also claimed that the acceleration of privatisation activity in the late 1990s was especially due to members of the EMU attempting to meet the convergence requirements of the Maastricht Treaty signed in 1992. Similarly, Yarrow (1999) asserts that the most common reason for privatisation has been fiscal pressure. Governments facing increased demand for public expenditure have divested many SOEs in an effort to keep their fiscal deficits and debt-to-GDP ratios within the limits set out by the Maastricht Treaty.

Since the economic case for privatisation is arguably to increase the efficiency of the enterprises being privatised and make the economy more productive in general, governments that use privatisation policy as a short-term means of raising money to tackle deficits and debt in order to meet EMU convergence criteria possibly do so at the expense of longer-run efficiency goals. Jeronimo *et al.* (2000) used country-level panel data on privatisation receipts and budget deficits for OECD countries from 1990 to 1997 to empirically analyse whether the concern with deficits in the 1990s is related to a shift from privatisation as a tool of economic restructuring, to privatisation as a tool of EMU convergence. Their results show that there was a statistically significant relationship for southern European states, but no such relationship in other EU member states. They concluded that their findings had 'important social welfare implications if the short-run gains from meeting the EMU criteria were lower than the long-run gains from the economic merits of privatization policies and from investing privatization receipts efficiently' (Jeronimo *et al.*, 2000: 330).

The criteria for EMU convergence were not the only factors encouraging privatisation in EU countries. European competition policy has also had a strong impact on member states' economic policies and, indirectly, the matter of public ownership, by intervening in the regulation of monopolies and at the same time limiting the amount of subsidies given to public enterprises. EU requirements concerning the liberalisation of markets in sectors like telecommunications and electricity have served as an important agent of change in these sectors. This is particularly evident in the telecommunications sector, where the introduction of competition in the market has been one of the key factors behind the privatisation of the national telecommunications company in virtually every EU member state.

While recognising the differences that apply across different member states, Parker (1999: 17–18) summarised the dominant arguments underpinning privatisation in the EU as follows:

1) Public enterprises are inefficient and privatisation will lead to improved efficiency;
2) Selling public enterprises is a legitimate method for reducing government debt and removes the risk of future capital injections into loss-making firms;
3) Privatisation is a necessary response to measures within the EU aimed at liberalising markets;
4) Privatisation can make a useful contribution to developing domestic capital markets.

The following section reviews the extent of privatisation activity in the EU15[7] and shows how the pace, content and economic significance of privatisation programmes varies considerably from member state to member state.

## 1.6    Privatisation in the EU: Extent of activity

Bortolotti and Milella (2008) estimated that in global terms, the cumulative value of privatisation proceeds raised by governments worldwide between 1977 and 2004 was approximately USD$1.35 trillion. Countries in Western Europe[8] accounted for 48 per cent of global proceeds, followed by Asia (24%) and Latin America (11%). After an increase in privatisation activity between 2004 and 2008, we estimate that the privatisation revenues generated globally from 1977 until 2008 totals almost USD$1.9 trillion.[9]

The scale of Europe's privatisation revenues relative to the rest of the world can be attributed to the large size of the public sector in most European economies prior to the 1980s, and to that fact that much of the privatisation activity during the 1990s involved the sales of ownership stakes in valuable former national monopoly operators in the telecommunications and utility industries. Given that the focus of this book is on the privatisation experience of a single Western European country, the remainder of the review of privatisation activity in this chapter focuses solely on the EU15.[10] The analysis carried out builds on the review of privatisation activity in the EU15 undertaken by Bortolotti and Milella (2008).

Figure 1.1 charts the extent of privatisation activity in the EU15, in terms of revenues raised and transactions over the period 1981–2008. There was little activity during the 1980s with the majority of sales in Europe accounted for by the UK. The principal exception was France, where a right-wing government privatised a number of large industrial and banking firms between 1986 and 1988 before the programme of divestiture was ended by the re-election of a socialist government in 1988 (Parker, 1998). Proceeds from privatisation increased considerably in the 1990s, particularly between 1994 and 2000, with the flotation of stakes in telecommunication and utility firms in many EU15 countries accounting for the majority of revenue raised during this period.

In general, a government's choice of privatisation method depends on a host of possible factors, such as the degree of importance attached to raising exchequer revenues, capital market conditions in the country, the importance of promoting wider share ownership and the competitive and financial position of the SOE (Megginson and Netter, 2001; OECD, 2003). Figure 1.1 shows that in terms of proceeds, public offerings of shares on the stock market have been the predominant method of sale in the EU. During the 1990s, public offerings, on average, accounted for over two-thirds of all privatisation proceeds. This share

*Figure 1.1*  Annual Privatisation Activity in the EU15, 1981–2008

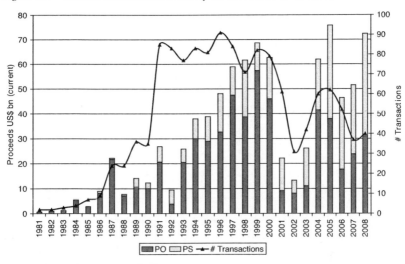

*Source*: *Privatization Barometer* database.
*Note*: PO refers to 'public offerings', i.e., the sale of company shares on the stock market; PS refers to 'private sales', whereby partial or entire stakes in firms are sold directly to another institution or consortium.

declined over the period 2000–03, mainly due to adverse equity market conditions. Although the revenues raised through public offerings picked up thereafter, private sales have, on average, accounted for the majority of proceeds generated since the turn of the century.

Figure 1.2 illustrates the total proceeds from privatisation in the EU15 between 1977 and 2008 broken down by sector. The total revenue generated during the period amounted to close to USD$890 billion, with the divestiture of SOEs operating in the telecommunications and utilities sectors accounting for almost 48 per cent of the total. This is to be expected given the size and importance of firms operating in these sectors. For example, the sale of approximately 57 per cent of France Telecom in different stages between 1997 and 2007 has already raised close to USD$27 billion, the sale of around 68 per cent of the Italian electricity company, Enel, has raised over USD$34 billion so far, while the sale of almost 49 per cent of shares in Deutsche Telekom has generated revenues of over USD$43 billion since 1996.[11]

Figure 1.3 displays the total proceeds from privatisation accrued by each member of the EU15 in constant prices.[12] As expected, the four largest countries in the EU15, namely France, Germany, Italy, and the

*Figure 1.2*  Breakdown of EU15 Privatisation Activity by Sector, 1977–2008

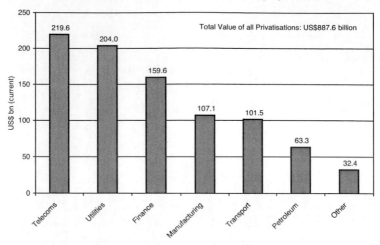

*Source*: *Privatization Barometer* database.
*Note*: 'Utilities' includes firms operating in the electricity, gas and water industries; 'Finance' includes mainly banking and insurance companies; 'Manufacturing' includes firms involved in various industries, including ship building, car manufacturing, steel, mining and chemicals; 'Other' includes firms involved in services, construction, trade, natural resources, public administration and agriculture.

*Figure 1.3*  Privatisation Revenues by EU15 Country, 1977–2008

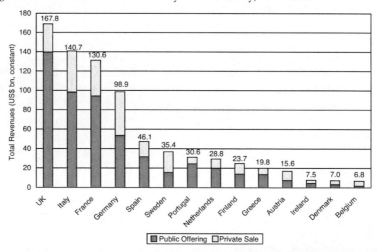

*Source*: Authors' calculation from data sourced from *Privatization Barometer* database and *OECD National Accounts*.
*Note*: Total privatisation revenues were converted to constant USD$ billions (2000=1) using a GDP price deflator derived from data on current and constant GDP in each country.

*Figure 1.4* Privatisation Revenues Relative to GDP by EU15 Country

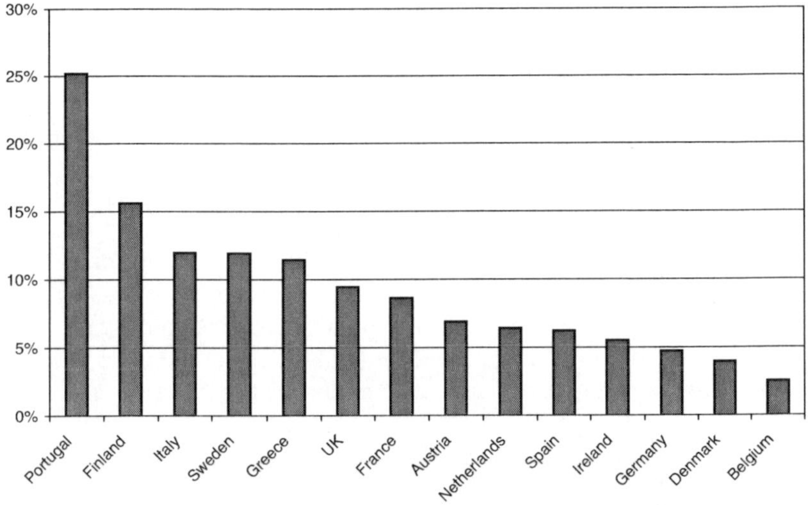

*Source*: *Privatization Barometer* database and *OECD National Accounts*.
*Note*: Privatisation Revenues relative to GDP was calculated as Total Privatisation
Revenues in constant USD$ billions (2000=1) as a percentage of 2008 GDP (in constant
USD$ billions (2000=1).

UK, have accrued the most revenue, with public offerings of shares
in their telecommunications and utility companies accounting for the
majority of the revenue raised. Smaller countries such as Ireland, Denmark and Belgium have generated the least amount of revenue, with
Belgium, Denmark and Sweden the only countries to have generated the
majority of revenue from private sales rather than public offerings.

Given the different sizes of each country, a more useful cross-country
comparison of the extent of privatisation is provided in Figure 1.4, which
presents the total privatisation revenue generated by each country as a
percentage of its GDP in 2008. The privatisation programmes of Portugal,
Finland, Sweden and Greece, which appeared relatively small in Figure 1.3,
are now shown to be significant, particularly in the case of Portugal,
where total privatisation revenues generated to date relative to GDP in
2008 amounts to just over 25 per cent. While the four largest countries in
the EU15 are now ranked comparatively lower, the scale of the revenue
raised in Italy, the UK and France is nonetheless considerable.

Figure 1.1 shows that privatisation activity declined significantly over
the period 2001–03. Parker (2003: 111) attributes this decline to factors
including: (a) weak stock markets, which diminished the prospects of

successful public offerings, (b) poor returns to investors in some privatisation issues, particularly in the telecommunications sector (for example,
Deutsche Telekom and France Telecom), (c) reluctance on the part of
some governments to consider selling majority stakes in strategic
industries, and (d) serious post-privatisation difficulties in some UK companies sold in the 1990s (for example, Railtrack and the National Air
Traffic Services). The slowdown in privatisation during the 2001–03
period prompted Bortolotti and Siniscalco (2004), in their analysis of
international privatisation in the 1990s, to conclude that privatisation
in Europe seemed 'exhausted' at the start of the new millennium. However, we can see in Figure 1.1 that the pace of privatisation activity subsequently picked up. Since then, the annual value of proceeds generated
in some years has in fact surpassed the peak values observed in the late
1990s. The following section turns attention to the surge in sales after
2003.

### 1.6.1 Privatisation in Europe post-2003

The recent increase in privatisation proceeds generated in Western Europe
can largely be attributed to activity in France, Germany and Italy. Indeed,
just over two-thirds of the total proceeds of USD$308.24 billion gener-
ated in the EU15 between 2004 and 2008 can be attributed to these countries. From 2004 onwards, all three countries began divesting partial
stakes in some major SOEs, with more favourable stock market conditions
facilitating a number of substantial seasoned public offerings. The rationale behind the increase in privatisation activity in each country would
appear to be largely due to financial pressures. Both France and Germany
were experiencing severe public finance problems and were struggling to
remain within the fiscal limits of the Stability & Growth Pact, while Italy
was still attempting to lower its debt/GDP ratio, which was the highest in
Europe at the time.

Since 2004, the privatisation revenues raised in France have dwarfed
all those of its European counterparts, accounting for over 38 per cent
of the total privatisation proceeds generated in the EU15 from 2004–08.
The establishment of an autonomous government shareholding agency,
the *Agence des Participations de l'Etat* (APE), during 2003 paved the way
for a considerable surge in privatisation activity from 2004 onwards. The
agency was created to act as shareholder for the government's public
sector enterprises and was charged with responsibility for optimising the
value of the government's portfolio of assets. Essentially, the main mis-
sion of the APE is to help prepare state companies for divestiture and
then to manage their privatisations as part of a stable and transparent

process.[13] In this regard the agency has been enormously successful, with France generating the highest privatisation proceeds in the EU15 every year from 2004 until 2008.

The French have raised appreciable sums of money from the sales of stakes in all of its major utility companies (Electricité de France, Gaz de France and France Telecom), the complete divestiture of its motorway networks, and the sale of stakes in some of its largest banks (such as CNCE). While the partial privatisation of the energy companies was politically controversial, the initial public offering (IPO) of stakes in both firms during 2005 was successful. Half of the shares in Gaz de France were reserved for domestic retail investors, and a further 15 per cent stake reserved for employees, with both tranches priced at a slight discount to the price charged to institutional investors. The IPO attracted 3.3 million new shareholders and was hugely oversubscribed, with the stock price increasing rapidly during the first days trading. While the IPO of Electricité de France was not as successful as its counterpart in the gas sector, the offering nonetheless attracted 4.8 million investors (Megginson, 2006a).

An important development in 2006 was the rise in popularity of privatisation by direct placement with private equity funds. Whereas before, privatising governments tended to favour floating stakes in large SOEs on the stock market, the increased interest of private equity groups in acquiring states assets, particularly in regulated utilities and real estate assets from 2006 onwards, presented governments with a choice between private sales or public offerings for even the largest of SOEs (Megginson, 2006b). Indeed, in 2006 alone, some 40 per cent of the total revenue raised in Europe stemmed from placements with private equity groups (Privatization Barometer, 2007a).

The turmoil in the financial markets that followed the subprime loan crisis in the United States in the latter half of 2007 led to a significant decline in investment activity and there was little appetite among private equity investors for state assets. During 2007, France was the only EU15 country that actively privatised, with the French government making a number of opportunistic sales of stakes in France Telecom, Electricité de France and the French bank, CDC (Privatization Barometer, 2007b). This pattern continued in 2008, with France again generating the majority of revenue, almost 40 per cent of the EU total, thanks largely to its merger of Gaz de France (in which the French government had a majority stake) and Suez (in which it had a partial stake) which netted the government over €15 billion. The merger also required Suez to divest its environmental subsidiary, Suez Environment, which was floated immediately after the merger, earning the French government another €4.65 billion (Privatization Barometer, 2008).

More recently, Sweden embarked on a significant programme of divestiture following the election of a new centre-right coalition government in 2006, which announced an ambitious privatisation plan. The government identified a number of SOEs that it would put up for sale and projected raising revenues of approximately €21 billion. After accruing revenues of just over €3.1 billion in 2007, the privatisation programme gathered pace in 2008, with proceeds of €13.7 billion generated from the sales of government stakes in OMX (stock exchange group), Vin & Spirit (alcohol) and Vasakronan (real estate). The programme of divestitures was suspended indefinitely at the end of 2008 due to the global collapse in stock market values (Privatization Barometer, 2008).

The onset of the global financial crisis has led to an extraordinary reversal of the privatisation trend observed over the past three decades. The Privatization Barometer (2008) estimates that over US$1.5 trillion in bank stocks and loans were transferred from the private to the public sector in 2008, with governments in many countries forced to partially or fully nationalise some of the biggest banks in their countries as a result of the global financial crisis. The amount of assets acquired in 2008 almost equalled the entire amount of revenue raised by privatising governments globally from 1977–2008. This trend continued in 2009, with government ownership of banking and insurance companies that had required state bailouts now common in many countries. We return to this important development in Chapter 8.

The sovereign debt crisis that has developed in a number of European countries (such as the so-called PIIGS countries: Portugal, Ireland, Italy, Greece and Spain) is likely to have significant ramifications for the development of privatisation programmes in these countries in the near future. Indeed, in June 2010 the Greek government announced a programme of planned SOE sales in an effort to raise revenues to help reduce the country's accelerating national debt. The plan, which was a condition of its €110 billion bailout by the EU and IMF, involves the divestiture of government stakes in a number of companies operating in the transport, postal and energy sectors, and is envisaged to raise approximately €1 billion a year from 2011–13.[14]

Similar to Greece, in March 2010 Portugal also announced a programme of divestiture in response to the severe fiscal problems that it currently faces. The plan, which involves the sale of stakes in 17 different companies operating in the transport, postal, defence, energy, financial and paper sectors, is expected to raise approximately €6 billion by

2013. This fire-sale of state assets has been justified by the Portuguese government on the grounds that the divestitures will contribute 'to the promotion of greater efficiency and productivity in the sectors concerned, and the essential reduction of general government debt'.[15]

The global financial crisis has had an enormous bearing on the extent and pattern of privatisation activity worldwide. On the one hand governments have been forced to acquire significant ownership stakes in financial companies, thereby reversing the pattern observed over the last 30 years or so. On the other hand, mounting fiscal deficits are creating pressures to sell other public enterprises in order to alleviate sovereign debt burdens. These developments are likely to lead to significant changes in the portfolio of state-owned assets in many countries. The implications of these developments for the future of the public enterprise sector in Ireland and beyond are discussed in further detail in Chapters 8 and 9.

## 1.7    Conclusion

Since coming into vogue in the late 1970s, privatisation policies have been a radical force in the redrawing of boundaries between the public and private sectors of economies around the world. Since its stealthy emergence as a minor tool of public policy in the UK in the late 1970s, privatisation has assumed global significance with the value of assets transferred from public to private ownership amounting to close to USD\$2 trillion. In regional terms, Europe accounts for the largest proportion of privatisation revenues raised to date. Although the extent of privatisation activity in Europe appeared to have slowed down in the early part of the new millennium, a number of factors, not least the current global financial crisis, have restored momentum to privatisation policies and raised the prospect for future divestitures.

The extent of privatisation activity and its precise nature has varied from country to country. Even within Europe, which commands the focus of this chapter, the experience has been heterogeneous in character, with important differences in the scale, methods and objectives of privatisation programmes across European countries.

The following chapter reviews the development of theories of privatisation, with an emphasis on the principal economic arguments in relation to enterprise efficiency. It also reviews the available empirical evidence concerning enterprise performance, as well as other aspects that contribute to the overall welfare impact of privatisation.

# 2
# Privatisation Objectives: Theory and Evidence

## 2.0 Introduction

The 1970s heralded the breakdown of the post-war Keynesian consensus. The problems of high inflation and unemployment (stagflation) as well as low economic growth and poor productivity led to disenchantment with the role of government in modern economies. At a macro-level, governments around the world turned to policies such as monetarism, whereas at a micro-level, market-based solutions to the problems of market failure came into vogue. The latter included a host of new arrangements that altered the boundaries between the public and private sectors, including deregulation, liberalisation, contracting out, the creation of quasi-markets, and different forms of privatisation.

In Chapter 1 we described a number of the reasons commonly put forward to justify the privatisation of SOEs. We noted how the motivations for privatisation could differ across countries and over time. For example, the initial adoption of privatisation policies in the UK was driven by the need to address the supposed poor enterprise performance associated with public ownership, whereas considerations in relation to raising exchequer proceeds were more prominent among other members of the EU. We also drew attention to how the analysis of privatisation policies is complicated by their multiplicity of objectives, as well as their internal inconsistency. For example, selling a public monopoly is likely to raise greater revenues than privatising the enterprise in the context of liberalising the relevant product markets. While our analysis of the Irish privatisation experience recognises these analytical challenges, the approach we adopt is to focus on three main objectives: the improvement in enterprise performance, the raising of revenues for the exchequer, and welfare-oriented objectives in relation to key stakeholders. Particular attention is paid to the question of enterprise performance. The importance of this aspect is emphasised by Yarrow (1986: 324), who asserts that it is on the issue of efficiency that privatisation should ultimately be assessed:

> Whilst a number of benefits have been claimed for privatization [...] many of its goals are better achieved by other policies and [...] it is on its contributions to economic efficiency that privatization must ultimately be judged.

Bearing these issues in mind, this chapter is mainly devoted to examining the economic case for privatising SOEs in terms of enterprise performance. It begins by considering the relevant economic theory that had been developed prior to the spread of privatisation policies in the early 1980s, before looking more closely at the literature on privatisation *per se*. This approach is necessary because the rise in popularity of privatisation policies owed little to developments in economic theory that explicitly made the case for transferring ownership of SOEs to the private sector. In fact, the theory of general equilibrium, which provides the foundation for modern microeconomic theory, places no emphasis on the ownership of firms. Competitive markets, rather, are the key to the attainment of an efficient allocation of economic resources. Where markets were characterised by failure, such as increasing returns to scale over the relevant range of demand in the specific market, the existence of more than one firm was shown to be inefficient. This natural monopoly argument justified public ownership in order to avoid private exploitation of monopoly power.

Earlier privatisation policies therefore drew support from theories that challenged the case for state intervention in economies for the purpose of correcting market failures. Developments in the fields of public choice and property rights theory shed light on the issue of 'government failure', and provided fertile ground for questioning the efficacy of government interventions, including public ownership, which had been in the ascendancy for much of the twentieth century. Economic theories of privatisation *per se* began to emerge in tandem with the growing popularity of privatisation from the early 1990s onwards. These perspectives were largely located in developments in economic theory, such as the economics of information and institutional economics. However, the development of these perspectives is still in its infancy and there are significant gaps in the economic literature on privatisation and ownership of firms (Roland, 2008).

## 2.1 Differences between public and private enterprise: A theoretical overview

Kay (1987) asserts that the European tradition of public enterprise theory, derived from writers such as Hotelling (1938) and Boiteux (1971), viewed the objective of public enterprise as one of welfare maximisation. If welfare could be described, public sector managers would implement the rules necessary to optimise it (Kay, 1987: 343). This apparently naive view of managerial behaviour was challenged by subsequently developed theories which focused principally on the issue of ownership and attendant concepts, such as objectives, incentives and monitoring under different models of ownership.

The theory of public choice developed by writers including James Buchanan, Anthony Downs and Gordon Tullock challenged the dominant orthodoxy of modern public administration and political science by questioning '[t]he mythology of the faceless bureaucrat following orders from above, executing but not making policy choices, and motivated to only forward the "public interest"' (Buchanan, 1978: 11). The precise motivations of bureaucrats came under scrutiny. A specific element of the theory of public choice is the assumption of '*Homo economicus*', meaning that individuals are assumed to maximise their own self interest. On this basis, the clearest theme of public choice theory is that elected representatives and bureaucrats pursue their own objectives rather than the public interest. In a world of uncertainty, the public sector is asserted to be wasteful as there are no incentives to control costs. Walsh (1995) summarises three fundamental sources of government failure identified by public choice theorists. Firstly, because politicians are assumed to maximise their own self-interest, they are not expected to demand the pattern of outputs that reflect the public interest. Secondly, even if politicians demand that the public interest be satisfied, the bureaucracy may not do so because it conflicts with their self-interest. Thirdly, it may be in the self-interests of bureaucrats to be inefficient. The ultimate conclusion is that the public sector will be characterised by both allocative inefficiency (the wrong mix of services), and X-inefficiency (failure to maximise output for a given level of inputs) (Leibenstein, 1966).

The property rights literature draws similar conclusions to the theory of public choice. Martin and Parker (1997: 10) state that the:

> ...standard property rights approach to public and private ownership acknowledges that there are agency problems in all forms of owner-

ship, but that because ownership is transferable through a competitive capital market in the private sector, a better use of resources results.

Alchian and Demsetz (1972) argue that the role of management is to monitor employees to ensure that higher productivity and lower costs are attained. In order to monitor workers effectively, however, managers require incentives. According to property rights theory, the incentive is profit (or the 'residual'). The core argument in the literature is that private organisations, where the rights to profits are well-defined, perform better than public organisations where rights are diffused and uncertain (Alchian, 1965; De Alessi, 1980). Most of the property rights literature is therefore concerned with the incentives to effectively monitor management behaviour under public and private ownership. In terms of enterprise performance, property rights theory argues that private sector enterprises will perform better since they are owned by shareholders who have an incentive to monitor managerial actions in order to ensure efficient decisions are made. In contrast, the 'owners' of public enterprises (the wider citizenry) do not recognise their rights to ownership in SOEs and have no incentive to monitor managerial decisionmaking. Property rights theory therefore argues that the privatisation of SOEs, which leads to a reallocation of property rights, will lead to an improvement in performance (Dunsire *et al.*, 1988: 365).

Despite their appeal, these theories of government failure do not adequately explain the reasons for supposedly superior performance by private sector organisations. Public choice theory arguably exaggerates the extent of the pursuit of self-interest on the part of bureaucrats and elected representatives. Furthermore, there is little empirical evidence in support of the predictions of public choice theorists (Lewin, 1991; Self, 1993, cited in Walsh, 1995). Property rights theory, while focusing on important ownership-related issues like objectives and incentives, understates the importance of market structure and the role of competition in ensuring the attainment of efficiency. The following section examines the claims of public choice and property rights theorists by reviewing empirical studies that seek to compare performance under public and private ownership.

## 2.2 Public vs. private enterprise performance: Empirical studies

### 2.2.1 Methodological issues

There have been a large number of international studies comparing the performance of public and private sector firms and most recognise that assessing organisational performance is not without problems, especially when conducted in a comparative context. One set of problems concerns the choice of performance indicator.[1] The standard measures of SOE performance employed in the literature include financial indicators, and measures of productivity and cost. Purely financial measures (for example, turnover, profitability, return on capital employed) are often inadequate insofar as they do not account for the non-profit-based objectives of SOEs. Whereas profit maximisation exists as a dominant objective of private enterprise, Gathon and Pestieau (1993) highlight the host of sometimes conflicting objectives generally ascribed to public enterprises. These include efficiency, equity (which is concerned, for example, with company performance in terms of government objectives regarding employment and pricing policy), and a variety of other macroeconomic objectives, such as inflation or the balance of payments. The use of SOEs as instruments of government policy with regard to these objectives limits the validity of single performance indicators, and undermines public-private sector comparisons.

As SOEs often operate in non-competitive markets, the prices which form a basis for most financial measures are not appropriate. This is a particularly significant factor if SOE performance is being assessed relative to that of privately-owned counterparts. Other standard measures like labour productivity and total factor productivity can also suffer from the problem of being price-based. Furthermore, if such indicators are being viewed over time, it is necessary to make adjustments for technological variation and control for trends in relevant industries or national productivity. Using an estimated cost function for comparing public and private sector performance on the basis of cost is also problematic. If the specification includes a dummy variable to account for the difference in average costs across the two sectors, the implicit assumption is that one of the sectors is efficient. This is not always the case (Martin and Parker, 1997).

Many comparative studies have been criticised insofar as they fail to control for all variables affecting performance, other than ownership. These include factors such as regulatory environment, size, market structure and incentive structure, which theory suggests are important determinants of performance. Furthermore, statistical tests have rarely been sophisticated enough to take account of these interacting but non-separable factors that impact on performance.

### 2.2.2 Empirical studies

Comparative studies have been reviewed by a number of writers (for example, Boardman and Vining, 1989; Borcherding *et al.*, 1982; Vickers and

Yarrow, 1988; Bös, 1991; Martin and Parker, 1997; Willner, 2001). Conclusions vary across studies and the literature fails to deliver a clear consensus regarding the superiority of either type of ownership. The findings of Borcherding *et al.* (1982) reflected the broad thrust of empirical comparisons prior to 1982. The authors concluded from the literature that (a) private production is cheaper than production in publicly-owned and managed firms, and (b) given sufficient competition between public and private producers (and no discriminative regulations and subsidies), the differences in unit cost turn out to be insignificant. Overall, they concluded that it is not so much the difference in transferability of ownership but the lack of competition which leads to the observed less efficient production in public firms. The majority of early studies examined firms in utility industries, such as electricity and water, and generally found no advantage or disadvantage associated with public ownership relative to private ownership.

Willner (2001) reviewed studies carried out on firms operating in service industries which are more labour intensive and concluded that while private ownership was found to be more advantageous, public ownership was no less efficient in more than half of the cases (Willner, 2001: 740). Bös (1991) reviewed studies published after 1982 and concluded that there was no systematic evidence that public enterprises were less cost efficient. Different case studies offered different conclusions regarding the more efficient form of ownership. This conclusion is supported by Boardman and Vining (1989) who found that early empirical work carried out on firms operating in utility industries provided weak support for the hypothesis that private firms are more efficient than state-owned firms, as they were limited by at least one of the following factors: (a) the firms studied had a natural or spatial monopoly, (b) the firms were part of a regulated duopoly, or (c) output could not be priced by competitive forces.

In their own empirical analysis, Boardman and Vining (1989) sought to account for the deficiencies of previous studies by explicitly comparing the effect of company ownership in a competitive market, while controlling for relevant factors such as industry and country. The authors used four separate profitability measures – the rate of return on equity (ROE), return on assets (ROA), return on sales (ROS) and net income – as well as two basic indicators of efficiency – turnover per employee and turnover per asset – in order to analyse the performance of the 500 largest (non-US) international industrial companies listed in *Fortune* magazine in 1983. After controlling for a wide variety of factors their results indicated that SOEs and mixed-ownership firms were less profitable and less efficient than similar private sector companies, with the ROE for state-owned firms 12 per cent lower on average than that of private firms, while ROS and ROA were approximately 2 per cent lower.[2] The authors found that the broad conclusion to be drawn from their study was that the case for private ownership is confined to sectors where markets are competitive and does not apply in the case of natural monopolies or heavily regulated industries. It must be noted, however, that the vast majority of the firms in their sample (409) were privately-owned, thereby biasing the results in favour of such enterprises.

Overall, the empirical evidence on the comparative performance of public and private sector enterprises fails to provide a clear-cut consensus regarding the superiority of either form of ownership. Empirical studies lend little support for the main performance-related propositions derived from theories of public choice and property rights. Despite the lack of clear-cut findings the literature does illuminate the complex set of factors that impact on enterprise performance. In particular, they draw attention to the importance of the degree of market competition as a key explanatory variable. In this regard a number of studies suggest that the lack of competition faced by many public sector firms is a more significant determinant of relatively lower efficiency levels than the issue of ownership (Borcherding *et al.*, 1982). It is particularly noteworthy that the inconclusive nature of empirical studies into the relative merits of public versus private ownership did little to deter policymakers from experimenting with privatisation policies. The advent of privatisation challenged scholars, and economists in particular, to further develop perspectives on this question and to offer insights into why a change in ownership might deliver improved performance. The following section examines subsequent developments and focuses on the emergence of theories of privatisation.

## 2.3   Economic theories of privatisation and performance

As we have seen from Chapter 1, privatisation has had various and complex objectives. From an economic perspective, the case for selling SOEs is usually based on supposed superior efficiency under private ownership. Economic analysis of privatisation therefore tends to focus on the question of efficiency. In this regard, it is important to distinguish between different concepts of efficiency. *Technical* efficiency is a supply-side concept, and firms are said to be technically efficient when they are maximising output for a given level of resources. Such an outcome is consistent with the minimisation of costs. *Allocative* efficiency is a broader, demand-side concept. It is concerned with 'prices that reflect the marginal economic cost of supply and therefore the optimal distribution of resources in society to maximise economic well-being' (Parker, 2000: xv).

Some of the earlier contributions to economic theories of privatisation offered perspectives on the trade-off between technical and allocative efficiency following privatisation. This trade-off was articulated by Bös (1987), who addressed the efficiency effects of a change in ownership by constructing a theoretical model based on the constrained optimisation approach common in the Boiteux tradition of public enterprise theory:

> The gains in productive efficiency from privatization argue in favor of selling as many shares as possible [...] On the other hand, selling shares leads to increasing profits for the firm and may well lead to increasing prices. These effects reduce welfare and argue in favour of keeping shares in public ownership, because then the remaining government representatives on the board of the firm are able to prevent unwanted profit or price increases.
>
> (Bös, 1987: 357)

This trade-off was also formally discussed by Vickers and Yarrow (1988) who adopted a principal-agent approach to the theoretical analysis of privatisation. This contractual perspective characterised much of the subsequent theoretical developments in the area (for example, Bös, 1991; Boycko *et al.*, 1996; Rees, 1988; Vickers, 1997). In its most basic form, principal-agent theory examines the relationship between one person (the principal) who delegates work to another (the agent). The agent then performs that work and makes decisions on behalf of the principal. The principal-agent relationship is characterised by problems that occur when the objectives of the principal and agent are different (*objective asymmetries*), and when it is difficult for the principal to observe what the agent is actually doing (*information asymmetries*). This leads to difficulties in designing contracts and incentives for the purpose of fostering economic efficiency.

Privatisation alters what Bös (1991: 92) refers to as the principal-agent setting within the firm. This may involve a reduction in the number of organisational layers, but an accompanying increase in the elements in the 'owner layer', with government now being replaced by a spread of ownership between financial institutions, private shareholders, and employees. Theoretically, such changes can impact upon efficiency through: (a) changes in organisational structure, (b) changes in owner and manager objectives, and (c) changes in monitoring, communication and incentive structures.

As more and more shares in an SOE are sold, the objectives of the owners change from welfare maximisation (allocative efficiency) to profit maximisation (technical efficiency) (Shapiro and Willig, 1990). This has obvious implications for performance, as measured in terms of technical and allocative efficiency, and points to a need for what Bös (1987: 356) argues is an optimal degree of withdrawal from an enterprise.

The difference between managerial characteristics and objectives in public and private sectors highlights the importance of incentives, information and monitoring in terms of shaping managerial behaviour. One way in which privatisation can impact on these variables is by enhancing the credibility of government commitments not to intervene in the operations of the company. If managers in SOEs make poor investment decisions, the government has an incentive and scope to bail them out using the public budget. The scope for intervention is reduced considerably following privatisation. Sheshinski and Lopez-Calva (2003) explain the rationale for government intervention under public ownership in terms of its ability to spread the cost of the bailout across taxpayers, who are likely to be less organised with more diversified interests than well-defined political groups like trade unions. In addition, bailing out the firm is likely to have a lower political cost than allowing it to go bankrupt. As governments do not have the opportunity to pursue such policies after privatisation, managers may face harder budget constraints and stronger incentives for efficiency (Vickers, 1997: 66).

A number of writers have pointed to the fact that the soft budget constraint problem is a general incentive problem that applies to SOEs and privately-owned firms. For example, Roland (2008) points out that hard budget constraints have, at times, been applied to state enterprises. However, governments and regulators employ a number of instruments to soften the budget constraints for private firms. These include subsidies, loan guarantees, trade protection and allowing increased prices. If these factors are taken into account, the distinction between public and private enterprise in terms of budget constraints is blurred.

The theories of government failure, discussed earlier in section 2.1, draw attention to supposed self-seeking behaviour by public sector managers which conflicts with the public interest. This is often attributed to weaknesses in the incentives to monitor on the part of public owners (for example, politicians and/or taxpayers). Where government-held shares are sold on the stock market, the pressure of capital markets is brought to bear and limits are placed on managerial discretion (Vickers and Yarrow, 1991: 115). Following privatisation, profit-maximising shareholders are incentivised to monitor managerial behaviour. Effective monitoring can overcome asymmetries in information between principals and agents and enable the design of efficient contracts aimed at ensuring that agents carry out the wishes of principals. The efficient market hypothesis proposes that efficient capital markets provide all relevant information, with share prices accurately supplying principals with information regarding the agent's performance.

Roland (2008) draws attention to two criticisms of this argument. Firstly, there is sufficient evidence to suggest that the efficient market hypothesis does not necessarily hold. The 2008 Nobel laureate in economics, Paul Krugman, points to the global financial and economic crisis that commenced in 2008 to support this argument.[3] Secondly, the efficient market hypothesis does not necessarily support the argument for full privatisation, as partial privatisation is all that is necessary if the useful information characteristics of stock markets are to be exploited. A third argument that undermines the case for privatisation in terms of improved monitoring and information via capital markets focuses on the issue of dispersed shareholdings. If shareholdings in a privatised company are dispersed (which is frequently the case), some groups may leave monitoring to those who they assume are better informed (for example, institutional investors). This free-rider problem has implications for the method of privatisation and could mean that there are advantages to selling shares in blocks to those who are viewed as being more likely to monitor managerial performance closely (Caves, 1990: 160).

The sale of government-held shares on the stock market introduces the threat of takeover, which rarely exists under public ownership. If a firm performs poorly, this is reflected in the share price and makes the firm attractive as a target for takeover. However, the impact of the takeover threat on managerial behaviour is weakened if the market for corporate control is inefficient. This occurs, for example, if small shareholders hold off on their decision to sell shares in the hope of exploiting the post-takeover increase in share price. It is also conceivable that the threat of takeover creates disincentive effects. Stiglitz (1991: 39) draws attention to the takeover frenzy in the USA during the 1980s where there were examples of managers who entrenched themselves in companies by devising 'golden parachutes'. This involved post-takeover owners being obliged to pay large amounts of compensation to dismiss incumbent managers. The effect was to divert takeover bids away from possibly inefficient companies. However, Roland (2008: 16) asserts that arguments in favour of privatisation on the basis of the takeover threat have 'little relevance in countries where corporate takeovers play a minor role, which is the case in most countries. Furthermore, takeovers in public utilities are quite rare even during periods of high takeover activity in other industries.'

One argument in favour of privatisation hinges on the assumption that firms operate in competitive product markets. Competition promotes internal as well as allocative efficiency by enabling comparison between firms:

> Imperfect information constrains the design of incentive contracts, and inefficiencies result. Information therefore has value insofar as it makes possible incentive schemes that are sensitive to more effort. Competition can act as a source of this kind of information, because rewards can be based on performance comparisons.
>
> (Vickers and Yarrow, 1988: 69)

The empirical evidence on the comparative performance of public and private enterprise also highlights the importance of competition in the firm's product markets in terms of determining outcomes. The evidence suggests that there is no economic case for privatising firms with market power. Where market power occurs, accompanying measures of liberalisation and regulation are necessary. Nevertheless, the policy options are not always straightforward. Yarrow (1986) argues that the introduction of competition may be inefficient if one or more sources of market failure exist. Furthermore, given the potential trade-off between allocative and technical efficiency, policies should ideally be framed in terms of a desired configuration of both concepts. Caves (1990: 150) argues that the 'simple and obvious choice – privatise for technical efficiency and liberalise for allocative efficiency – is unlikely to be optimal'. An optimal combination of privatisation and liberalisation may, however, exist. Take the example where liberalisation can reduce allocative efficiency due to economies of scale. A degree of privatisation might allow for marginal gains in technical efficiency to offset any losses in allocative efficiency. The issue is a normative one which policymakers must decide on, but the possibility of an optimal mix of both policies does exist and varies from case to case.

Developments in incomplete contract theory provide further perspectives on the question of privatisation. Roland (2008) explains that the contracting perspectives discussed above focus mainly on information differences between public and private ownership. In contrast, the incomplete contracting perspective focuses on differences in control rights. Incomplete contracts arise where parties cannot fully design, execute and/or enforce contracts that account for all contingencies. Ownership of assets confers control rights and bargaining power, which are important in circumstances where contracts are incomplete. The incomplete contracting perspective adds considerable sophistication to the analysis of privatisation. One of the particular strengths of the approach is that it demonstrates how ownership does matter. Bortolotti and Siniscalco (2004) argue that the incomplete contracting approach provides valuable insights into how the behaviour of privatised firms differs from those under state ownership. This should not be interpreted as an argument in favour of privatisation. Depending on the precise aspect of incomplete contracting examined, contributions offer different conclusions in relation to the most desirable form of ownership.

Examples from the incomplete contracting perspective include contributions from Laffont and Tirole (1991) and Sappington and Stiglitz (1987), who focus on the question of government retention of residual rights of control. Under public ownership this can lead to expropriation of managerial investments and the redeployment of assets to achieve social goals. To illustrate, Bortollotti and Siniscalco (2004) use the example of where the government might reduce the value of investment in a facility, such as a telecommunications network, by granting *ex post* access to the wider population. Although this expropriation may be socially optimal, it dampens the public manager's incentive to invest. Private ownership is therefore superior if the gains from optimal investment outweigh the gains of wider access. But where a monopoly is privatised and regulation is required, the welfare effects depend on the effectiveness of regulation.

The trade-off between technical and allocative efficiency is also addressed from the incomplete contracting perspective. Schmidt (1996) and Laffont and Tirole (1991) develop models that highlight the costs that arise after privatisation. These costs occur due to the need for regulation under conditions of asymmetric information. Competition is therefore necessary if net gains are to be realised under privatisation.

The incomplete contracting perspective has also shed light on the question of the trade-off between reduced costs and deterioration in service quality. Focusing on the differences between public and private production, Hart *et al.* (1997) examine the cases of schools, healthcare, foreign policy and prisons. While it is assumed that cost reductions have a negative effect on service quality, in general, they conclude that public production is more likely to be superior in the case of prisons, as the quality spillover is strong. Unfortunately, they fail to arrive at strong conclusions for the other sectors.

Overall the nature of the analysis of privatisation has become more sophisticated and valuable insights can be drawn from perspectives such as incomplete contracting. Nevertheless the policy prescriptions fail to come down unequivocally in favour of privatisation. Stiglitz (2008) goes so far as to say that:

> ...the theoretical case for privatization is, at best, weak or non-existent. It is strongest in areas in which there is by now a broad consensus – areas like steel or textiles, conventional commodities in which market failures may be more limited. But by the same token, these are precisely the sectors in which abuses can most easily be controlled, appropriate incentives can best be designed, and benchmarks can most easily be set.
>
> (2008: xii)

It is striking that the UK launched the world's first large-scale privatisation programme largely on the basis of faith, and that theoretical developments in the field of privatisation paralleled, rather than preceded, the spread of privatisation policies (Bortolotti and Siniscalco, 2004). While there have been considerable theoretical developments in the field of privatisation over the last 20–30 years, findings remain equivocal on the key question of privatisation and microeconomic performance. The following section therefore turns to the relevant empirical evidence in search of illumination.

## 2.4   Privatisation and enterprise performance: The evidence

Numerous empirical studies on the effects of privatisation on the financial and operating performance of divested firms have been carried out in recent years. As in the case of studies that compare the performance of public and private enterprises, the evidence from these studies is generally inconclusive. In general, the empirical literature can be divided into two main groups: broad-based international studies which by and large find that privatisation leads to improved performance, and more in-depth country-specific studies that find more ambiguous results, and suggest that privatisation does not automatically lead to an improvement in company performance. The findings of some of the main empirical works to-date are summarised in Table 2.1 and a number of these studies are discussed in more detail below.

Among the early assessments of privatisation of SOEs in the UK are those by Yarrow (1986) and Bishop and Kay (1989). Both studies focused on productive efficiency. Yarrow (1986) used performance indicators based on financial data (profits, margins and share price), and concluded that for companies operating in competitive markets, private ownership was generally to be preferred to public ownership. In cases where firms operated in markets characterised by market failure there was no evidence of improved performance. Yarrow (1986: 341) therefore concluded that 'there was little support for the view that privatization has made a major contribution to microeconomic policy goals'.

Bishop and Kay (1989) examined the performance of a sample of UK-based companies, some of which were privatised and others that remained in state ownership. On the basis of the financial performance indicators they adopted, it was concluded that 'causality runs from growth and profitability to privatization rather than the other way around' (Bishop and Kay, 1989: 653). In addition, the results from their analysis of productivity using a total factor productivity (TFP) measure denied 'any simple views about the relationship between ownership and performance', the greatest gains being in companies not privatised (Bishop and Kay, 1989: 653). Their conclusions also pointed to the positive impact of the threat of privatisation and commercialising reforms directed toward making SOEs more efficient.

Bishop and Thompson (1992) studied the performance of British utilities between 1970–80 and 1980–90. They found improvements in labour productivity in most of the ten companies examined, while their results using a TFP measure were more mixed. They found that productivity gains (using both measures) were higher in the 1980s compared to the 1970s and concluded that changes in the regulatory environment rather than privatisation had a greater impact on performance in the 1980s.

There were three major broad-based empirical studies of the impact of privatisation on company performance conducted during the 1990s. Studies by Megginson *et al.* (1994), Boubakri and Cosset (1998) and D'Souza and Megginson (1999) all used the same methodology and tested similar hypotheses. Specifically they tested whether privatisation will: (a) increase profitability, (b) increase operating efficiency, (c) increase capital investment spending, (d) increase output, (e) increase dividend payments, (f) decrease employment, and (g) decrease leverage. The three

studies collectively analysed 211 firms from 42 countries and 56 industries. Twenty-six of the countries were classified as 'developing'
and represented 103 of the firms in the sample, with the remaining
108 firms coming from 16 developed countries. Each study compared
the pre- versus post-privatisation financial and operating performance,
using standard performance indicators for the three years prior to and
following divestiture. Profitability was measured using the rate of return
on sales, return on assets and return on equity ratios, while operating
efficiency was measured using sales per employee and net income per
employee ratios.

The main findings of the three studies are summarised in Table 2.1.
In general, all three studies found that privatisation leads to an improvement in profitability and efficiency and yielded remarkably consistent
results, despite the fact that the years analysed varied across the studies
and the fact that Boubakri and Cosset (1998) concentrated solely on
privatised firms in developing countries. D'Souza and Megginson (1999)
found that significant levels of the improvement in the profitability,
output and efficiency variables observed in their study were greater
than those calculated by Megginson *et al.* (1994), and similar to those
in Boubakri and Cosset (1998).

Boubakri and Cosset (1998) recognised that some of the differences
between pre- and post-privatisation performance in their study could
have been due to economy-wide factors. They used both raw and
market-adjusted performance indicators '[t]o take account of this possibility and to isolate the effect of privatization from the impact of macroeconomic changes on the financial and operating performance of SOEs'
(1998: 1083). While Megginson *et al.* (1994) did not use market-adjusted
performance indicators, they did examine whether their results were
driven by changes in the macroeconomic environment by computing the
average Gross National Product (GNP) growth rate, inflation rate and
change in industrial production index for each country. On this basis
they concluded that performance was not affected by the macroeconomic
environment.

D'Souza and Megginson (1999) made no allowance for the business
cycle in their analysis. Their sample of companies included a sizeable
representation of electricity and telecommunication firms, the result of
'massive technological change, a worldwide trend towards deregulation
of utilities, and a desire among policy-makers to privatize and modern-
ize suddenly dynamic and increasingly vital industries' (1999: 1426).
These factors also contributed to the remarkable performance improvements observed in these companies and call into question whether the

**Table 2.1  Main Findings of Empirical Studies on Privatisation and Performance**

| Study | Country | Industry | # Firms | Measures | Findings | Summary |
|---|---|---|---|---|---|---|
| Bishop and Kay (1989) | UK | Various | 12 | Financial, TFP | Ambiguous | Find significant increases in profitability but that much of growth occurs pre-privatisation. TFP results do not suggest private ownership is superior. |
| Bishop and Thompson (1992) | UK | Various | 9 | LP, TFP | Ambiguous | Analyse productivity growth over two decades. Results show that rate of productivity growth in 1980s significantly higher than 1970s. Authors argue this is due to regulatory rather than ownership changes. |
| Megginson et al. (1994) | Various | Various | 61 | LP, financial | Private superior | Find that privatisation led to: increased profitability, dividend payments and capital investment; reduced debt-to-equity and debt-to-sales ratios. Also find employment levels do not fall after sale. |
| Galal et al. (1994) | Various | Various | 12 | TFP, welfare | Private superior | Compare post-privatisation performance with counter-factual predicted performance of firms had they remained in public sector. Find net welfare gains in 11 of the 12 cases; productivity increases in 9 of the 12 cases. |

44

Table 2.1  Main Findings of Empirical Studies on Privatisation and Performance – *continued*

| Study | Country | Industry | # Firms | Measures | Findings | Summary |
|---|---|---|---|---|---|---|
| Martin and Parker (1995) | UK | Various | 11 | Financial | Ambiguous | Mixed results. Less than half of firms performed better post-privatisation. Several firms improved performance prior to sale but not afterwards. |
| Martin and Parker (1997) | UK | Various | 11 | Financial, LP, TFP, DEA | Ambiguous | Mixed results. LP growth was greater post-privatisation in 6/11 cases but TFP growth greater in only 2/11 cases after divestiture. 8 firms recorded greater profitability under private ownership. |
| Boubakri and Cosset (1998) | Various | Various | 79 | Financial | Private superior | Use same method as MNR. Document significant increases in profitability, operating efficiency, capital investment, output, total employment and dividend payments post-privatisation; decrease in leverage ratios. Insignificant changes in employment. |
| Frydman *et al.* (1999) | Various | Manuf. | 209 | Financial, LP | Ambiguous | Document significant improvements for firms controlled by outsider-owners but insignificant for insider-owners in Central European transition economies. |

**Table 2.1** Main Findings of Empirical Studies on Privatisation and Performance – *continued*

| Study | Country | Industry | # Firms | Measures | Findings | Summary |
|---|---|---|---|---|---|---|
| D'Souza and Megginson (1999) | Various | Various | 85 | Financial | Private superior | Use same methodology and test same hypotheses as MNR. Significant increases in profitability, sales, operating efficiency and dividend payments; decrease in leverage ratios. Insignificant changes in employment. |
| Dewenter and Malatesta (2001) | Various | Various | 63 | Financial | Ambiguous | Similar methodology to MNR. Find significant increases in profitability prior to privatisation but not after. Document significant decreases in leverage and labour intensity after divestiture. |
| Bortolotti *et al.* (2002) | Various | Telecoms | 31 | Financial | Private superior | Find that privatisation is significantly related to higher profitability, output and efficiency and significant decreases in leverage. Authors admit that a sizable fraction of documented improvement results from regulatory changes rather than privatisation alone. |

*Note:* Megginson *et al.* (1994) = MNR; LP = labour productivity; TFP = total factor productivity; DEA = data envelopment analysis.

privatisation of these companies was responsible for any improvement in performance. In terms of employment, D'Souza and Megginson (1999) surprisingly found that average employment rose following privatisation, and that employment levels increased in almost two-thirds of all cases. These findings were consistent with those of Bishop and Kay (1989) who found little reduction in employment in the British privatised companies they examined.

Dewenter and Malatesta (2001) used a similar methodology to Megginson *et al.* (1994) in their analysis of the pre- versus post-privatisation performance of 63 firms in various countries. However, the authors examined a longer time period both before and after divestiture and also controlled for the business cycle. Their results showed that 'much of the firm performance improvement associated with privatization actually occurs over the three years before government reduces its ownership' (Dewenter and Malatesta, 2001: 321). The authors concluded that pre-privatisation performance improvements cannot be attributed to the change of ownership, rather they are driven by the political impetus behind privatisation which impelled SOEs to operate more profitably. The privatisation of these firms then helped to perpetuate efficiency gains in the post-privatisation environment.

The findings of the studies reviewed here are subject to a number of limitations. For example, the studies by Yarrow (1986) and Bishop and Kay (1989) were conducted shortly after privatisation and thus precluded definite conclusions regarding the impact of privatisation. Bishop and Kay (1989) failed to control for national productivity growth in the period they examined. In addition, the time periods covered did not coincide with the ownership change so it is difficult to relate their figures to the act of privatisation as against other possible factors (Martin and Parker, 1997: 88). More generally, few studies have examined the links between privatisation and changes in organisation/management structure, which public choice theories suggest may act together to improve efficiency. One exception is the Megginson *et al.* (1994) study, which examined the association between privatisation and change in the composition of management and board of directors. The authors concluded that 'the greater the change in a firms control structure, the greater the improvement in its operating performance after privatisation' (Megginson *et al.*, 1994: 445).

A study of the privatisation experience of 11 UK companies by Martin and Parker (1997) represents one of the most comprehensive studies of the impact on performance to date. It also addresses most of the weaknesses evident in previous studies discussed above. The impact of privatisation on the efficiency of the firms under review was examined with reference to labour productivity and TFP. Average figures were provided for various periods before and after privatisation and the authors controlled for national productivity trends. The authors concluded that the change in ownership was associated with improved labour productivity in a majority of cases and improved TFP in only two cases. This was:

> ...consistent with the view that state ownership is primarily associated with overstaffing, consequent upon managerial slackness and inefficiency resulting from political intervention [...] The relative TFP results are particularly poor and do not support the view that privatisation will necessarily lead to a major change in the use of all inputs leading to higher efficiency.
>
> (Martin and Parker, 1997: 110–11)

The exercise was repeated using two accounting ratios – return on capital employed (ROCE) and value-added. The writers concluded that 'it is difficult to sustain unequivocally the hypothesis that private ownership is preferable to nationalisation on efficiency grounds' (Martin and Parker, 1997: 124). The ROCE figures displayed general improvement after privatisation but the value-added figures were more mixed.

Further examination of the impact of privatisation on the technical efficiency of the firms was conducted using data envelopment analysis (DEA). This is a linear programming method 'used to derive the relative efficiencies of decision making units, where the presence of multiple inputs and outputs makes it difficult to derive a summary measure of efficiency' (Martin and Parker, 1997: 147). Three different models were used and the results were broadly similar across the three. Although there was evidence of efficiency improvements in three of ten companies following privatisation, there was 'no systematic evidence that public enterprise was less technically efficient than private firms' (Martin and Parker, 1997: 149).

Finally, the authors examined the impact of business restructuring on performance in the context of privatisation and changes in competition. They argued that the effects of the latter two factors tended to work via changes in the internal structure of the organisations. Overall, Martin and Parker found that despite considerable differences across the sample of companies examined, there were features common to all. In summary, they found that privatisation was associated with increased emphasis on the objective of profits and focusing on consumer needs, the introduction of more flexible working practices, a flattening of the organisational structure and introduction of profit centres, and increased activity in disposals and acquisitions as companies become more internationalised (Martin and Parker, 1997). While these changes have occurred at the level of association, it is unlikely that ownership is irrelevant. Although these findings are not as definite as those derived from hypotheses based on more conventional economic analysis, they do draw attention to the relevance of the role of factors inside the 'black box' of organisations. Probing how public sector reforms like privatisation works through the internal processes of organisations can deepen the understanding of policies that are mainly driven by an economic rationale.

## 2.5   Privatisation and social welfare

Whereas the studies reviewed above concentrate on the key question of enterprise performance and efficiency, it is important to recognise that economic efficiency accounts for only one part of overall social welfare. From a policymaking perspective, the social welfare consequences of privatisation are paramount, and a consideration of this wider dimension requires an examination of distributional issues. However, the international literature has paid little attention to the social welfare aspect of privatisation policy. This is largely due to methodological difficulties, since a proper examination of social welfare effects would require a cost-benefit analysis, with identification of the winners and losers, measurement of gains and losses, and some form of social weighting of the gains and losses (Parker, 1999). Consequently, most studies that have examined the social welfare aspects of privatisation tend to be partial analyses that focus on one particular stakeholder or a group of stakeholders. In general these studies have analysed the impact on groups such as workers (in terms of employment and wages), shareholders (in terms of share prices and profits), and consumers (in terms of prices and services). We return to some of these analyses below, but first we draw attention to two studies that have adopted a more comprehensive approach to measuring the overall welfare and redistributive effects of privatisation.

Galal *et al.* (1994) and Florio (2004) have provided the most complete analyses of the winners and losers from privatisation. Galal *et al.* (1994) assessed the impact of ownership change on all relevant actors and stakeholders in the privatisation of twelve companies in three developing countries and the UK. The authors adopted a counterfactual approach in order to isolate the effects of ownership change from broader economic shifts and events, and reported net welfare gains in eleven of the twelve cases. Despite the fact that their analysis is comprehensive, the small size of their sample means that their results cannot be generalised.

Florio (2004) used a social cost-benefit analysis framework to examine the welfare impact of the UK privatisation programme between 1979 and 1997. The author estimated the change in welfare for consumers, taxpayers, firms, shareholders and workers and concluded that privatisation *per se* had little overall impact on welfare. The redistributive effect was, however, far from negligible, with the net beneficiaries of privatisation belonging to the wealthiest 10–20 per cent of the population, and the net losers belonging to the bottom 10–20 per cent cohort. Net beneficiaries gained from factors including the purchase of discounted shares, regressive tariff rebalancing, and price discrimination in favour of high users. Net losers incurred losses due to increased tariffs, job losses and greater job insecurity.

Returning to studies that have focused on specific sets of stakeholders, a number of authors have examined the impact of privatisation on labour. Haskel and Szymanski (1992, 1993) examine the employment effects of the privatisation of fourteen UK public enterprises. While employment fell following the change to more commercial objectives, wages were only slightly affected. However, if the firm lost market power, there was a corresponding decrease in wages. Martin and Parker (1997) found mixed evidence in relation to the impact of privatisation on employment levels in the 11 UK privatised SOEs in their study. The authors also found ambiguous evidence in relation to wages per employee relative to the economy as a whole, with no common trend in wage relativities observed in the pre- versus post-privatisation periods. The mixed nature of the results from the above studies suggests that effects on labour are industry-specific and that privatisation will not automatically result in major changes in employment.

Proponents of privatisation commonly cite reduced consumer prices and improved service. This is attributed to efficiency gains being passed on to consumers in the form of lower prices. The experience with privatisation of utilities in the UK suggests that price reductions are dependent on ownership in conjunction with competition, regulation and technological change. The post-privatisation experience has been one of falling prices in privatised utilities in the UK, reflecting gains in productive efficiency. Parker (2003) provides some examples: in telecommunications, average charges fell by around 40 per cent (in real terms) between 1987 and 1997; in the gas sector, domestic gas bills fell by an average of 2.6 per cent per year after privatisation (in real terms); and in electricity, a decline of 26 per cent in charges to domestic users was recorded. The exception to this trend was the water and sewerage industry where domestic charges rose sharply after privatisation, by over 40 per cent (in real terms). It is noteworthy that Parker stresses that the price reductions observed in the telecommunications industry result 'from changes in technology and competition in addition to ownership change and regulation' (2003: 13). Moreover, the price increases recorded in the water sector reflect the lack of competition in water services since privatisation.

An important objective of the UK privatisation programme, as well as those of other European countries, has been to promote wider share ownership or 'popular democracy' along with employee share ownership. Share issue privatisations of many of the largest utilities and banking companies across Europe have often involved significant transfers of wealth from general taxpayers to small shareholders and employees. Parker (1999) states that, although many European governments view privatisation as a useful means of promoting wider share ownership and developing domestic capital markets, the extent to which new small shareholders are investing for the long-term or for short-term speculative gains is unclear. For example, of the two million German citizens that bought Deutsche Telekom shares in 1996, approximately one-half had sold their shareholdings within one year (Parker, 1999). A similar pattern of 'stagging' was recorded for early UK privatisations: for example, within one year of flotation, the number of small shareholders in British Aerospace fell from 158,000 to 27,000 (Vickers and Yarrow, 1988: 189). Later UK privatisations did more to increase the number of shareholders by offering significant incentives to retain shares.

While there was evidence that share ownership was widened as a result of the UK programme, it failed to deepen. A survey conducted by the Confederation of British Industry in 1990 estimated that only 14 per cent of 10.6 million shareholders owned shares in four or more companies, while 61 per cent of shareholders held shares in just one company. Moreover, a separate survey conducted in 1988 found that the owners of shares were drawn disproportionately from the middle classes, in particular males and the middle-aged (Saunders and Harris, 1994: 144). The same authors also conducted their own examination of the impact of privatisation on share ownership and found evidence that share ownership was more widespread than indicated by the aforementioned studies.

The implications of privatisation for wider social welfare are of enormous importance, but conducting a comprehensive analysis of these issues poses considerable methodological challenges. Many of the available studies covering welfare or distributional impacts of privatisation tend to focus on certain stakeholders such as employees and shareholders. In later chapters we follow the latter approach by focusing on the welfare effects of Ireland's privatisation experience in relation to employees, citizens and the exchequer.

## 2.6   Conclusion

This chapter has reviewed the arguments and evidence with regard to the objectives commonly ascribed to privatisation policies. Overall, the empirical evidence with regard to the impact of privatisation on enterprise performance mirrors the thrust of relevant economic theories. Notwithstanding problems with performance measurement, which can have a significant bearing on results, the general conclusion we can draw is that privatisation leads to improved enterprise performance in some, but not all, cases. As Parker (2000: xx) points out, this poses a challenge for economists to 'investigate the conditions under which privatisation is most likely to succeed or fail.' While there is strong evidence concerning the positive role played by competition in relevant product markets, there remains scope for detailed examination of how institutional factors such as the regulatory framework and the characteristics of capital markets contribute to changes in enterprise performance in the context of privatisation.

The wider impact on social welfare is also considered. Privatisation and related policies such as liberalisation have wide ranging implications for the economy and society. Despite the methodological difficulties involved, a number of studies have sought to illuminate impacts of privatisation beyond those concerning enterprise performance. These include the redistributive impacts of privatisation that arise when key stakeholders lose or gain following the sale of state assets, and which can have a significant bearing on the wider welfare of society. We turn our attention to such aspects of privatisation in the Irish context in later chapters. To lay the contextual ground for these chapters, Chapter 3 describes the extent of privatisation activity in Ireland and seeks to understand the key factors that have shaped the evolution and implementation of privatisation policies.

# 3
# Public Enterprise and Privatisation in Ireland

## 3.0 Introduction

When measured in terms of the number of divestitures or the size of revenues, privatisation activity in Ireland has been low in international terms. This, however, is a reflection of the size of the Irish economy rather than the scale or reach of privatisation activity in Ireland. As we show in this chapter, the Irish state has withdrawn from direct activity in a number of key sectors of the economy including telecommunications, air transport, shipping and banking (though this was reversed following the banking crisis in 2008). Besides altering the composition and structure of these sectors, divestitures have had a considerable impact on the exchequer as well as different stakeholders. Nevertheless, the history of privatisation in Ireland differs significantly from that of the UK and other comparable countries in terms of the timing and rationale for sales, as well as the details of divestitures. In addition, the state continues to play an important and sometimes dominant role in key areas of economic activity such as energy, airports and transport.

This chapter describes the details of Ireland's programme of privatisation to date. It looks to commonly accepted explanations for the adoption of privatisation policies and demonstrates that Ireland fails to fit neatly with such explanations. Instead, the pursuit of privatisation in the case of Ireland owes more to pragmatism and a peculiar mix of forces that are unique to the Irish case.

## 3.1 The development of state-owned enterprise in Ireland

Before dealing with the question of privatisation it is necessary to explore the original rationale for creating SOEs in Ireland. This creates a context for understanding privatisation policies, but also to highlight the continued importance of the SOE sector in Ireland. Chapter 1 (section 1.2) provided a brief overview of the common factors that underpinned the growth of public enterprise in Europe up until the 1980s. These factors included post-war political ideologies, industrial reconstruction, the rationalisation of key sectors in the economy, regional development, and national wealth development. While a number of these factors apply at different points in Ireland's history, a number of unique internal factors assist in explaining the precise rationale for the extent of SOE development in the Irish case.

The evolution of a significant SOE sector in Ireland dates back to the foundations of the state. Breen *et al.* (1990: 22) state that following independence in 1922, the balance of forces favoured an auxiliary state which was 'supplementary, though not necessarily subordinate, to other institutions within the society'. However, pressures to adopt substantial interventionist measures also existed. Breen *et al.* (1990: 24) quote Sinn Féin's Democratic Programme of 1919, which promised each citizen the right to 'an adequate share of the produce of the Nation's labour'. The authors argue that the development of public enterprises over subsequent decades was a creeping legacy of this document and represented an exception to the minimalist approach to state activity adopted prior to the opening up of the economy in 1958.

The scheme to generate electricity from the river Shannon during the 1920s marked the beginning of the Electricity Supply Board (ESB), the first major commercial public enterprise development in the fledgling Irish state. The scheme was initiated amid enormous controversy, with objections based on issues ranging from the socialist dimension of nationalising the 90 existing private electrical utilities, to the fact that the contractor (Siemens) was German. Ironically, the champion of the scheme in government was the Minister for Industry and Commerce, Patrick McGilligan, who was noted for his conservatism and opposition to interventionist policies. In fact, McGilligan's stance provides a revealing insight into the motivations for state control of the scheme. He originally travelled extensively around the USA to canvass companies to run the scheme, but concluded that electricity was too important to be controlled by interests whose only objective was the maximisation of profit (Sweeney, 1990). In 1925, the *Shannon Electricity Bill*, which legislated for the provision of electricity by the state, was published and the state-owned ESB was established through the 1927 *Electricity (Supply) Act*. Once the Shannon scheme commenced in 1925, it was used to play a role in government policy to control wages and working conditions. This was detailed by Manning and

McDowell (1984) who explain how McGilligan not only succeeded in extracting cheap labour, but placed strict limits on the profits accrued by the main contractor Siemens.

After this precedent was set, successive governments used public enterprise as an instrument for securing the economic development of the newly independent state. The specific rationale varied from case to case, but the establishment of SOEs was primarily driven by the necessity for the extraordinary needs of the new state to be satisfied through state efforts. The first transfer of power in the history of the Free State followed the 1932 general election, when Eamon de Valera's first Fianna Fáil government embarked on the ushering in of a new era of protectionism directed towards self-sufficiency and economic independence from Britain.

A number of SOEs were established in the drive towards self-sufficiency in agriculture, industry, investment and production. Sweeney (1990) charts the growth of these enterprises during the era of import-substitution development, with the establishment of the Irish Sugar Company in 1933 representing a prototype SOE. The Industrial Credit Corporation (ICC) was also established in 1933 to counter the shortage of funds, particularly long-term credit for industry. The Agricultural Credit Corporation (ACC) had been established in 1927 to provide a similar service for agriculture. Ceimici Teo was originally set up in 1939 to manufacture industrial alcohol from surplus potatoes and later expanded its operations to all kinds of chemicals. The government entered aviation transport in 1936, with the establishment of Aer Lingus, the national airline. In 1937, Aer Rianta, the airports authority, took over the management of Dublin Airport (on an agency basis), from the Department of Transport.

The drive towards self-sufficiency was a necessity rather than an option during World War II and the proliferation of SOEs continued apace. Irish Shipping was established in 1941 to ensure the security of the import and export of essential goods. Córas Iompair Éireann (CIE) was formed in 1944, after the nationalised Great Southern Railway and United Dublin Tramway Companies were merged with the Grand Canal Company. Irish Steel and Arramara Teo (a seaweed processing company) were formed after the nationalisation of private companies in financial difficulty in 1946 and 1949 respectively. In the financial sector, the Irish Life Assurance Company was established in 1939 after the nationalisation of five UK insurance companies which the state had already invested in, and in 1957 the Voluntary Health Insurance company was founded to cater for those not covered by the Health Acts.

The establishment of these SOEs between 1927 and 1958 was one of a number of examples serving to highlight the increasing autonomy

Table 3.1    Commercial State-Owned Enterprises in Ireland by the 1980s

| Company | Established | Sector |
|---|---|---|
| Agricultural Credit Corporation | 1927 | Banking & Finance |
| Electricity Supply Board | 1927 | Electricity |
| Industrial Credit Corporation | 1933 | Banking & Finance |
| Irish Sugar | 1933 | Sugar Production |
| Aer Lingus | 1936 | Air Transport |
| Aer Rianta | 1937 | Airports |
| Ceimici Teo (closed 1986) | 1939 | Chemicals |
| Irish Life | 1939 | Insurance |
| Irish Shipping (closed 1984) | 1941 | Sea Transport |
| Córas Iompair Éireann | 1944 | Rail and Road Transport |
| Bord na Móna | 1946 | Peat Production |
| Irish Steel | 1946 | Steel Production |
| Arramara Teo | 1949 | Seaweed Processing |
| Voluntary Health Insurance | 1957 | Health Insurance |
| Raidió Teilifís Éireann | 1960 | Broadcasting |
| Nítrigin Éireann Teo – IFI | 1961 | Fertiliser Production |
| B&I Line | 1965 | Sea Transport |
| Foir Teo | 1972 | Banking |
| Bord Gáis Éireann | 1976 | Gas Distribution |
| Irish National Petroleum Corporation | 1979 | Oil Refining & Supply |
| Bord Telecom Éireann | 1984 | Telecommunications |
| An Post | 1984 | Postal Services |
| Coillte Teo | 1989 | Forestry |

and capacity of the new state in terms of its ability to formulate and pursue its own objectives over this period. It also demonstrates the active rather than passive role of the state in this period. SOEs were a crucial instrument in the more active state's arsenal. When the era of economic planning and outward orientation was embarked upon in 1958, SOEs were positioned to implement the broad policies advanced by government departments.

The rate at which SOEs were established continued to increase over the period of economic planning (1958–72). The dismantlement of protection and adoption of outward-looking policies with an emphasis on exports and the attraction of foreign direct investment led to the creation of state agencies 'mostly confined to servicing the needs of private capital, providing advice and information on matters such as export marketing and investment opportunities and the expenditure plans of the public sector' (O'Malley, 1989: 86). These agencies included Córas Tráchtála, the Irish Export Board, and three agencies responsible for the encouragement of foreign investment: the Shannon Free Airport Development Company, the Industrial Development Company and An Foras Tionscail. Gaeltarra Éireann (now Údarás na Gaeltachta) was founded in 1959 for the development of Irish speaking areas (Gaeltachta), the National Building Agency was set up in 1960 to provide housing near newly built industrial estates, and Bord Iascaigh Mhara was established in 1952 to develop the fishing industry. Among the more commercial SOEs founded after 1958 were: Raidió Teiliefís Éireann, the national broadcasting agency (1960); the fertiliser company Nítrigin Éireann Teo (1961); and B&I Line, the ferry company, which was formed in 1965 following the nationalisation of an ailing UK private company.

SOE creation continued during the 1970s. In 1972, a state rescue bank, Foir Teo, was established to aid industrial firms with credit difficulties. Bord Gáis Éireann, the monopoly distributor of natural gas, was set up in 1976. Three companies were corporatised from the civil service during the 1980s: Telecom Éireann and An Post in 1984, and Coillte Teo, the state forestry company in 1989. Of the 100 or so bodies in existence at the beginning of the 1980s, the great majority were established during the planning era (1958–72). Approximately 23 of these bodies fell into the 'commercial SOE category' at the beginning of the 1980s. These bodies (see Table 3.1) were set up to engage in the production of goods and services for sale, while the remainder were active in administrating or regulating some area of social or economic activity, or carrying out developmental activities associated with industry (Chubb, 1982: 271). Their formation was often *ad hoc* but principally owed to the urgency of the task of developing the national wealth of a state lacking in basic industries (Parris *et al.*, 1987: 21). This urgency, allied to the accompanying dearth of private enterprise and the conditions necessary to foster private initiative (for example, access to risk capital), bolstered the state's growing autonomy (Lee, 1989; O'Malley, 1989), thereby mobilising the formation of SOEs in the pursuit of state goals.

## 3.2   Different explanations of privatisation

To what extent, if any, does the history of privatisation in Ireland fit with explanations for the adoption of such policies offered in the relevant academic literature? As we noted in Chapter 2, the initial rise in the popularity of privatisation policies was attributable to theories of government failure such as property rights and public choice theory. Whereas discussions on the relevance of public choice theory in the context of privatisation normally concentrate on the comparative performance of public versus private enterprise, Foster (1994), for example, draws on the Chicago and Virginia schools of public choice to examine the course of privatisation in the UK. He explains how George Stigler's economic theory of politics (or Chicago theory) postulates that 'all parties to a political or legislative change are moved by their financial self-interest' (Foster, 1994: 494). In the context of privatisation, the hypothesis to be drawn from this perspective is that SOE managers have an incentive to lobbyrelevant ministers and politicians in favour of privatisation when they associate a change in ownership with significant personal gains. Virginian political economy sees relations between government ministers and SOE managers as based on levels of bargaining which allow certain levels of political interference at the expense of economic efficiency. It is proposed that political interventions in relation to issues such as pricing or the provision of non-economic services are tolerated if they do not cause damage to the fundamental interests of SOE managers. Virginian political economy provides explanations for privatisation where such policies are driven by political or non-economic objectives, such as reducing trade union power, widening share ownership or seeking to increase support for the sponsoring political party.

As privatisation policies became more popular, they were accompanied by rapid growth in the analysis of such policies. Although much of the earlier analytic work was driven by normative agendas and was aimed at improving the formulation and implementation of privatisation programmes (Yarrow, 1999: 157), there was significant growth in the number of positive theories of privatisation which are reviewed in Chapter 2. As we have seen, most of these theoretical contributions adopt a mainly economic perspective, focusing on the relationship between privatisation and efficiency. The thrust of these perspectives is neatly captured by Clifton *et al.* (2003: 1) who, in a critical sense, argue that explanations of privatisation have been driven by a dominant discourse that describes a global shift from state to market, due to the assumption that a change of ownership from public to private status would release enterprises from the 'shackles of bureaucracy' and lead them via the 'cold winds of market forces' to economic efficiency. Both Yarrow (1999) and Clifton *et al.* (2003) have sought to address the shortcomings they perceived in relation to available explanations of privatisation.

Yarrow (1999) seeks to understand questions such as why countries characterised by different institutional structures, and at different stages of development, have pursued similar policy strategies. More specifically, given the extensive evidence in favour of privatisation as a means of improving enterprise performance, he investigates why so many countries (particularly developing countries) have engaged in low levels of privatisation. Yarrow does not dismiss the importance of positive theories of privatisation, such as those in the principal-agent tradition which explain privatisation in terms of the efficiency benefits that arise following the change to private ownership. He does, however, argue that such a factor 'is likely to be relatively stable over time' (1999: 167) and his focus is therefore on developing a dynamic model of privatisation. He proposes that privatisation should be seen as a natural stage in the life cycle of an SOE. Over time, shifts in factors such as institutions, political influence and technologies can be expected. As a consequence, it is natural for the portfolio of state activities to adjust over time.

Yarrow's model predicts that privatisation is triggered by fiscal crises that arise due to high levels of government expenditure and rising rates of taxation. In such circumstances, the budget allocated to an SOE is squeezed. This may be manifested in terms of a reduction in the amount of finance made available for new investment, but, over time, the typical sequence is for tighter budgets to be followed by privatisation. In relation to the type of activities to be privatised, Yarrow (1999: 166) predicts that the most likely candidates will be those producing outputs 'whose benefits rise less slowly than national income and which are not subject to counteracting reductions in costs'. Examples of SOE activities that fall into this category might include those that are subsidised to protect the development of a sector (for example, infant industries, or networks such as those in the telecommunications sector which are less of a development priority as an economy develops). A further prediction derived from Yarrow's model is that privatisation is more likely in recessionary times.

Clifton *et al.* (2003) seek to articulate an alternative to perspectives such as public choice theory, which they believe have dominated the discourse on privatisation and underscored privatisation policy in countries such as the UK (the generally accepted pioneer of privatisation), as well as in powerful multilateral organisations such as the World Bank and the International Monetary Fund (IMF). They explore the logic of integration to illuminate privatisation in the EU. They highlight how some European countries (for example, the UK, France, Italy and Spain) embarked on privatisation policies in the 1980s, but how:

> ...the bulk of privatisation activity across the EU occurred during the 1990s, specifically from 1993. This suggests that the need to implement sectoral liberalization in the light of the Single Common Market and the Maastricht Treaty in 1992 were far more influential factors for

governments when introducing privatisation reforms than pro-market discourse (Clifton *et al.*, 2003: 3).

EU directives that have shaped approaches to privatisation policy in member states cover issues such as state aids, liberalisation and monetary union. Parker (1999), in his review of privatisation within the region, noted that EU policy on the ownership of industry has traditionally been neutral. Instead, the emphasis is on competitive markets rather than ownership. This had particular implications for SOEs in terms of state aids to companies. Article 92 of the Treaty of Rome forbids state aid that distorts competition between member states, although in practice, derogations have been granted by the EC to allow for other policy objectives, such as regional development. This prohibition on state aids has had implications for individual country policy on SOEs, particularly those that are loss making.

The Single European Act which came into force on 1 July 1987 brought about significant changes that had implications for government policy on state-owned utilities. As the Act was intended to remove remaining non-tariff barriers to trade within the European Community by 1992, it led to the EC applying pressure on member states to open utility markets up to competition. The adoption of a 'vertical approach' meant that progress in this respect varied across sectors with some markets (for example, telecommunications and electricity) moving more rapidly towards liberalisation compared to others (for example, the gas and postal sectors). Although moves towards liberalisation do not necessitate accompanying measures of privatisation, Parker (2003: 118) notes that privatisation 'to the extent that Member states judge it compatible with their objectives could further progress already made' in the direction of liberalisation.

The progressive integration of the EU has also influenced privatisation policies in member states by creating fiscal reasons to privatise. The Maastricht criteria for membership of the single European currency set targets for reductions in deficit and debt levels. Receipts from the sale of SOEs were an attractive proposition for governments seeking to meet these criteria. Although the EC does not allow privatisation receipts to be included in the calculation of deficits, it is possible to use these receipts to retire government debt, which will indirectly reduce budget deficits via lower interest payments. Hence, there is an incentive to privatise in order to pursue fiscal objectives.

## 3.3 Privatisation activity in Ireland

Bearing these explanations in mind we now turn to the extent of privatisation activity in Ireland and examine the nature of privatisation

Table 3.2   Privatised SOEs in Ireland and Exchequer Proceeds

| Company | Year of sale | Exchequer proceeds (€'000s) |
| --- | --- | --- |
| Irish Sugar | Apr. 1991 | 210,650.8 |
| Irish Life | Jul. 1991 | 601,930.8 |
| B&I Line | Jan. 1992 | 10,792.8 |
| Irish Steel | Apr. 1996 | 0 |
| Telecom Éireann | Jul. 1999 | 6,399,907.9 |
| Industrial Credit Corporation | Feb. 2001 | 322,274.8 |
| Trustee Savings Bank | Apr. 2001 | 408,350.3 |
| Irish National Petroleum Corporation | Jul. 2001 | 20,000.0 |
| Agricultural Credit Corporation | Feb. 2002 | 154,603.0 |
| Aer Lingus | Oct. 2006 | 240,902.3 |
| **Total** | | **8,369,412.7** |

*Source*: Authors' own calculations from Exchequer Statements.
*Notes*: (1) The table above details direct proceeds accruing to the exchequer only. Indirect proceeds that accrued to the privatised company are excluded. For example, when Aer Lingus was floated on the stock exchange in 2006, the government allowed the airline to issue new shares which raised over €530 million for the company.

policy in the context of explanations offered in the privatisation literature. Table 3.2 shows that, to date, ten Irish SOEs have been privatised raising gross proceeds of over €8.36 billion. In international comparative terms the scale of the Irish privatisation programme has been small, but in domestic terms the privatisation programme, along with measures in relation to liberalisation and regulation, has brought about significant changes in the structure and composition of key sectors of the Irish economy such as telecommunications, banking, air and sea transport.

The history of privatisation in Ireland has been shaped by a host of factors, some of which apply to other European countries (for example, rules in relation to state aids to industry) and others that are unique to the Irish context. In the following section, we examine the factors that explain the privatisation programme to date, and the extent to which the explanations for privatisation described earlier apply in the Irish case. To gain an understanding of these issues, it is necessary to examine government policy on the SOE sector in the years before privatisation.

## 3.4   SOE policy in the 1980s: Commercialisation before privatisation

Although privatisation policies gained international popularity in the mid to late 1980s, the option was eschewed in Ireland until 1991.[1] This is particularly noteworthy when one considers that Ireland experienced an acute fiscal crisis in the 1980s and privatisation would have presented an attractive opportunity to raise exchequer revenues. Instead, government policy on SOEs in the 1980s was largely focused on improving the commercial performance of the sector. Poor financial performance in many SOEs became a matter of significant concern as the public finances deteriorated in the early 1980s. This was highlighted in a number of official reports and policy documents in the early 1980s, all of which advocated commercialisation with 'primary emphasis [...] to be placed on commercial viability and profits' (*Building on Reality*, 1984: 67). Most SOEs adopted an increased business focus from the mid-1980s onwards. Sweeney (1990, 1998) analysed the financial performance of the SOE sector since the early 1980s and concluded that:

> ...state-owned companies, including the monopolies have been commercialised. Several of them had been unprofitable, poorly managed, and some made poor investments. All shifted into a far more commercial mode in the period under review (1987–96). Most are now profitable.
>
> (Sweeney, 1998: 96)

This emphasis on commercialisation rather than changes in ownership can be viewed in terms of the wider institutional context which shaped the formulation of economic and social policy in Ireland from the late 1980s. Drawing on the strategic programme for economic recovery provided by the National Economic and Social Council (NESC) in their report *A Strategy for Development, 1986–1990*, a series of negotiated agreements between government and key interest groups (primarily trade unions, employer and business organisations, farming organisations, and later the voluntary sector) were initiated in 1987. Allen (2000: 14) asserts that when the first agreement, the *Programme for National Recovery*, was approved in 1987, the then Taoiseach (Prime Minister), Charles Haughey, promised the trade unions that the main government party, Fianna Fáil, would not sell off any commercial SOEs. As a consequence, the agreement enunciated policies that aimed to expand rather than privatise the SOE sector.

This institutional check on privatisation policy was, however, short-lived. The early 1990s witnessed a gradual shift in policy concerning the ownership of SOEs. This coincided with a significant change in the political context, with the pro-privatisation Progressive Democrats (PDs) entering government for the first time as the minor party in the new coalition formed in 1989. The second social partnership agreement, the *Programme for Economic and Social Progress* (PESP), which was signed in 1991, set out a number of principles in relation to SOEs, including agreed principles on the question of private involvement in the shape of joint ventures and the sale of shares (PESP, 1991: 51). These developments coincided with the decisions to privatise two SOEs, the Irish Sugar Company (now Greencore) and the state-owned insurance company, Irish Life Assurance, by initial public offering (IPO) in 1991. While this wider institutional context certainly paved the way for the introduction of privatisation policies, the key factor in the case of the first two sales was the ability of top management in both companies to successfully pursue their pro-privatisation agendas.

### 3.4.1   The first sales: Top management driving the agenda

The privatisation of both the Irish Sugar and the Irish Life Assurance Companies in 1991 represented a break with the traditional approach to government policy on SOEs that consistently fell short of considering changes in ownership. In both companies the decision to privatise was driven by key decisionmakers within the company. Their success in bringing both companies to the stock market lends support for the Chicagoan explanation of privatisation in terms of the preferences of top management and their ability to lobby relevant government ministers and officials.

Sweeney (1990) details how Irish Life was the first Irish SOE to mention privatisation, when the directors in the 1980 annual report hinted at the possibility of a change in ownership. A year later, the then managing director, R.P. Willis, stated that he found the government's involvement with Irish Life a hindrance to the company's marketing in both Ireland and the UK, and that the company did not wish 'to be associated with the stigma of state bodies' (Sweeney, 1990: 27). In the late 1980s, Irish Life began looking to expand in North America, however this was hindered by the fact that approximately half of the States in the USA had legal objections to companies controlled by other governments. Irish Life was also constrained by limited access to funds for growth due to its capital structure. The company felt that there would come a time when extra funds would be needed for expansion and that it was unlikely that the state would be of any help. All of these factors led to the proposal for privatisation by the board of directors of Irish Life to the government.

The critical role of top management in driving the privatisation agenda is particularly evident in the case of the Irish Sugar company, where the company's chief executive, Chris Comerford, and chairman,

Bernie Cahill, drove the privatisation initiative from its inception to fruition, despite a significant degree of opposition and scepticism from other stakeholders, including members of the company's board of directors. The case articulated for the privatisation of Irish Sugar can be traced back to the increasingly poor financial performance of the company towards the end of the 1970s. Persistently low profits and the requirement for an ongoing capital investment programme to modernise its sugar factories, financed in the main from borrowings, resulted in a serious deterioration in the financial structure of the company. Concern over resultant high debt-equity ratios was therefore a recurring issue in the annual reports of Irish Sugar for a decade before privatisation, as is evident from the following chairman's statement:

> In previous annual reports I have expressed my concern at our Company's inadequate capital base. The financial situation of the group dictates that I must highlight forcefully the basic weakness in this area [...] It is imperative that our equity base be strengthened and that a crippling factor in our operation be removed.
>
> (Irish Sugar, 1980: 8)

Despite two injections of equity into Irish Sugar in the mid-1980s, which raised equity share capital from €8.9 million in 1980 to €83.8 million in 1990, the need for access to non-debt capital continued as a persistent theme in the company's annual reports throughout the decade. Direct references to privatisation were, however, avoided. In fact, minutes of the meetings of directors indicate a degree of conflict within the board on the issue. For example, minutes dated May 1989 record a statement by the chairman, Bernie Cahill, saying that 'as far as he was aware the known policy [of the board] would not favour privatisation'.[2]

Despite recognising this opposition, however, Cahill proceeded to independently argue for privatisation. In his statement in the company annual report of September 1989, the chairman replaced previous pleas for additional government equity with arguments in favour of access to the stock market and privatisation:

> ...it must be recognised that to be successful in acquiring or investing in new enterprises and/or joint ventures, one must be competitive in the type of package that can be offered. Access to sufficient funds is an important pre-requisite to any major development. It is neither reasonable nor practical to expect the government to fund further acquisitions. It is not commercially feasible to fund significant

purchases by recourse to increased borrowing alone. The Group could only be expanded slowly if it was dependant on funding from internal sources. Indeed, it is arguable that in these circumstances it could not make significant investments as by their nature such opportunities will not wait until the Group has accumulated sufficient cash. The development plan must therefore, be financed by alternative methods and this, in effect, means access to the stock market.

(Irish Sugar, 1989: 10)

The chairman's views with regard to privatisation were in accord with those of another key figure in the process – managing director, Chris Comerford. The preference for privatisation expressed by both the chairman and managing director continued to conflict, however, with at least some members of the board of directors. Indeed, minutes from a meeting of the board of directors in February 1990 indicate that some members of the board felt they were being dealt a *fait accompli*:

Concern was expressed that this was the first opportunity that the board was given to discuss privatisation. The media was dealing with it on a daily basis and the Chairman's Statement in the Accounts was taken as the Board's view on the matter.[3]

The same minutes recorded that in response to this concern, the chairman stated that his comments in the annual report were his personal observations on the company and its future development. Despite the expressed reservation of some board members with regard to privatisation, developments continued apace. Minutes of meetings in February and March 1990 recorded discussion of privatisation-related topics such as retention of the sugar quota, a cap on the amount of equity that could be held by any shareholder, the use of a golden share and possible government veto of the disposal of assets in the sugar business.

Minutes recorded in March 1990 further highlight the division of board opinion on the issue of privatisation, with a proposal that the board indicate its view to the Minister on the likely share sale rejected on the basis of the inability 'to form a cohesive opinion largely because of a lack of knowledge of all issues involved'.[4] By December 1990, any opposition was futile as copies of the *Sugar Bill 1990*, which paved the way for the company's privatisation under the new name Greencore, were circulated to the board of directors. The wishes of the key players, in other words, the chairman and managing director, were realised.

Whereas top management played an undoubted role in ensuring that both Irish Life and Irish Sugar were privatised, the attraction of exchequer revenues should also be recognised as an important determinant of the final government decisions in this regard. In both cases, government statements mainly justified privatisation in terms of ensuring the survival of the companies, but, as Yarrow (1999) suggests, securing exchequer revenues also played a part. For example, prior to the sale of Irish Sugar the Minister of Finance, Albert Reynolds, stated in his budget speech that he had

> ...made a prudent provision in the White Paper on Receipts and Expenditure for a further increase in sales [of state assets] in the current year. This is the first phase of a new five-year programme of such sales so as to reduce the national debt.
>
> (Budget Book, 1990: 34)

This objective gained greater prominence in the sale of the government's remaining shares in Irish Sugar/Greencore.[5] In the second public offering of Greencore shares, a 15 per cent stake was placed on the stock market at a fixed price in February 1992, despite government undertakings after the initial public offering (IPO) that there would be no further offerings for two more years. The sale generated revenues of over €40 million that helped to meet commitments under the second social partnership agreement – the PESP – which required the Minister to seek savings of around €127 million. If the Greencore receipts had not been included in the budgetary figures, this would have increased the exchequer borrowing requirement (EBR) to over €760 million, thereby risking a negative reaction in the market for sovereign debt.

The remaining 30 per cent of government-held shares in Greencore were also sold to financial institutions at a fixed price. The government did consider selling to an international food company (Archer Daniels Midland) in keeping with the expressed desire of the company, but yielded to political objections on the grounds of selling to a foreign investor. The placement of these shares in 1993 yielded revenues of almost €89 million. In effect, this meant that Irish Sugar/Greencore was fully private-owned within two years of the initial flotation of shares, despite the initial justification of partial privatisation on the grounds that it was in the interest of employment and beet growing in Ireland.

### 3.4.2   No room for loss makers – The sales of B&I Line and Irish Steel

The policies of successive governments towards SOEs in the early 1990s continued to be characterised by a large degree of pragmatism. Although the sales of Irish Sugar and Irish Life set a precedent for privatisation, the thrust of government policy remained cautious in this regard, with the emphasis mainly placed on improving commercial performance rather than necessarily changing ownership.

This commercial imperative had become increasingly evident during Ireland's fiscal crisis of the 1980s, when successive governments adopted 'get tough' policies in relation to poorly performing SOEs. This approach was exemplified by decisions to place two SOEs into liquidation. The first such company was Irish Shipping, which was put into liquidation in 1984. The company entered into speculative long-term chartering agreements which were greatly above market prices. This resulted in a rapid escalation of debt that the company could not service. Rather than propping up the poorly managed enterprise, the government took the unprecedented decision to put the company into liquidation in 1984. This was followed by the closure of a smaller SOE, Ceimici Teo, in 1986.

Poor financial performance and high levels of indebtedness raised the spectre of liquidation for two other SOEs in the 1990s. However, in the cases of B&I Line and the Irish Steel Company, privatisation by selling the enterprises as going concerns presented a more acceptable alternative that was no longer blocked by social partnership agreements or any lack of precedent for changing ownership. In the case of the ferry company, B&I Line, which was sold in 1992, accumulated losses stood at €170.71 million in 1991 and the company remained heavily reliant on exchequer funding to service its debt. This was the main factor behind the decision in 1990 to examine the future options for the company, with the government eventually opting for privatisation rather than liquidation or further exchequer funding. After examining a number of proposed bids from interested parties, including a consortium of B&I Line management and Danish backers, the government decided to sell the company to Irish Continental Group (ICG). On 31 January 1992, B&I Line was acquired for €10.79 million and, as part of the deal, the government agreed to pay off existing accumulated debt of some €44.4 million.[6]

The Irish Steel Company, which was sold in 1996, had been in financial difficulty for a number of years and had become heavily reliant on government funding. Between 1980 and 1993, Irish Steel received €234.9 million in funding from the government but continued to incur heavy losses.[7] After incurring a net loss of €16.48 million in 1993, Irish Steel attempted to implement cost reduction measures. Protracted resistance by trade unions had ended when it became apparent that the board of directors made a recommendation to government that the company be liquidated if agreement was not reached. Even with the eventual acceptance of a viability plan, Irish Steel was still in an extremely poor financial position. The board of directors submitted a final survival plan in November 1994, which included a request for some €63.5 million in state aid. Rather than put the company into liquidation, the government decided to follow the board's recommendation with a view to finding a buyer for the company.

After receiving a number of applications, the government sold Irish Steel to ISPAT International in April 1996. At the time, the company, founded in India, was the world's largest producer and consumer of iron produced from iron ore, and one of the world's largest producers of liquid steel. ISPAT had a track record of acquiring state-owned steel enterprises and turning them around.[8] Irish Steel was sold for a nominal sum of IRP£1[9] due to the large amount of debt on the company's balance sheet.

The privatisation of both B&I Line and Irish Steel, as well as the liquidation of other poorly performing SOEs, signalled the clear imperative of satisfactory commercial performance for Irish SOEs. Moreover, decisions in relation to these companies demonstrated the growing influence of increased European integration on SOE policy. The requirement for greater fiscal discipline built into the Maastricht criteria for membership of a single European currency, as well as obstacles to state aids to failing enterprises were relevant to the privatisation of both Irish Steel and B&I Line. Another aspect of increased integration, namely the liberalisation of markets dominated by state-owned utilities, had a significant bearing on the next privatisation, that of Telecom Éireann, the national telecommunications company.

### 3.4.3   Privatising the first utility – Telecom Éireann

The privatisation of Telecom Éireann represents the most significant divestiture in Ireland to date, and the decision to fully privatise the company in 1999 can be attributed to a number of the explanations for privatisation described in this chapter. Telecommunications services in Ireland had been run by the civil service since independence in 1922. Poor financial performance allied to sub-standard service quality led to the establishment of a commercial SOE, Telecom Éireann, in 1984. Within six years of corporatisation, the company had successfully transformed itself from a loss-making bureaucratic government department to a commercial and profitable SOE seeking to diversify and expand. The commercial focus that characterised the company as it entered the 1990s was stressed in its 1990 annual report which articulated the objectives of:

> ...responding effectively to the challenge of competition emerging in various areas of the business [...and...] using the Company's

increasing business strengths to increase shareholder value and contribute to the growth of the economy.

(Telecom Éireann, 1990: 54)

Even at this early stage in the company's history it was apparent that influential parties within the company were in favour of privatisation. In his statement in the 1991 annual report, the then chairman, Michael Smurfit, stated:

I am on record personally on the subject of privatisation and I have been criticised in some quarters for it. I recognise, of course, that this is first and foremost a matter for the Government as the Company's shareholder. My own motivation in this respect is purely my concern that Telecom should be in the best possible position to meet the competition which is inevitable and which we would have no way of averting even if we wished to. The Board must be left to motivate and reward all employees in the competitive environment that will emerge.

(Telecom Éireann, 1991: 8)

Although subsequent annual reports did not mention privatisation explicitly, they did refer to the extremely dynamic nature of the international telecommunications market, which was built around rapidly evolving technology, and the fact that, given the rapid pace of change, a small national monopoly supplier such as Telecom Éireann could ill-afford to isolate itself. In this context, the prospect of a strategic alliance or joint venture became an ever more important part of corporate strategy. Part-privatisation in the form of a strategic alliance materialised in late 1996, when 20 per cent of Telecom Éireann's shares were sold to the Comsource consortium (which consisted of PTT Telecom BV and Telia AB[10]). Comsource also acquired an option that entitled it to increase its shareholding to 35 per cent in the future.

While the preferences of top management along with impending market liberalisation were undoubted drivers of this sale, an additional critical factor was the endorsement of the trade unions. McCarthy (2007) details how the company's main trade union, the Communication Workers Union (CWU), reviewed its traditional opposition to privatisation. In 1994, the CWU made the decision to support the company's pursuit of a strategic alliance on the grounds that some form of privatisation was inevitable. On this basis, they agreed to support the strategy in exchange for employee participation and employee share ownership. Although an Employee Share Ownership Plan (ESOP) was not officially established until 1998, moves in this direction were afoot once the unions gave the strategic alliance their approval.

The establishment of a strategic alliance paved the way for full privatisation which was completed in July 1999. By divesting the state's remaining shareholding, the Fianna Fáil-led government (elected in June 1997) sought to follow a worldwide trend of privatising telecommunications companies. The official justification for full privatisation was couched in terms of the necessity for the company to compete in the newly liberalised EU telecommunications market. Private ownership was viewed as the most appropriate ownership structure in the context of competitive markets. When introducing legislation to enable the sale of the company, the Minister for Public Enterprise, Mary O'Rourke, stated that Telecom Éireann could 'only achieve its commercial mandate by being able to operate freely in pursuance of its own commercial strategic goals'.[11] O'Rourke was also a supporter of granting employees a significant shareholding and this approach diminished any worker opposition to full private ownership. After two years of negotiation with two different governments, the company's trade unions secured a 5 per cent stake in exchange for agreement to firm restructuring and significant changes in work practices. A further 9.9 per cent stake was then purchased at a fair price.

Once the ESOP was established in 1998, the momentum towards privatisation was unstoppable. In the run-up to the flotation of the government's remaining 50.1 per cent stake in July 1999, government officials also justified the divestiture on the grounds that it would promote 'popular capitalism', with shares available to small investors. Allen (2007: 219) quotes Minister O'Rourke's promises that privatisation would mean 'a company that is literally owned by the people through the widest possible share ownership'. The flotation of the company, under the new name Eircom, was heavily advertised along the lines witnessed when public utilities were sold in the UK during the 1980s. The advertising campaign was hugely successful with 1.2 million people registering for shares, and 575,000 eventually purchasing. However, the enthusiasm of small shareholders was short-lived as the share price subsequently deteriorated, with tens of thousands of small investors incurring considerable losses. Nevertheless, the first privatisation of a major state-owned utility in Ireland was complete and the stage was set for a number of other divestitures over the next few years.

### 3.4.4   Privatising the banks

At the end of the millennium the Irish state continued to hold ownership of three commercial banks, the Agricultural Credit Corporation (ACC), the Industrial Credit Corporation (ICC) and the Trustee Savings Bank (TSB). These banks were, however, small players in the Irish retail banking sector. Their privatisation had been on the agenda since the early 1990s, as successive governments sought to increase competition in the banking sector. In 1992, the possible privatisation of the ICC and ACC was mooted with the government seeking bids for both banks. No deal materialised, however. A possible merger of all three state banks along with the Post Office Savings Bank as a 'third banking force' was also proposed in 1992 as part of the *Programme for a Partnership Government 1993 to 1997* put forward by the Fianna Fáil/Labour coalition government. In April 1994, the TSB approached the government with a request to approve its sale to National Australia Bank, but the coalition government collapsed before any decision was reached.

The Fine Gael-Labour-Democratic Left coalition government that was formed in 1994 retained the proposal to merge the three state banks with the Post Office Savings Bank in its *Programme for Government*, however, the purchase offer for the TSB led the government to appoint consultants to advise on the future options for the three state banks. Subsequently, in 1995 it was suggested that the ICC and ACC would be merged and the TSB sold off, with the proceeds being used to recapitalise the ACC and ICC. A change in government in 1997 effectively shelved any decisions on the future of the state banks until July 1998, when the Minister for Finance formally announced that the government had decided to sell the ICC and allocate a 14.9 per cent stake to employees through an ESOP. This provided the impetus for the Minister for Finance to push the other two banks to examine their future options and begin looking for potential buyers.

All three banks were eventually sold between 2001 and 2002. The ICC was sold to Bank of Scotland (Ireland) which had commercial operations in Ireland that were entirely focused on the SME business sector, a market the ICC already commanded a large share of. Bank of Scotland (Ireland) put a valuationof €349 million on the ICC and the bank was officially sold in February 2001. After receiving a number of bids, the TSB recommended to the Minister for Finance that the bank be sold to Irish Life & Permanent Group plc (IL&P), after the group made an offer of €430 million. The sale would lead to a merger between IL&P and the TSB to form Permanent TSB. IL&P planned to make use of the TSB's extensive branch network to establish itself in the retail banking sector and the bid was seen as the best option for maximising the TSB's future development. Prior to the merger, Irish Permanent had been one of the leading residential mortgage lenders on the Irish market. The integration of the TSB's retail banking activities gave the new bank 25 per cent of the mortgage market and 10 per cent of current accounts (IL&P, 2000).

With the ICC and TSB banks successfully sold off in early 2001, the ACC was under pressure to find a buyer. Interest from domestic and foreign financial institutions proved to be very low, primarily due to a large net loss of €23.3 million incurred by the bank in 2000, a result of exceptional costs related to its restructuring plan and penalties in relation to its DIRT[12] tax arrears. In late 2001, Rabobank Nederland, the Dutch co-operative bank, signalled its interest in the bank, and the ACC was sold for €165 million in February 2002.

The exit of the state from the Irish banking sector was a drawn out process over a ten year period. However, the protracted nature of the state's withdrawal was mainly attributable to practical difficulties involved in finding buyers rather than issues in relation to opposition to privatisation. Successive governments shared the common objective of increasing competition in a concentrated banking sector. Privatising three small players was seen as a means to this end. With the precedent of significant employee share ownership set in the case of Telecom Éireann, the traditional source of opposition to privatisation policies was removed, with workers and trade unions persuaded to cooperate with the sales in return for 14.9 per cent stakes in all three cases.

### 3.4.5 Appetite for privatisation diminishes

The period 2001–02 was particularly busy in terms of the privatisation of Irish SOEs, with the Irish National Petroleum Corporation (INPC) sold in addition to the sales of the three state banks. The INPC had been established in 1979 in order to ensure security in the supply of oil. The decision to sell the company was prompted by concerns about the cost of the capital investment required to upgrade its refinery facilities, as well as concerns about the company's operation of a mandatory 'off-take regime', which effectively raised oil prices.[13] After a year of negotiations, the INPC was sold to the US oil company Tosco Corporation for €116 million. As part of the deal, Tosco agreed to operate the company's refinery and terminal on a fully commercial basis for at least 15 years, as well as undertake any capital investment that might be necessary under future EU Auto Oil programmes. Tosco also agreed to preserve existing jobs and employment conditions as part of the 15-year commitment.

Following the sale of the state banks and the INPC there was a noticeable lull in privatisation activity. Nor was there any evident appetite for further sales despite sustained economic growth, low unemployment, and the stability of the coalition government (which included the pro-privatisation Progressive Democrats) that had overseen the majority of sales to date. This lack of privatisation activity is partly explained by the fact that those enterprises that remained under public ownership were largely utilities or companies that held considerable market power. Although the electricity market was partly liberalised in 2001 and fully liberalised in 2007, new players were slow to enter a market that continued to be dominated by the state-owned ESB. Powerful SOEs also dominated public transport (rail and urban bus services), airports (where attempts to stimulate competition were also unsuccessful) and postal services. Privatising these enterprises is not a realistic proposition in the absence of competition in the relevant markets.

A high degree of disenchantment arising from the privatisation of Eircom was also a factor that dampened the appetite for future sales among policymakers and the wider public. Significant losses among small shareholders in Eircom, in addition to low levels of investment in telecommunications infrastructure and attendant low levels of service quality (discussed in Chapter 7), influenced policymakers to adopt a cautious approach to future privatisations. This cautious approach was particularly evident in the case of the most recent divestiture to date, that of the state-owned airline, Aer Lingus.

Like most state-owned airlines, Aer Lingus has faced enormous challenges over the last 25 years in aviation markets that have been characterised by ever increasing volatility. Aer Lingus responded to crises at the beginning of the 1990s and 2000s with rationalisation plans. The first plan, which followed the Gulf War of 1990–91, included significant reductions in employment, the sale of assets and ancillary companies, an injection of state capital, and the granting of a 5 per cent shareholding to employees. The rationalisation plan restored the company to profitability and it became a candidate for privatisation at the end of the 1990s, as the challenge of funding fleet renewal became more acute. The decision to privatise the company was made in December 1999, but six years were to pass before the company was eventually transferred to private ownership.

Legislation to allow for privatisation was introduced in 2000, however, this was withdrawn following a deterioration in company performance after the outbreak of foot and mouth disease in the UK and Ireland, as well as industrial unrest. Further delays in the sale process followed the terrorist attacks on New York and Washington in September 2001. Like other airlines Aer Lingus, stood on the verge of bankruptcy and responded by implementing its second major rationalisation plan in a decade, which involved some 2,000 redundancies, a pay freeze and new working practices, along with the sale of non-core assets and subsidiaries.

Employees received a further 9.9 per cent of the company's equity as part of the plan bringing their stake in the company to 14.9 per cent in total. Crucially, further injections of state capital were ruled out. This decision was officially justified on the grounds that further capital injections by the government would break EU rules on state aid. This argument, however, has been shown to be spurious. Sweeney (2004: 10) explains how the market investor principle, which underpins the EU rules on state aid, states that:

> ...if a prudent investor would not invest in a company (for fear they would lose their money), then such an investment would be a state aid [...] If the company is viable, the state can invest in it, without reference to anyone.

Although Aer Lingus was profitable, the government nonetheless persisted with the argument that equity injections were disallowed, and the *Aer Lingus Bill 2003* enabling the sale of the airline was passed in the spring of 2004. The government, however, was slow to make decisions on how or when the airline would be sold. This was attributable to a degree of political sensitivity around the future of Aer Lingus, which was based in the electorally important constituency of Dublin North.

The move to privatise had full support from management at Aer Lingus, and, in September 2003, the airline's board indicated to the government that it favoured an institutional placement of a stake in the company rather than flotation on the stock market. In June 2004, the then CEO of Aer Lingus, Willie Walsh, and two colleagues announced a surprise management buyout bid for the airline. The government responded by appointing Goldman Sachs to advise on the possible future ownership options for the airline. They subsequently recommended that the airline be floated on the stock market with the government retaining a minor stake of at least 20 per cent. With the government delaying over any decision on the future of the airline, the company's top management team[14] controversially resigned in November 2004, claiming that they believed the then Taoiseach, Bertie Ahern, had no appetite to sell part of the airline and that they had done as much as they could with the company. The decision to finally float the airline on the stock market was taken in early 2006, with the government opting to retain a 25 per cent stake in the company. Despite some delays in the sale due to a dispute with trade unions over future pay and conditions, the airline was floated on the stock exchange in October 2006.

The case of Aer Lingus exemplifies the many factors that shape the decision to privatise a major SOE in Ireland. There was clearly no ideological objection to the privatisation of Aer Lingus, as the same government had presided over a number of SOE sales over the previous nine years. Despite the official emphasis on EU rules on state aid, the privatisation of Aer Lingus owed little to the logic of European integration explanation offered by Clifton *et al.* (2003). The willingness to privatise was principally driven by government policy on SOEs that required commercial viability. Support in the form of subsidies or capital injections were no longer considered an option. Whereas the transition to private ownership was given impetus by managerial support and employee cooperation, it was constrained by political considerations. These related to the political sensitivity attached to Aer Lingus and, more importantly, the negative controversy surrounding the privatisation of Telecom Éireann. The latter has altered Irish public opinion on the question of privatisation and had considerable influence on the path dependence of Irish privatisation policy.

## 3.5 Conclusion

The last 20 years have witnessed enormous change in the Irish SOE sector, with the advent of liberalisation in a number of hitherto protected sectors, such as telecommunications and electricity, the development of a comprehensive regulatory framework and a significant degree of privatisation. The Irish state withdrew from involvement in sectors such as banking (pre-2008 banking crisis), air and sea transport, sugar and steel production and telecommunications services. While this withdrawal from direct government production of goods and services is similar to that witnessed in other European countries, the Irish experience has been characterised by a number of distinctive features. Commonly accepted explanations for the development of privatisation policy have a degree of resonance in the case of some sales but not others. Whereas economic theories of privatisation that emphasise the potential for improved enterprise performance help to explain most divestitures, other economic perspectives that point to fiscal pressures as an explanation for privatisation have only some relevance.

The logic of EU integration explanation for privatisation offers a useful perspective in cases such as Irish Steel, Telecom Éireann/Eircom and Aer Lingus. However, one of the key factors shaping general policy on SOEs, as well as privatisation, has been the requirement for SOEs to perform on a commercially viable basis. Perennial loss-makers have been put into liquidation and privatisation has been adopted without any great ideological impetus. The most distinctive feature of the Irish privatisation programme has been the cooperation of trade unions and employees who have taken ownership stakes in privatised companies that are well in excess of international norms. This suggests a stakeholder approach to privatisation that mirrors the 'social partnership' approach to wider economic policy, which has been a key institutional feature of policymaking in Ireland since 1987. This is set to change, however. The national economic crisis that has emerged since late 2008 has increased the likelihood of future sales, as the Irish government seeks to raise revenues in order to cope with serious fiscal difficulties. However, the social partnership model has been severely destabilised in the context of the crisis. It is therefore likely that future privatisations will meet with greater levels of resistance from employees and trade unions compared to past divestitures. The future course of privatisation in Ireland is uncertain and we return to this issue in Chapter 9.

# 4
# Privatisation and Performance in Ireland

## 4.0 Introduction

Of the various reasons put forward in support of privatisation, the goal of improving enterprise efficiency is the most prominent. In general, empirical studies of privatisation have utilised measures of profitability and productivity in order to determine whether or not privatisation results in an improvement in performance. In line with studies such as Megginson *et al.* (1994), D'Souza and Megginson (1999) and Dewenter and Malatesta (2001), this chapter examines the performance of privatised Irish SOEs using a number of standard measures of profitability and productivity. The use of accounting ratios in the measurement of performance, while open to criticism, can still provide valuable information. Financial indicators may be unsuitable where enterprises operate in imperfectly competitive markets and/or are prone to changes in accounting practices across time periods, but they are still widely used indicators of performance. Although more sophisticated performance measures (for example, total factor productivity indices) are generally preferred to accounting ratios, the use of these indicators is not possible for a number of the companies covered here, and they are therefore omitted in the interests of meaningful comparisons of performance.

While the goal of this chapter is to measure the impact of changes in ownership on performance, it is important to bear in mind the role of product market competition in this respect. As discussed in Chapter 2, economic theory suggests that competition leads to improved firm efficiency. Where companies are exposed to increased competitive pressures, management are incentivised to minimise waste and maximise efficiency in order to survive. Therefore, any analysis of the pre- versus post-privatisation performance of a public enterprise must take into account any significant changes in product market competition that may have occurred at or around the time of privatisation. Disentangling the effects of ownership change and competition on company performance is, however, problematic and usually requires in-depth case-study analysis that, for example, includes an examination of how changes in the firm's external environment impact on its internal organisation structure (see Dunsire *et al.*, 1988, 1991).

For most of the privatised SOEs analysed in this chapter, there were no significant changes in product market competition during the pre- and post-privatisation periods examined. The three state banks were all small players in the Irish banking market and faced considerable competition from the larger domestic and international banks operating in the banking industry. Irish Life faced competition in the life insurance markets up until the company's flotation on the stock market. The INPC operated in the highly competitive international oil refinery and storage markets which were subject to considerable volatility both pre- and post-privatisation. The national airline, Aer Lingus, experienced strong competition from its domestic rival Ryanair, and other major European airlines for many years prior to divestiture and, like the INPC, was also forced to deal with considerable volatility in its trading environment. Irish Steel faced strong competition from other European and international steel producers, especially after Ireland joined the European Economic Community (EEC) in 1973. B&I Line also experienced considerable competition from other ferry companies, as well as from increases in air travel in the late 1980s as a result of the liberalisation of the industry.

Both Irish Sugar and Telecom Éireann were privatised while strongly dominant in their respective core product markets. Prior to divestiture, Irish Sugar held a near monopoly position in the Irish sugar market, with little or no increase in competition post-divestiture. However, the continued expansion and diversification of Irish Sugar's food division after privatisation did expose the company to significant increases in competitive pressures. An analysis of the pre- versus post-privatisation performance of Telecom Éireann is complicated by the fact that the Irish telecommunications market was fully liberalised in the year preceding the flotation of the firm. Since these two companies experienced significant changes in product market competition at or around the time of privatisation, our analysis of performance in each case includes discussion of the likely impact of competition.

For the non-financial public enterprises examined in this chapter, profitability is measured using the rate of Return on Sales (ROS) and the rate of

Return on Assets (ROA). Operating efficiency is measured using Sales Efficiency (SEFF) and Value-Added per Employee hour (VAE). Sales Efficiency is a gross measure of labour productivity and is calculated as turnover divided by the number of employees whereas VAE provides a net measure of employee productivity by using employee-hours as a denominator (Martin and Parker, 1997). Table 4A1 in the appendix provides further information on data sources and the formulae used in the calculation of the aforementioned performance indicators.

Given the nature of the business activities for companies operating in the financial sector, most of the performance and efficiency indicators used for non-financial companies are not appropriate measures for the performance of the financial SOEs privatised to date. Consequently, a number of more instructive performance indicators are adopted in the case of the three state-owned banks privatised, with separate indicators relevant to the life insurance industry also adopted in the case of Irish Life. The indicators used for each of the privatised financial SOEs are discussed in further detail later in the chapter. Our analysis of performance for each company is designed to test the theoretical prediction that privatisation will lead to improved company performance.

For each company we present performance results in both tabular and graphical format. Tables present our performance indicators as three- or four-year averages. A limitation to the use of annual averages is that they can conceal important year-on-year movements in any indicator. To compensate for this shortcoming we also use graphs to present the year-on-year variations in a selected number of key indicators. The results in each graph are normalised to equal '1' in the year of privatisation, thus providing a clear visual presentation of trends in performance indicators both before and after privatisation.

## 4.1   Irish Sugar/Greencore

Irish Sugar was one of the first public enterprises to be established in Ireland after the government took the decision, in 1933, to nationalise a private sugar production company that had been heavily reliant on state assistance. Up until the 1940s, sugar production was the sole business of Irish Sugar, however, in the late 1940s and early 1950s, in response to financial difficulties that arose during World War II, Irish Sugar diversified into ancillary activities such as the production of agricultural machinery, fertiliser distribution and limestone quarrying. Further diversification occurred in the early 1960s when Irish Sugar established a food processing subsidiary, Erin Foods, which went on to become the largest food processing company in the country.

The pre-privatisation history of Irish Sugar provides an instructive case study of changing government policy on SOEs in the late 1970s and 1980s. This period was characterised by a significantly increased emphasis on commercial objectives, and consequent tensions at political and social levels as wider social objectives, such as maintenance of employment, were relegated in terms of importance. Up until the late 1970s, Irish Sugar reported profits in all but three of the years since it had been established in 1933. By 1980, however, the company was experiencing severe financial difficulties. The food division, which had incurred heavy losses during the 1970s, continued to perform poorly and was a major drain on company resources. The company had invested over €50 million on modernising its factories between 1976 and 1980, and had financed this from its own resources and borrowings. The high cost of servicing its increasing debt coupled with the need for further capital investment led to a request for a significant government capital injection.

The government convened a Joint Oireachtas Committee[1] on State-Sponsored Bodies (JOCSSB) to analyse Irish Sugar's operations and make recommendations on the future development of the company. The review was completed in December 1980 and recommended rationalisation of the company's sugar production facilities through the closure of unviable plants, as well as considering the closure of some factories in the loss-making food division. The committee also recommended that the government assist Irish Sugar by providing an immediate capital injection (JOCSSB, 1980a).

In response to its financial difficulties, Irish Sugar implemented a significant rationalisation and cost-cutting programme and began placing greater emphasis on becoming commercially viable. In September 1981, the board recommended the closure of the smallest of the company's four sugar plants (in Tuam), as maintaining operations at the plant would lead to annual losses of over €3 million.[2] The government, however, refused to accept the board's recommendation following strong local opposition to the closure and consequent job losses.[3] This decision imposed a considerable cost on Irish Sugar for which it received no compensation. An effective stand-off between government and enterprise management ensued, with little invested in the plant over the following years. In December 1986, the government finally relented to its closure. The cost of keeping the Tuam plant open since 1983 had amounted to some €16.25 million (Irish Sugar, 1986).

Further rationalisation measures were announced in October 1987, when Irish Sugar management recommended to the board that operations be ceased at the Thurles sugar plant within two years, and production would be expanded at the remaining two factories in Carlow and Mallow. The Thurles factory was smaller than the other two plants and had received less capital investment over the years. Irish Sugar formally announced the closure of the Thurles plant in January 1989, after the government accepted the company's proposal.

The impact of factory closures, labour shedding[4] and other rationalisation measures in both the sugar and food divisions contributed to considerable efficiency gains. Table 4.1 and Figure 4.1 show these improvements as measured by SEFF and VAE. Similarly impressive improvements are evident in the profitability indicators. After incurring net losses of over €10 million on average per annum between 1980 and 1985, the company began making healthy profits from 1987 onwards. By the end of the 1980s, the company had made the transition from serving as a tool of government policy to operating as a profitable commercial SOE focused on growing the company's business.

There were, however, significant obstacles to expansion. The European Commission (EC) quota system precluded Irish Sugar and all other European sugar companies from growing their sugar processing operations. Since input (sugar beet) and output (white sugar) prices were effectively fixed by the EC,[5] the only option for increasing rates of return was to reduce operating costs through the concentration and rationalisation of

Table 4.1   Summary of Results for Irish Sugar

| | Pre-privatisation | | Post-privatisation | |
|---|---|---|---|---|
| Indicator | 1984–87 | 1988–91 | 1992–95 | 1996–99 |
| Real Sales | −1.25 | 16.86 | 7.79 | 12.08 |
| Employment | −10.18 | 0.69 | −1.96 | 20.69 |
| ROS | 7.22 | 9.57 | 10.77 | 11.75 |
| ROA | 11.33 | 14.30 | 14.25 | 13.34 |
| SEFF | 127.65 | 197.57 | 262.14 | 263.76 |
| VAE | 17.50 | 22.99 | 29.58 | 29.46 |

*Source*: Authors' calculations from Irish Sugar and Greencore annual reports.
*Notes*: (1) Results for Real Sales and Employment are presented as average annual percentage changes; (2) Results for ROS and ROA are presented as average annual rates of return; (3) Results for SEFF are presented as average annual turnover per employee (in €'000s); (4) Results for VAE are presented as average annual value added per employee hour (in €s).

*Figure 4.1*  Irish Sugar/Greencore Performance, 1984–99

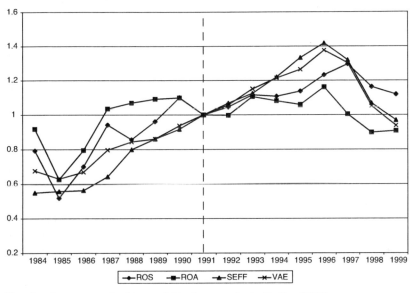

*Note*: Results are normalised to equal 1 in the year of privatisation (1991).

sugar processing operations. With plant closures completed, and investment in the modernisation and expansion of the remaining plants executed, Irish Sugar's scope for improving rates of returns through the
achievement of cost reductions was largely exhausted by the start of the
1990s.

In order to grow its business, Irish Sugar turned to diversification into
non-sugar activities. Similar strategies were pursued by other European
sugar companies faced with uncertainty around the European sugar
regime (van der Linde *et al.*, 2000). In 1990, the company purchased a
50 per cent stake in the largest flour milling group in Ireland. It further
expanded its food operations by acquiring a 65 per cent stake in a food
preparation company and also diversified into fertiliser production. By
the time Irish Sugar was privatised (see discussion in Chapter 3), it had
evolved from operating as a loss-making entity dominated by its sugar
activities, to a profitable and commercial agri-food company. In April
1991, the company was floated on the stock market under the new name
Greencore.

The newly branded company continued to seek opportunities for
expansion and diversification of activities in the post-privatisation period.
Through acquisitions in Ireland, Belgium and the UK, by 1998 Greencore

had become the fifth largest malt producer in the world. In 1998, it also acquired Paramount Foods, a leading producer of pizzas and sauces in the UK. This signalled Greencore's intention to significantly grow its food division and diversify into convenience foods. By virtue of these acquisitions, the contribution of Greencore's food division to group turnover surpassed 50 per cent in 1999. Acquisitions were not, however, confined to the food division. In 1996, it acquired 26.9 per cent of Imperial Holly, the largest sugar producer in the USA. Subsequent substantial losses incurred by the company resulted in its closure in 2000, with Greencore forced to write off its investment at a cost of over €63 million.

In terms of enterprise performance, Figure 4.1 indicates that the strong improvement in all indicators recorded before privatisation continued in the first five years after divestiture. However, Greencore's strategy of increased acquisitions and diversification did not lend itself to sustaining this trend of improved performance. Figure 4.1 illustrates the decline in all performance indicators from 1996 until the end of the period under review. The shifting of Greencore's activities into highly competitive malting and international food markets exposed the company to new competitive pressures and tighter profit margins. In particular, the consolidation and restructuring of the company's various malting operations under one integrated division and the rationalisation of a number of smaller and less efficient malting plants took time to implement, and the division also suffered from weak global malt markets in the late 1990s.

In summary, the period of commercialisation heralded a marked improvement in the performance of Irish Sugar across all indicators. Improved performance continued after privatisation, until the food division accounted for the dominant proportion of the company's activities. The case of Greencore follows the trend observed for British companies by Bishop and Kay (1989), who found that the pattern was for improved performance to lead to privatisation rather than the other way around.

## 4.2   B&I Line

B&I Line was established as a commercial SOE in 1965 after the nationalisation of the British and Irish Steam Packet Company, a private UK ferry operator which had run into financial difficulties by the early 1960s. During the 1970s and 1980s, B&I Line required significant capital funding from the government in order to survive. Between 1971 and 1991, the exchequer injected some €134.6 million worth of equity, with €67.2 million of that paid in from 1985 onwards.[6] Even with such large capital injections, the company still performed poorly during the 1980s, and in 1985 the government decided to appoint a new chief executive who would also serve as chairman of the board. Under his stewardship, two separate restructuring and rationalisation programmes were implemented in an attempt to restore the company to viability. Although the second of these programmes led to a return to profitability after years of heavy losses, B&I Line's continued reliance on exchequer funding to service its existing debt led to the decision to privatise the company in 1992. The performance of B&I Line during the restructuring programmes implemented during the pre-privatisation period is examined below along with the post-privatisation performance of the company.

The results presented in Table 4.2 utilise the performance indicators for non-financial SOEs described earlier and are expressed as three-year averages for four separate periods. The pre-privatisation years are split into two separate time periods corresponding with two separate restructuring programmes implemented by B&I Line. The first pre-privatisation period covers the years following the restructuring programme introduced in 1985. This programme involved a large reduction in staff numbers and a route sharing agreement with another ferry operator (B&I Line, 1985). The failure of this plan to restore the company to profitability is evident from the poor profitability and productivity results recorded for the 1986–88 period in Table 4.2. In addition, B&I Line recorded net losses of €29.6, €15.4 and €19.9 million for the years 1985–87 respectively. The poor performance of the company during this period, along with the

Table 4.2   Summary of Results for B&I Line

| Indicator | Pre-privatisation | | Post-privatisation | |
|---|---|---|---|---|
| | 1986–88 | 1989–91 | 1992–94 | 1995–97 |
| Real Sales | −17.89 | 3.36 | −0.17 | 4.20 |
| Employment | −18.96 | −1.90 | −6.49 | −2.97 |
| ROS | −0.12 | 2.73 | 4.40 | 12.76 |
| ROA | −0.13 | 7.11 | 9.15 | 8.11 |
| SEFF | 72.32 | 67.50 | 74.83 | 114.07 |
| VAE | 10.45 | 9.96 | 10.39 | 20.75 |

*Source*: Authors' calculations from B&I Line and Irish Ferries annual reports.
*Notes*: (1) Results for the 1995–97 period relate to Irish Ferries Group; (2) Results for Real Sales and Employment are presented as average annual percentage changes; (3) Results for ROS and ROA are presented as average annual rates of return; (4) Results for SEFF are presented as average annual turnover per employee (in €'000s); (5) Results for VAE are presented as average annual value added per employee hour (in €s).

impact of the liberalisation of the Irish air transport industry in 1986 (which led to lower air fares in general) and industrial disputes which halted services for a number of weeks, led to the introduction of a second rationalisation plan in December 1987.

The new plan of action introduced by B&I Line succeeded in halting the heavy losses incurred by the company and brought about some relative improvements in performance, as can be seen in Table 4.2. However, B&I Line's significant accumulated losses (which stood at €170.71 million by the end of 1991) and the fact that it remained heavily reliant on exchequer funding led to the government's decision to sell the company to Irish Continental Group (ICG) in January 1992.[7] Upon completion of the sale, ICG immediately set about separating the newly acquired B&I Line into three separate business divisions, namely Ferries, Container Services and Dublin Ferryport. The three divisions were restructured so that they could then fund their own investment programmes and a voluntary redundancy programme was also put in place (ICG, 1991).

The positive impact of these changes is evident from the post-privatisation results for 1992–94 displayed in Table 4.2 and Figure 4.2, registering

*Figure 4.2*   B&I Line Performance, 1986–97

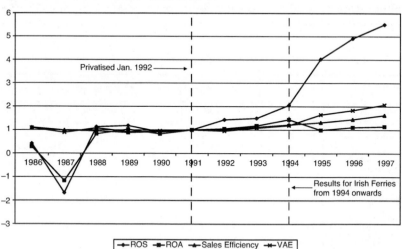

*Notes*: (1) Results are normalised to equal 1 in the year of privatisation. Although B&I Line was sold in January 1992, the company's financial year end was December 31st and 1991 is therefore taken to be the year of privatisation. (2) Results for the 1994–97 period are for Irish Ferries as a whole.

improvements across the profitability and efficiency indicators. In 1995, B&I Line was officially amalgamated with Irish Ferries Limited, a separate subsidiary of ICG. Financial results for B&I Line as a separate entity are thus only available up until 1994. Nevertheless, the Irish Ferries results for 1995–97 provide useful insights into the performance of B&I Line as it accounted for the most of the newly amalgamated entity's business over that period.[8] These results demonstrate that the pattern of improvement observed in the early years after privatisation was sustained. The case of B&I Line therefore lends support to the hypothesis that privatisation is associated with improved enterprise performance. After years of poor results and consequent reliance on exchequer funding, the company turned itself around following divestiture and performed well in a very competitive trading environment.

## 4.3   Irish Steel[9]

Irish Steel was established in 1947 after the nationalisation of a private company, Irish Steel Ltd, which went into receivership in 1946. As a commercial SOE, Irish Steel performed reasonably well during the 1950s and 1960s. It benefited from a government ban on the export of domestic scrap metal that provided the company with cheaper raw material, and, by 1971, employment reached a high of over 1200 workers. However, after Ireland's entry into the EEC in 1973 the company began to suffer losses for a number of reasons which included: 1) increased competition due to the free trade conditions it now had to operate under as part of the EEC; 2) its outdated steel plant and equipment; and 3) a downturn in the European steel industry after the first oil crisis of 1973. A project to restructure the company's operations by replacing the old plant with a modern efficient steel mill began in 1978 and was completed in 1981 at a cost of €101.58 million.[10] Nonetheless, the company continued to experience severe financial difficulties during the 1980s. In the two decades prior to 1995, the company made a profit in just three out of the 20 years.

The poor performance of Irish Steel during the 1980s and 1990s can be attributed to several factors, including a costly overhead structure and uncompetitive labour costs. Irish Steel's position as a small player on the European and international steel industry was not helped by a downturn in the worldwide steel market. In the 1980s selling prices were driven lower than they had been for over 20 years. In addition, a rise in the price of raw material put immense pressure on profit margins. Most European steel companies suffered from the downturn in the industry during the late 1980s and early 1990s and, as a result, the EC implemented a large-scale restructuring of the European steel industry.

In June 1994, Irish Steel's accumulated losses stood at €176.5 million, with the company incurring a net loss of €26.25 million in that year alone. As discussed in Chapter 3, the government followed the board's recommendation to seek a buyer for the company, and Irish Steel was sold to the Indian steel company, ISPAT, in April 1996 for a nominal sum of IRP£1 due to the large amount of debt on the company's balance sheet.[11] As part of the sale, the government agreed to write off a substantial amount of debt and provide an exchequer contribution to compensate ISPAT for future restrictions on production and sales imposed by the EC.[12] ISPAT, in turn, agreed to employ a minimum of 300 workers for at least five years and to invest approximately €30 million in the company in the first six years.

The poor performance of Irish Steel in the nine years prior to privatisation is evident from Table 4.3 and Figure 4.3. In Table 4.3, the pre-privatisation era is split into three separate three-year periods with the third period corresponding to the years after the introduction of the 1994 viability plan. Although the company generated minor profits in 1989 and 1990, performance deteriorated significantly thereafter. Despite implementing rationalisation measures in 1994, there was no marked improvement in the performance indicators for the 1994–96 period relative

Table 4.3   Summary of Results for Irish Steel

| Indicators | Pre-privatisation | | Post-privatisation | |
|---|---|---|---|---|
| | 1988–90 | 1991–93 | 1994–96 | 1997–99 |
| Real Sales | 20.14 | –13.97 | 0.01 | –0.15 |
| Employment | 7.40 | –4.97 | –9.19 | 0.25 |
| ROS | –1.56 | –10.50 | –10.47 | –6.57 |
| ROA | –0.81 | –10.47 | –13.44 | –8.08 |
| SEFF | 151.19 | 124.43 | 149.44 | 170.35 |
| VAE | 15.94 | 12.29 | 8.93 | 11.62 |

*Source*: Authors' calculations from Irish Steel annual reports.
*Notes*: (1) The results for Real Sales and Employment in the 1988–90 period are two-year averages while the subsequent three periods are all three year averages; (2) Results for Real Sales and Employment are presented as average annual percentage changes; (3) Results for ROS and ROA are presented as average annual rates of return; (4) Results for SEFF are presented as average annual turnover per employee (in €'000s); (5) Results for VAE are presented as average annual value added per employee hour (in €s).

*Figure 4.3*  Irish Steel Performance, 1988–99

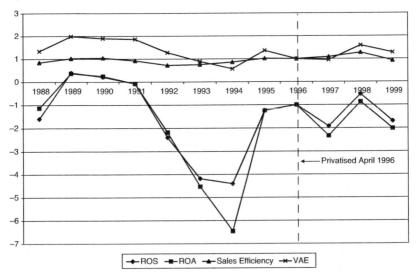

*Notes:* (1) Results for Sales Efficiency and VAE are normalised to equal 1 in the year of privatisation (1996); (2) ROA and ROS results were normalised to equal '–1' in the year of privatisation, since the company made a loss in every year except for 1989 and 1990; (3) Results were reported for 1997 as a 19-month financial year and were annualised to allow comparison with figures for 1998–99.

to previous years, with the ROS remaining static while ROA and VAE actually deteriorated further.

Post-privatisation results, which are only available up until 1999, do not show any turnaround in performance after the change in ownership. Despite a slight improvement in labour productivity as measured by VAE, the company continued to incur operating losses and, consequently, ROS and ROA remained negative. In June 2001, only days after the terms of its five-year deal with the government expired, ISPAT announced that it would be closing its Irish operation with the loss of over 400 jobs. The company blamed the closure on increasing labour and electricity costs and the mounting losses incurred as a result.[13] Another significant factor was the imminent introduction of new pollution controls to be imposed by the Environmental Protection Agency (EPA) that would have required significant investment on the part of ISPAT in order to clean up its plant in Cork. A last-minute rescue package proposed by unions consisting of substantial cost-cutting measures was rejected by management and the company was put into receivership with workers only left with statutory redundancy payments. ISPAT was also accused of asset stripping after it sold a large portion of land just prior to its closure.[14]

The privatisation of Irish Steel failed to turn around the company's performance and was marred by controversy. ISPAT failed to invest in the plant as promised and had a poor safety record, with a number of tragic deaths occurring during its period in ownership.[15] In addition, the liquidation of Irish Steel by ISPAT left the government with a large environmental clean-up bill of approximately €30 million, after the government lost a High Court bid in 2004 to have the ISPAT liquidator pay the cost of cleaning up the 20-acre former factory site on Haulbow-line Island in Cobh, Co. Cork.

In conclusion, the case of Irish Steel does not provide support for the hypothesis that privatisation results in improved enterprise performance, even taking into account Irish Steel's extremely poor performance under public ownership. The small scale of company operations allied to the severity of market conditions faced in the 1980s and 1990s were such that a change in ownership was not sufficient to engineer a turnaround in the company's fortunes.

## 4.4   Telecom Éireann/Eircom

Telecom Éireann was established as Ireland's national telecommunications operator in 1984 after it was recommended that the operation of the national telecommunications service be corporatised from the civil service and transferred to a commercial SOE (see Chapter 3 for further details). Upon its establishment, Telecom Éireann inherited severe financial problems that were mainly due to inadequate capital investment in previous years and a management structure unsuitable to commercial operation. The telecommunications service had last made a profit in 1969/70 and the company was also severely hampered by huge debts, which stood at €1.228 billion in 1985 (Telecom Éireann, 1985).

The newly established SOE immediately set about commercialising the telecommunications service and investing significant amounts in modernising the national telecommunications network. A five-year corporate plan outlined in 1985 set targets of improving the quality and performance of the network, reducing financial losses to the point where the company hoped to break even in 1988 and go on to make reasonable profits in subsequent years. By the end of the 1980s, the company had succeeded in transforming the telecommunications service from a perennial loss maker to a profitable operation. The turnaround in performance was mainly achieved through a large reduction in staff numbers and strong business growth.

From 1990 onwards, there was a discernible shift in the company's objectives as articulated in a second five-year plan. While original concerns about profitability and network performance retained importance, the five-year plan announced in 1990 emphasised the imperative of coping with the emergence of competition in different areas of the business. Responding to increased competition required the company to transform from operating as an inward-focused monopolist to one that was externally-focused, customer-driven and competitive. To meet the challenges of rapid technological advances in the increasingly globalised telecommunications market and the move towards full market liberalisation in 1998, Telecom Éireann actively pursued the strategy of entering possible alliances with international telecommunications companies. In 1996, it sold 20 per cent of the company to the Comsource consortium (consisting of the Dutch and Swedish national telecommunications operators). This was followed by full privatisation in 1999 when the remainder of government-held shares were floated on the stock exchange.

In order to examine the impact of privatisation on enterprise performance we use 1996, the year of the strategic alliance, as the year of privatisation. Since post-privatisation data is unavailable after 2001 as the company was split up and sold off, focusing on 1996 allows a sufficient number of years to examine post-privatisation performance. Table 4.4 and Figure 4.4 show performance indicators for the period 1990–2001.

**Table 4.4    Summary of Results for Telecom Éireann/Eircom**

| | Pre-privatisation | | Post-privatisation | |
|---|---|---|---|---|
| Indicators | 1990–92 | 1993–95 | 1996–98 | 1999–2001 |
| Real Sales | 9.91 | 3.60 | 15.87 | 16.56 |
| Employment | –1.78 | –2.53 | –1.57 | 2.82 |
| ROS | 25.17 | 18.98 | 18.21 | 15.18 |
| ROA | 11.39 | 9.25 | 13.04 | 10.95 |
| SEFF | 71.10 | 84.10 | 129.08 | 190.08 |
| VAE | 26.76 | 30.44 | 40.62 | 41.95 |

*Source*: Authors' calculations from Telecom Éireann/Eircom annual reports.
*Notes*: (1) Results for Real Sales and Employment are presented as average annual percentage changes; (2) Results for ROS and ROA are presented as average annual rates of return; (3) Results for SEFF are presented as average annual turnover per employee (in €'000s); (4) Results for VAE are presented as average annual value added per employee hour (in €s).

*Figure 4.4*   Telecom Éireann/Eircom Performance, 1990–2001

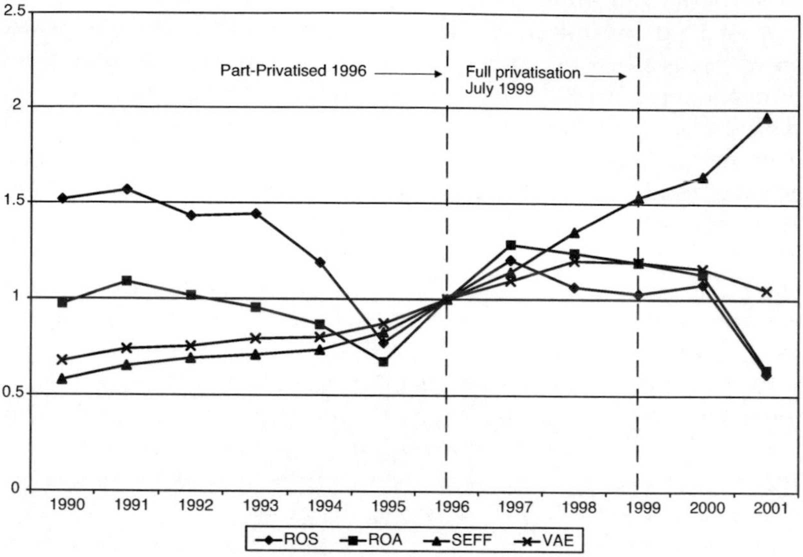

*Note*: Results are normalised to equal 1 in the year that Telecom Éireann was part privatised.

The pre-privatisation period, 1990–96, was characterised by consistent year-on-year improvements in SEFF and VAE. These productivity gains were mainly attributable to a programme of large-scale labour shedding which commenced in the 1980s and continued into the 1990s. Employment levels were reduced by 13.1 per cent over the period 1990–96. These improvements however failed to translate into sustained improvements in profitability. The ROA and ROS measures deteriorated over the same period as the company incurred large increases in operating costs.

After the partial privatisation of the company in 1996, there were gains across all profitability and efficiency indicators; however, VAE, ROS and ROA followed a declining trend after full privatisation in 1999. The only exception in this regard was SEFF, which continued the trend of improvement that began in the 1980s. Overall, the performance indicators used in this analysis fail to provide conclusive evidence that changes in ownership were associated with improved enterprise performance. On the other hand, it is important to note that the company was privatised during a period when the Irish telecommunications market was undergoing full liberalisation. To better understand the trends in the performance measures adopted it is therefore necessary to look beyond the simple relationship between performance and ownership, and examine changes in the degree of competition faced by the company.

Throughout the period examined (1990–2001), Telecom Éireann experienced significant changes in its operating environment, with the prospect of competition driving enterprise strategy up to 1998, when effective competition became more of a reality following full liberalisation of the telecommunications market. The extent to which the company faced actual competition was, however, limited during the period under review. Telecom Éireann held a statutory monopoly of the Irish telecommunications market throughout the 1980s and early 1990s. Despite some diversification into other activities, up until the mid-1990s the company's business was dominated by its fixed-line division. During the late 1990s, its mobile subsidiary, Eircell, became an increasingly important part of the company's business due to the phenomenal growth experienced by the mobile industry in Ireland. In 1999, Eircell contributed 19 per cent of total revenue and by 2001 this had risen to approximately 33 per cent, with the division becoming the most profitable part of the company's business.

Despite full market liberalisation in December 1998,[16] competition in the fixed-line telecommunications market was slow to develop with Telecom Éireann's share of the market remaining stubbornly high. By September 2001, almost three years after full liberalisation the company maintained an 86 per cent market share in the domestic call market and a 76 per cent share of the international call market. With regard to competition in the mobile market, Eircell was the sole operator in the mobile market from 1986 until the late 1990s. The company first faced competition in 1997, when a second operator, Esat Digifone, entered the market. Competition in the market developed further when a third operator (Meteor) was launched in February 2001.

While it does not appear that Telecom Éireann faced considerable increases in the level of *actual* product market competition prior to privatisation, there is evidence to suggest that the threat of competition was a significant driver of the improvement in company performance in the run up to divestiture during the 1990s with the company 'in a race to become cost competitive' (Telecom Éireann, 1996: 14). Telecom Éireann's preparation for increased competition was evident from the considerable price reductions implemented by the company after the introduction of a regulated price cap in 1997.[17] During the first four years of the price cap, Telecom Éireann's price reductions were far in excess of the required reductions suggesting the company was gearing up for the competitive pressures it would face in the newly liberalised market.

Moreover, the threat of competition is associated with the impressive improvements in productivity measures since the late 1980s. In international comparative terms this improvement has been noted in a number of studies. For example, in an analysis of the productivity of major European telecoms operators, Daßler *et al.* (2002) found that productivity growth in Ireland surpassed that of every country over the period 1979–98. In addition, a study on the operational efficiency of the main European telecoms firms by Pentzaropoulos and Giokas (2002) found Telecom Éireann to be fully efficient relative to its peers in the year it was privatised (1999).

Overall, it is clear that changes in ownership at Telecom Éireann coincided with marked changes in its competitive environment and disentangling the effects of both changes is problematic (Palcic and Reeves, 2010b). Whereas the evidence indicates that the threat of competition has been associated with efficiency gains since the late 1990s, the data does not indicate a structural break in performance as a result of privatisation. This case illustrates the elusive nature of performance and warns against simplistic associations between privatisation and performance.

As the first privatisation of a major utility industry in Ireland, the case of Telecom Éireann/Eircom has been an important part of the history of privatisation to date. Whereas the analysis presented in this section focuses solely on enterprise performance, it is important to recognise that this divestiture has had major effects in terms of the wider strategic objectives of the Irish economy. These issues are addressed in Chapter 7 when we return to the case of Eircom and examine developments in the telecommunications industry in Ireland since privatisation.

## 4.5 Irish National Petroleum Corporation

The INPC was established in 1979 during the second oil crisis in order to improve security in the supply of oil. In 1982, it acquired the Whitegate oil refinery in Co. Cork when a consortium of private oil companies decided to close their operation. In 1986, the INPC also acquired an oil terminal operation in Bantry, Co. Cork, which had not been in operation since 1979 after a major explosion. In 1995, the National Oil Reserves Agency (NORA) became a subsidiary of the INPC with responsibility for the maintenance of Ireland's strategic oil reserves.

The government began considering the sale of the INPC in the late 1990s when it became clear that the company would have to invest heavily in upgrading the Whitegate refinery to meet new EU emission standards. The INPC also relied on a mandatory 'offtake regime', whereby all oil companies operating in Ireland were required to purchase a proportion of their oil from the INPC at a premium price. The INPC was thus instructed by government to conduct an examination of its future options. In the summer of 2000 it was announced that Tosco Corporation[18] had submitted a bid for the Whitegate refinery and Bantry terminal operations. The sale of the two operations for €116 million was agreed in July 2001.

Table 4.5 and Figure 4.5 present the pre- versus post-privatisation results for the INPC. Pre-divestiture results are split into two four-year periods, the first of which coincides with a corporate plan introduced at the end of 1993 in order to put the enterprise on a commercial footing by the beginning of 1997. Prior to 1993, the company had only focused on the maintenance of the mandatory offtake from the Whitegate refinery, which operated at two-thirds capacity (INPC, 1995). No major investment projects had been undertaken since the 1970s and the Bantry terminal had been effectively dormant since the company had acquired it in 1986.

Between 1994 and 1997, the company implemented measures to reduce the cost of processing crude oil and increase levels of throughput while also undertaking a number of significant investment projects. The jetty at Whitegate was deepened to allow the intake of larger cargoes of crude oil, reducing freight costs, while modifications were made to plant equipment to increase capacity. In 1995, a project to construct a new single

Table 4.5  Summary of Results for INPC

| Indicator | Pre-privatisation | | Post-privatisation | |
|---|---|---|---|---|
| | 1994–97 | 1998–2001 | 2002–05 | 2006–08 |
| Real Sales | 7.68 | 11.66 | –2.57 | 14.91 |
| Employment | 0.66 | 1.06 | –4.97 | 0.55 |
| ROS | 1.03 | 3.71 | 0.72 | 0.76 |
| ROA | 3.18 | 10.10 | 2.55 | 1.92 |
| SEFF | 2,065.40 | 2,872.80 | 2,572.69 | 3,977.58 |
| VAE | 35.69 | 93.85 | 64.57 | 73.08 |

*Source*: Authors' calculations from INPC and ConocoPhillips annual reports.
*Notes*: (1) Results for Real Sales and Employment are presented as average annual percentage changes; (2) Results for ROS and ROA are presented as average annual rates of return; (3) Results for SEFF are presented as average annual turnover per employee (in €'000s); (4) Results for VAE are presented as average annual value added per employee hour (in €s).

Figure 4.5    INPC Performance, 1994–2008

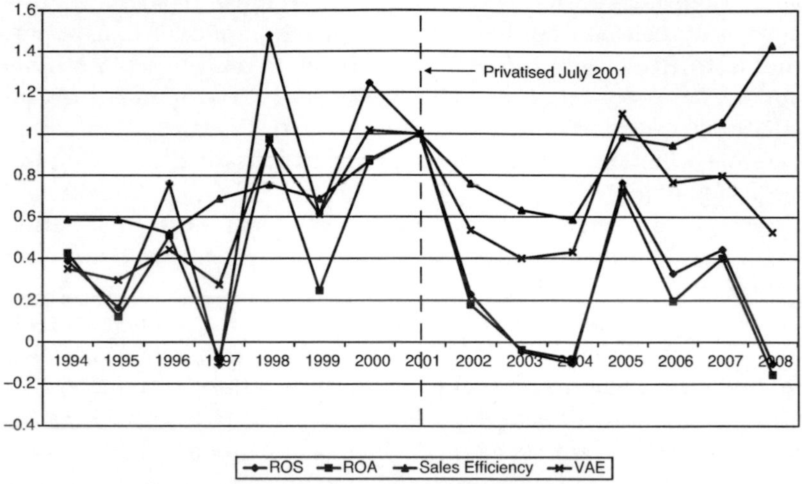

*Note*: Results are normalised to equal 1 in the year of privatisation (2001).

point mooring at the Whiddy terminal was approved and the company invested in new tankage and roadloading facilities, improving processing efficiency and logistics.

The second pre-privatisation period coincides with a number of other significant investment projects in the company. The single point mooring system at the Whiddy terminal was completed and began operating in 1998, allowing the long dormant terminal facilities to operate actively for the first time since an explosion in 1979. The storage capacity of the terminal was expanded with the refurbishment of three 75,000 tonne tanks and the Whiddy terminal began handling and storing product on a commercial basis. The reactivation of the terminal effectively gave the INPC a secondary supply source for refined oil in Ireland (INPC, 1999).

Another significant investment project that was approved in 1999 was the upgrading of the Whitegate refinery to meet the EU Auto Oil 1 emission standards that were to become effective in 2000. Although initially estimated to cost over €80 million, it ended up costing approximately €60 million, with most of the work carried out in 1999. The upgrade expanded the crude oil processing capacity of the refinery and improved the quality of the finished product. In total, some €152 million[19] was invested in fixed assets between 1995 and 2000 in order to improve the commercial operations of the company. As is evident from the results in

Table 4.5, the benefits of the investments detailed above contributed to a general improvement in performance across all indicators between 1995 and 2001. Although the ROS and ROA results displayed in Figure 4.5 fluctuate widely during this period, this is largely explained by the considerable volatility in the global oil market within which the company operates, and the underlying trend in performance is clearly upwards.

The post-privatisation results presented in Table 4.5 and Figure 4.5 are those reported by ConocoPhillips for its Irish operations, namely the Whitegate refinery and Bantry terminal. These results are, however, comparable with those for the pre-privatisation period.[20] The post-privatisation results do not reveal any improvements in efficiency or profitability. The results displayed in Table 4.5 and Figure 4.5 show that performance deteriorated considerably in the seven years after divestiture. The temporary improvement in 2005 was the result of a number of factors: 1) improved market margins due to the effects of Hurricane Katrina on the east cost of the USA; 2) a cost reduction programme consisting of labour shedding implemented in 2004; and 3) significant investment in an upgrade of the Whitegate refinery in 2004 which allowed the production of 10ppm diesel (ConocoPhillips, 2005). Performance again deteriorated post-2005, with the company recording exceptionally poor results in 2008 as a result of the global recession that reduced energy demand and depressed refinery processing margins.

In general, the results presented for the INPC do not support the hypothesis that privatisation leads to improved performance. However, it must be noted that the INPC's main activities – the refining, storage and trading of petroleum products – are subject to considerable volatility in the global petroleum market. Profitability in a given year is largely influenced by movements in crude oil prices, global refinery margins and international market conditions for the petroleum storage market. The question of company ownership is therefore unlikely to have a discernible impact on performance in the context of markets characterised by such volatility.

## 4.6    Aer Lingus

Aer Lingus, which was privatised in October 2006, was originally established in 1936 to provide air services to and from Ireland. The airline started as a very small operation but expanded rapidly from the 1950s onwards. The company diversified considerably during the 1970s in an effort to offset the cyclical swings of its air transport activities, acquiring hotels in the UK, USA and Europe, establishing subsidiaries in aircraft maintenance and engineering, helicopter operations and many other businesses. By 1991, Aer Lingus had 12,261 staff worldwide, with almost half of them employed in non-core activities.

In the early 1990s, the airline incurred heavy losses in its core air transport activities. This was in line with the economic downturn experienced across the air transport market at the time, largely a result of increases in fuel prices due to the Gulf War. Further losses in subsequent years led to the implementation of a radical restructuring plan in 1993. The plan, which primarily consisted of cost-cutting measures, was eventually successful with the airline returning to profitability by 1995. This section examines the performance of Aer Lingus following the return to profitability in the mid-1990s, through privatisation in 2006, and up to 2009.

The performance measures presented in Figure 4.6 show some improvement in the company's commercial performance in the late 1990s. The return to profitability in this period (apart from poor results in 1998) strengthened the company's candidature for privatisation, especially given the airline's reliance on exchequer funding for fleet renewal and overall expansion. In December 1999, the government took the decision to float the airline on the stock exchange and introduced legislation to allow for this in 2000. This was subsequently withdrawn due to a number of events that adversely affected Aer Lingus and the wider airline industry. These included industrial unrest and the outbreak of foot and mouth disease in the UK and Ireland, which resulted in a marked deterioration in performance that continued after the September 11th attacks on New York. In 2001, the company reported an operating loss of €50.36 million

Table 4.6 Summary of Results for Aer Lingus

| Indicator | Pre-privatisation | | Post-privatisation |
|---|---|---|---|
| | 1996–2000 | 2001–05 | 2006–09 |
| Real Sales | 3.09 | –11.89 | 6.35 |
| Employment | –7.83 | –11.17 | 2.66 |
| ROS | 4.70 | 5.82 | 0.19 |
| ROA | 4.15 | 3.70 | 0.05 |
| SEFF | 178.02 | 217.30 | 305.15 |
| VAE | 28.17 | 40.49 | 44.40 |

*Source*: Authors' calculations from Aer Lingus annual reports.
*Notes*: (1) Results for Real Sales and Employment are presented as average annual percentage changes; (2) Results for ROS and ROA are presented as average annual rates of return; (3) Results for SEFF are presented as average annual turnover per employee (in €'000s); (4) Results for VAE are presented as average annual value added per employee hour (in €s).

*Figure 4.6* Aer Lingus Performance, 1995–2009

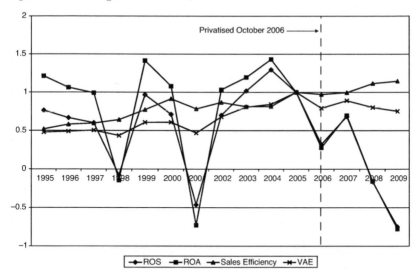

*Note*: Results are normalised to equal 1 in 2005, the year prior to privatisation, since there was a major change in company accounting policies in that year. Up until 2005, Aer Lingus prepared its accounts in accordance with Irish Generally Accepted Accounting Principles (GAAP). In 2006, the airline began producing its accounts using International Financial Reporting Standards (IFRS). The post-2005 results above are therefore not strictly comparable with pre-2005 results, however, they still provide a strong indication of relative company performance.

compared to an operating profit of €79.93 million in the previous year (Aer Lingus, 2001). Once again Aer Lingus, like many other airlines, stood on the verge of bankruptcy and was forced to implement its second major survival plan in a decade.

The survival plan (detailed in Chapter 3) included a reduction in employment by almost one-third and heralded a radical change in business strategy, with the company adopting the low-cost, low-fares model successfully pursued by its main rival airline, Ryanair. These measures had a markedly positive impact and contributed to a significant turnaround in profitability and a sustained improvement in efficiency (see Table 4.6). Although turnover fell compared to the late 1990s, the reduction in staff numbers as well as other cost-cutting measures led to an improvement in SEFF and VAE, while ROS and ROA increased considerably from 2001 onwards, before dipping after 2004. This general improvement in performance paved the way for the re-emergence of plans to privatise the company which were implemented in October 2006.

The three-year period since privatisation witnessed the airline continuing to grapple with the challenges of a volatile and competitive market place. The improved performance recorded in the years prior to divestiture was not sustained. The airline has experienced a serious deterioration in results since 2007 and an operating loss of €80 million was reported in 2009, which represented a four-fold increase in losses over a 12-month period (Aer Lingus, 2009). Among the factors underlying this deterioration were the global economic downturn (which contributed to the collapse of transatlantic business traffic), a decline in overall passenger revenues between 2008–09, significant increases in fuel and oil prices (which more than trebled between 2005–09) and losses at a new base at Gatwick Airport. In addition, the company incurred considerable exceptional charges due to redundancy payments under its cost reduction programme. While these factors underpin the deterioration in profitability measures such as ROS and ROA (see Figure 4.6), it is worth noting that efficiency-based measures have remained relatively stable in the turbulent post-privatisation period. Moreover, in 2010 the airline agreed a far-reaching cost-reduction programme which is expected to contribute to improved performance over the coming years.

To summarise, in the case of Aer Lingus, the available evidence fails to support the basic hypothesis that privatisation leads to improved corporate performance. Performance in the aviation sector is a function of a host of factors that create a particularly volatile business environment. Ownership is but one of this complex amalgam of factors and offers little in the way of explaining performance in the pre- and post-privatisation periods.

## 4.7    The state banks

As discussed earlier, the performance indicators utilised in our analysis of the non-financial SOEs privatised are not suited to financial SOEs. Consequently, a number of more appropriate indicators are adopted in the case of the three state-owned banks privatised between 2001 and 2002. The profitability indicators utilised are Return on Equity (ROE) and Return on Assets (ROA). In addition, profit margin and asset utilisation measures are also calculated. The asset utilisation indicator provides an indication of how much income is generated from existing assets, while ROE, ROA and profit margin relate profits generated to shareholder's funds, assets and operating income respectively. Table 4A2 in the appendix provides the formulae used in the calculation of each indicator.

The efficiency measures used to analyse bank performance are income efficiency (IEFF) and cost/income ratios. Income efficiency is a basic measure of labour productivity, whereas the cost/income ratio is an important measure of cost efficiency. The ratio illustrates how efficient a bank is in terms of the costs incurred to generate income. In contrast to the other performance indicators used in this chapter, a lower cost/income ratio indicates higher efficiency and vice versa. The next three sections examine the pre- versus post-privatisation performance of each of the three (pre-banking crisis) state banks.[21]

### 4.7.1    Industrial Credit Corporation

The ICC was originally established in 1933 in order to provide medium- to long-term credit to private industry, particularly in the case of newly established or expanding enterprises. While the scale of the ICC's activities was modest up until the 1960s, it nevertheless played an important role in providing capital to private industry during the formative years of the state. Rapid economic growth in Ireland during the 1960s and 1970s led to a significant expansion in the ICC's business activities. At the same time, however, the bank faced new competition from major UK, USA and European commercial banks who began taking an interest in providing finance to the rapidly developing industrial sector and consequently established subsidiaries in Ireland (JOCSSB, 1980b). During the 1980s and 1990s, the ICC began refocusing its activities towards the small-to-medium sized business (SME) sector, where it established a distinct niche. The ICC established a venture capital fund, and over the years it became a major part of its core business, with the bank becoming one of the leading venture capital providers in the country.[22]

The events leading up to the sale of the ICC are outlined in detail in Chapter 3. The government initiated a sale process in 1999, but the process was temporarily suspended due to a general decline in the value of financial stocks and a subsequent lack of satisfactory bids for the bank. After a renewed search for a potential bidder in 2000, it was announced that Bank of Scotland had made an offer for the bank. Prior to the purchase, Bank of Scotland's Irish commercial operations were focused on the SME business sector where the ICC already commanded a large market share. The ICC was sold to Bank of Scotland (Ireland) for €349 million in February 2001.

Results for ICC are only available up until December 2001 as the bank was merged with Bank of Scotland (Ireland) Limited (BoSI) in March 2002. Thereafter, results are only available for BoSI as a whole and do not include a breakdown for ICC. However, where the separate accounts of both banks can be compared for 2001, ICC's contribution to BoSI's reported figures for gross income, total assets and profit before tax was 64.17, 63.72 and 66.60 per cent respectively.[23] Moreover, at the time of sale, ICC Bank had a 13 per cent share of the SME sector, its core business area. When the two banks merged in 2002, their combined market share of the SME sector was 15 per cent. This highlights the significant contribution of ICC to BoSI's operations, particularly given its core objective of targeting the business banking sector. Given that the ICC was evidently such a large part of the post-privatisation combined entity, there is some justification for comparing post-privatisation performance indicators derived from BoSI accounts with those recorded for the ICC pre-divestiture.

Table 4.7 and Figure 4.7 present the pre-privatisation results for ICC and post-privatisation results for BoSI. Prior to divestiture, there was an improvement across all indicators with the exception of ROA and asset utilisation. The fall in ROA was consistent with the prevailing trend in the Irish banking sector. Moreover, the decline in ROA was not surprising in the case of the ICC, given that total assets more than tripled between 1994 and 2001. The improvement in ICC's cost/income ratio is impressive given that the Irish banking sector average over the same period was approximately 60 per cent (CBFSAI, 2005).

Table 4.7   Summary of Results for ICC

| Indicator | Pre-privatisation | | Post-privatisation |
|---|---|---|---|
| | 1994–97 | 1998–2001 | 2002–05 |
| Real Operating Income | −1.55 | 17.49 | 20.85 |
| Real Total Assets | 4.28 | 21.93 | 28.12 |
| Employment | 0.58 | 3.20 | 13.02 |
| ROE | 23.55 | 24.99 | 27.22 |
| Profit Margins | 17.98 | 21.05 | 27.73 |
| Asset Utilisation | 7.92 | 6.23 | 4.36 |
| ROA | 1.42 | 1.36 | 1.23 |
| Cost/Income ratio | 51.18 | 41.95 | 37.24 |
| Income Efficiency | 173.87 | 237.52 | 316.14 |

*Source*: Authors' calculations from ICC and BoSI annual reports.
*Notes*: (1) Results for Real Operating Income, Total Assets and Employment are presented as average annual percentage changes; (2) Results for Profit Margin, Asset Utilisation, ROA and Cost/Income are presented as average annual rates; (3) Results for Income Efficiency are presented as average annual Income Efficiency (in €'000s).

*Figure 4.7* ICC Performance, 1993–2005

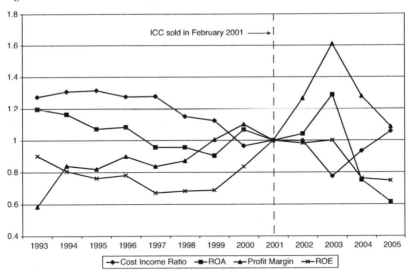

*Notes*: (1) Results are normalised to equal 1 in the year of privatisation (2001); (2) Results for 2002–05 are for Bank of Scotland (Ireland).

The results after divestiture indicate that pre-privatisation improvements in performance were sustained on average (see Table 4.7), although ROA decreased further. The continued decline in ROA after privatisation is again consistent with an overall decline in the Irish banking sector, and also reflects the fact that total assets increased from over €9.5 billion in 2002 to €23.5 billion in 2005 due to a considerable increase in lending. The increase in loans advanced by BoSI was facilitated by the ease of access to funds from its parent group. Bank of Scotland (UK) merged with Halifax into one entity, HBOS, in the summer of 2001 making it the fourth largest bank in the UK.

In conclusion, the case of ICC lends some, albeit limited, support for the hypothesis that privatisation is associated with improved performance. The improvements observed prior to divestiture were sustained but post-privatisation performance was largely unremarkable. A further point of relevance should be noted in relation to the ICC in the context of its takeover by Bank of Scotland. While it is impossible to determine the degree to which ICC's individual performance improved after privatisation given that its operations were subsumed into a larger banking group, its operations appeared to have benefited from the change in ownership and greater access to funds.

The lessons that have been learned in the context of the current banking crisis demonstrate that increased lending and business growth facilitated by greater access to funds is not necessarily indicative of improved performance if the increased lending is not productive. The continued fall in the asset utilisation and ROA measures post-privatisation, shown in Table 4.7, are indicative of unprofitable growth in the case of BoSI. It is now evident that BoSI was one of the most aggressive and highly competitive lenders during Ireland's recent property boom, with the bank the first to offer borrowers 'tracker' mortgages, forcing down margins across the industry as competitors followed suit. BoSI has since incurred considerable losses and has closed its Halifax branch network. The underlying performance of ICC under private ownership is much less impressive when these issues are taken into account.

### 4.7.2   Trustee Savings Bank

The Trustee Savings Bank (TSB) was a unique form of SOE in that the bank had no share capital and was effectively funded by its depositors. The structure of the TSB that existed prior to privatisation in 2001 was only formalised in 1989 by the Trustee Savings Banks Act of that year. The Act merged the activities of a number of separate trustee savings banks as one entity and removed a number of severe restrictions on the operations of the trustee savings banks. Prior to this, the activities of the banks had been very much constrained, with the banks only allowed to take deposits and make loans to individuals and not businesses. They were also prevented from engaging in fund management and corporate finance activities. In addition, 80 per cent of deposits had to be lodged with the exchequer, with only the remainder available for lending activity.

The events leading up to the privatisation of the TSB have been previously outlined in Chapter 3. After the proposed merger with the ACC failed, the board of trustees sought proposals from parties interested in acquiring or entering into a joint venture with the bank. After receiving a number of bids, the TSB recommended to the Minister for Finance that the bank be sold to Irish Life & Permanent Group plc (IL&P).[24] The TSB was officially acquired for €430 million by IL&P in April 2001. The TSB's operations were merged with IL&P's existing banking division, Irish Permanent, in 2002, and was renamed Permanent TSB. Prior to the merger, Irish Permanent had been one of the leading residential mortgage lenders on the Irish market. The integration of TSB's retail banking activities gave the new bank 25 per cent of the mortgage market and 10 per cent of current accounts (IL&P Annual Report, 2000).

Table 4.8 and Figure 4.8 display the pre-privatisation results for the TSB. After merging the Dublin and Cork/Limerick savings banks in 1992, the newly integrated TSB was very much a small player in the Irish banking sector. The bank had total assets of €1,401.7 million in 1992, half of which were held on deposit with the Minister for Finance, with lending of only €385 million. Between 1992 and 2000, the bank developed its operations considerably, expanding its loan book year-on-year and generating healthy profits in a highly competitive retail banking environment. By 2000, total assets stood at almost €3.1 billion, over €2.5 billion of which was made up of loans and advances. While the TSB expanded considerably in the pre-privatisation period, its performance as measured by the profitability and efficiency indicators presented in Table 4.8 and Figure 4.8 remained relatively static.

Since the operations of the TSB were merged into the IL&P group, results are not available post-privatisation. However, an examination of the results for Permanent TSB reveal considerable improvements in performance after 2001, with the bank establishing a significant presence in the retail banking sector. By 2007, the bank had accumulated over half a million current account customers and registered considerable growth in bank lending and mortgage lending, with Permanent TSB competing strongly in this highly competitive sector. Total lending increased from almost €13 billion in 2001 to over €39 billion in 2007, and the bank

**Table 4.8  Summary of Results for TSB**

| Indicator | Pre-privatisation | |
|---|---|---|
| | 1993–96 | 1997–2000 |
| Real Operating Income | 2.25 | 11.01 |
| Real Total Assets | –1.14 | 12.44 |
| Employment | –1.51 | 4.46 |
| ROE | 26.26 | 21.58 |
| Profit Margins | 29.99 | 32.76 |
| Asset Utilisation | 12.51 | 11.30 |
| ROA | 3.74 | 3.70 |
| Cost/Income ratio | 70.01 | 67.24 |
| Income Efficiency | 90.38 | 105.50 |

*Source*: Authors' calculations from TSB annual reports.
*Notes*: (1) Results for Real Operating Income, Total Assets and Employment are presented as average annual percentage changes; (2) Results for Profit Margin, Asset Utilisation, ROA and Cost/Income are presented as average annual rates; (3) Results for Income Efficiency are presented as average annual Income Efficiency (in €'000s).

*Figure 4.8*   TSB Performance, 1992–2000

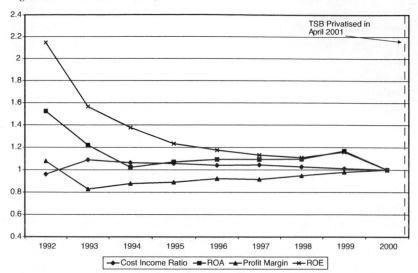

*Note*: Results were normalised to equal 1 in the year prior to privatisation (2000).

recorded strong growth in profits year-on-year (IL&P Annual Report, 2007).

While no accurate post-privatisation data is available it is evident that the privatisation of the TSB and its merger with Irish Permanent allowed the bank to significantly expand its activities. Although the bank improved its efficiency and profitability in the run up to divestiture, it was very much a small player in the retail banking sector and would arguably not have had the funding and scale necessary to develop its business and compete with the larger banks in the highly competitive Irish banking market had it remained within the public sector.

### 4.7.3   Agricultural Credit Corporation

The ACC was established in 1927 in order to provide medium- to long-term loans to farmers and to facilitate the development of co-operatives. The bank was very much a small operation up until 1960. However, a number of Acts passed by the government during the 1960s allowed it to expand its activities significantly. This was further aided by Ireland's entry into the EEC in 1973, which led to an increase in investment in agriculture and a considerable expansion in the ACC's business. Up until the 1980s, little importance was placed on ACC's profitability, with the bank mainly used as a means of providing finance on reasonable terms to farmers without a major emphasis on obtaining a high return on capital. During the late 1980s, however, the ACC struggled due to severe financial difficulties experienced by the agricultural sector at the time. The bank incurred a loss of approximately €19 million in 1987, and was dependent on a government guarantee against losses on its loans to survive. In recognition of its vulnerability to conditions in the agricultural sector, the ACC began to diversify after 1989 and entered the mortgage and business lending markets.

During the 1990s, the ACC developed rapidly and performed relatively well, expanding its business sector and mortgage operations. The bank was embroiled in the DIRT tax[25] evasion scandal uncovered by the Public Accounts Committee in 1999 and was forced to pay €22.7 million to the Revenue Commissioners in settlement of unpaid tax liabilities dating back to 1986. After a proposed merger with the TSB failed, a new CEO and senior management team were appointed in January 2000 in order to bring about improvements in efficiency and organisational control. A restructuring plan involving voluntary redundancies aimed at reducing operating costs was put in place, and the new management team refocused the bank's business away from retail banking and mortgages towards more profitable business banking activities (Annual Report, 2002).

In October 2001 it emerged that Rabobank Nederland, the Dutch co-operative bank, was prepared to make an offer for the ACC and, in December of the same year, a sale price of €165 million was agreed upon. The sale of ACC to Rabobank was completed in February 2002 and a comprehensive change management programme was immediately put in place by the new owners (Annual Report, 2002). A new board of directors was appointed and set about targeting the provision of banking services to SMEs and agricultural customers. Table 4.9 and Figure 4.9 present the pre- versus post-privatisation results for ACC's performance. The pre-privatisation years are split into two separate four-year periods while post-privatisation data is only available for four years after divestiture.

Although total assets increased steadily in the two pre-privatisation periods, it must be borne in mind that ACC's total assets were relatively low in the early 1990s. Between 1994 and 2001, total assets increased from €1,182.9 million to €3,313.5 million. ACC benefited from its privatisation as the ease of access to funding from the much larger Rabobank Group enabled it to significantly expand its lending, increasing its loans to customers and businesses from €564.6 million and €2,318.7 million respectively at the end of 2001 to €2,254.5 million and €6,844.9 million by the end of 2005. This increase in business was funded through borrowings from other Rabobank Group members as well as from an increase in customer accounts (ACC, 2005).

The rapid increase in total assets post-privatisation is not reflected in an increase in profitability as measured by ROA. The fall in ROA evident in Table 4.9 and Figure 4.9 both before and after privatisation is consistent with the general trend in the Irish banking sector. Since the Central Bank began keeping records, ROA for the Irish banking sector decreased from 2 per cent in 1993 to 1.1 per cent in 2005 (CBFSAI, 2006a). The reduction in ROA across the industry was due to a decrease in asset utilisation driven by a decline in net interest margins. The experience at ACC has thus been no different to the rest of the banking industry. While profit margin remained relatively static prior to privatisation, and increased after divestiture, ACC's asset utilisation ratio has fallen continuously since 1994.

There was a significant improvement in the cost/income ratio post-privatisation with the bank successfully limiting its cost growth while simultaneously increasing operating income leading to an improvement in efficiency. By 2005, ACC's cost/income ratio had fallen to 54.66 per cent, bringing the bank very much in line with the average for the banking sector. Overall, the analysis lends some support to the hypothesis that the privatisation of ACC was associated with improved enterprise performance. Whereas the pre-privatisation period was char-

Table 4.9　Summary of Results for ACC

| Indicator | Pre-privatisation | | Post-privatisation |
| --- | --- | --- | --- |
| | 1994–97 | 1998–2001 | 2002–05 |
| Real Operating Income | 2.72 | 7.47 | 8.73 |
| Real Total Assets | 18.28 | 6.15 | 22.34 |
| Employment | 4.98 | 0.79 | 1.59 |
| ROE | 25.29 | 16.55 | 17.45 |
| Profit Margin | 32.96 | 32.19 | 37.40 |
| Asset Utilisation | 8.17 | 6.69 | 4.33 |
| ROA | 2.71 | 2.16 | 1.59 |
| Cost/Income ratio | 67.04 | 67.81 | 62.01 |
| Income Efficiency | 117.66 | 134.85 | 175.55 |

*Source*: Authors' calculations from ACC annual reports.
*Notes*: (1) Results for Real Operating Income, Total Assets and Employment are presented as average annual percentage changes; (2) Results for Profit Margin, Asset Utilisation, ROA and Cost/Income are presented as average annual rates; (3) Results for Income Efficiency are presented as average annual Income Efficiency (in €'000s).

*Figure 4.9* ACC Performance, 1994–2005

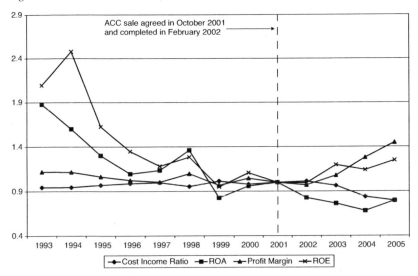

*Note*: The financial year end for ACC's accounts is 31 December. Therefore, although the company was officially sold in February 2002, 2001 is taken to be the year of privatisation and the results above are normalised to equal 1 in that year.

acterised by a declining or flat trend in most indicators, the evidence suggests that change in ownership was followed by stronger performance in the years covered.

## 4.8    Irish Life

Calculating profitability for any life assurance company is complicated by virtue of the nature of the business. Although the company receives an income in the year a policy is sold, that income is offset by payments of commissions to brokers, administration costs and the amount that must be set aside to cover future payouts to policyholders. Various actuarial methods of measuring value and performance can be used and each method differs in the way the value of an insurance policy sold in one year is shown in the profit and loss account and balance sheet. Since Irish Life used different valuation methods pre- and post-privatisation,[26] it is not possible to compare performance using a consistent actuarial method of valuation. Instead, a number of basic measures of performance specific to the life insurance industry are adopted in order to provide an overall picture of post-privatisation performance.

The growth in real income, real funds (total funds under management), real sales (new business) and employment are all expressed as average annual percentage changes. Profitability is measured using return on investment (ROI) and the claim/premium ratio, and both measures are presented as average annual rates. The claim/premium ratio relates outgo to income and, unlike most performance indicators, the lower the ratio is, the more profitable the company. Labour productivity is measured using income efficiency (IEFF) and assets per employee, and both are expressed as average annual rates. Further information on the formulae used to calculate each indicator is included in Table 4A3 in the appendix.

The analysis of pre-privatisation performance in Table 4.10 is split into two four-year periods. The 1980s was a decade of significant expansion for Irish Life. Between 1980 and 1990, funds under management increased from just over €800 million to €5,696 million, while income from premiums and investments increased from €291.74 million in 1981 to €1,090.29 million in 1990. Irish Life's UK subsidiary expanded rapidly and, by 1990, it was contributing some 14 per cent of total premium income. The company also established a presence in the US, French and Norwegian markets. The impact of these developments is evident from the improvement in most of the indicators in Table 4.10 prior to 1991. Although the average return on investment fell slightly in the 1987–90 period, this was mainly due to the considerable increase in total assets in the late 1980s.

Table 4.10    Summary of Results for Irish Life

| Indicator | Pre-privatisation | | Post-privatisation | |
|---|---|---|---|---|
| | 1983–86 | 1987–90 | 1991–94 | 1995–98 |
| Real Income | 15.36 | 5.73 | −1.07 | 7.49 |
| Real Sales | 26.81 | −0.02 | 2.76 | 10.96 |
| Real Funds | – | 16.96 | 9.42 | 15.05 |
| Employment | 5.11 | 6.19 | 0.73 | 0.71 |
| ROI | 6.11 | 5.40 | 5.56 | 4.76 |
| Claim/Premium | 56.55 | 63.37 | 84.92 | 91.49 |
| IEFF | 576.90 | 650.90 | 518.84 | 636.92 |
| Assets per Emp. | 2,394.13 | 3,001.92 | 2,760.44 | 4,221.75 |

*Source*: Authors' calculations from Irish Life annual reports.
*Notes*: (1) The average growth in employment for 1983–86 is a two-year average since staff numbers were not available pre-1984; IEFF and Assets per employee are three-year averages for the same period; (2) The Real Income, Sales, Funds and Employment indicators are expressed as average annual percentage changes; (3) Results for the remaining indicators are expressed as average annual rates.

*Figure 4.10*    Irish Life Performance, 1984–98

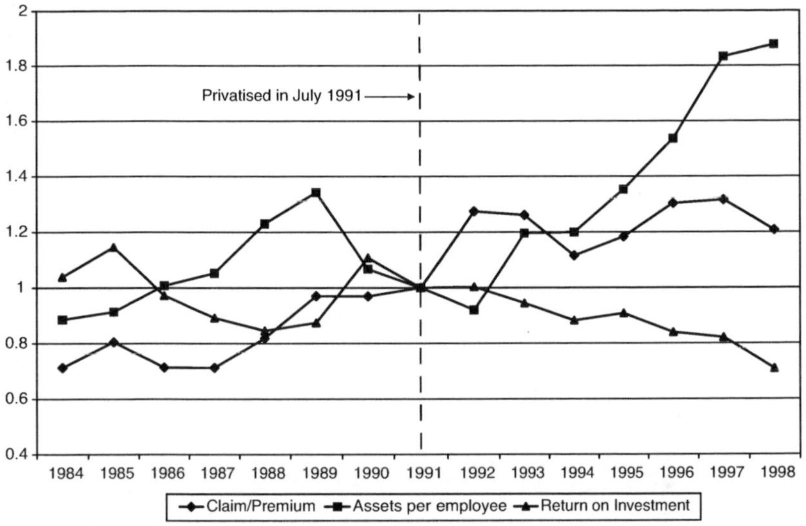

*Note*: Results are normalised to equal 1 in the year of privatisation (1991).

The deterioration in the claim/premium ratio experienced before divestiture continued after 1991 although the ratio began to improve slightly after 1997. The high claim/premium ratio recorded by Irish Life during the 1995–98 period was in line with the rest of the Irish life insurance industry, with average ratios of over 80 per cent experienced by the industry in 1997 and 1998 (CBFSAI, 2006a). The fall in return on investment in the post-privatisation period is also consistent with that of the industry as a whole. Despite a slight decrease in the indicator between 1991 and 1994, the assets per employee ratio improved significantly after privatisation.

In general, Table 4.10 and Figure 4.10 show that pre-privatisation performance improvements in Irish Life were generally sustained following divestiture. These improvements were reflected in the company's share price, which remained above its IPO level from 1993 onwards, and by the time it merged with the Irish building society, Irish Permanent, in 1999 the company was trading at 317 per cent above its IPO price. It must be noted that at the time of the merger, Irish Life was outperforming the ISEQ index, which had increased by 272 per cent since Irish Life's flotation in 1991.[27]

## 4.9   Conclusion

By focusing on the question of enterprise performance, this chapter addresses one of the key issues in the privatisation debate. As the number of privatised enterprises in individual countries is rarely of a sufficient size to allow statistical analysis, single country studies generally focus on detailed cases of privatised companies (for example, Martin and Parker, 1997). The analysis conducted in this chapter faces the same constraint as only ten enterprises have been privatised in Ireland to date. Nonetheless, as the most recent divestiture dates back to 2006, sufficient scope exists for an analysis of the impact of privatisation over time that allows us to draw some reliable conclusions.

Parker (1999) asserts that 'static efficiency gains' are commonly observed in privatisation programmes and are generally associated with rationalisation programmes that include measures such as labour shedding and plant closures. With the exception of one enterprise (Irish Steel), all of the former SOES examined in this chapter accrued static efficiency gains in the run up to privatisation. Most companies implemented large-scale reductions in employment along with other cost-cutting measures in the drive towards commercialisation in the 1980s.

Post-privatisation performance has, in the main, been less impressive. Focusing on the six non-financial SOEs, the results fail to support the hypothesis that privatisation *per se* leads to an improvement in performance, with B&I Line proving the only exception. Irish Steel was closed five years after being acquired by a bigger player, having incurred continuous losses in the post-privatisation period. Although Eircom and Greencore did record improvements in the years following divestiture, these were not sustained. In both cases, the former SOEs were dominant players in their core markets (sugar and fixed-line telecommunications). Following privatisation, they faced increasingly competitive market environments and struggled to maintain the same rates of improved performance. A similar story arose in the cases of Aer Lingus and the INPC, where the competitive environments in the aviation and oil sectors have been characterised by high volatility. Overall, the pattern for non-financial companies has been the accrual of impressive static efficiency gains through the reduction of operating costs before privatisation. Once these gains have been exhausted, the challenges of operating in competitive markets have resulted in the rate of improvement slowing down or, in some cases, being reversed.

Turning to the four financial companies (Irish Life and the three state banks), we find that in each case the pre-privatisation period was characterised by a large expansion in business. All four companies recorded strong growth in their asset bases, with the ACC and ICC tripling the size of their businesses in this regard. Moreover, all four companies recorded general improvement in most key efficiency indicators. While the post-privatisation period was characterised by limited improvements in some indicators, it is necessary to sound some cautionary notes. First, all three banks were subsumed into bigger organisations and benefited from greater access to funds. In this regard, privatisation has provided benefits to the organisations and contributed to much needed competition in the Irish banking sector. Second, the years covered in the analysis of each financial institution preceded the crises in the global financial system and the Irish banking sector. Whereas the performance measures we adopt are commonly used in the banking sector and serve our needs in terms of comparing pre- and post-privatisation periods, the onset of the Irish banking crisis has illuminated the caution that ought to be taken when subjecting performance indicators to interpretation. We return to this point in Chapter 8.

On balance, the Irish privatisation experience provides little evidence to support the fundamental hypothesis that a change to private owner-ship is performance enhancing. Ownership is but one of a complex set of factors that impact on performance. Other important factors include market structure and factors internal to the relevant organisation, such as structure, management and governance. An important question con-cerns what would have happened in the absence of privatisation. The vast majority of cases analysed in this chapter demonstrate that public ownership is compatible with significant improvements in perfor-mance. Our conclusion is that these improvements were largely static in nature and there was no clear indication that sustained dynamic efficiencies would have followed under public ownership. Such efficien-cies are more likely to be determined by the degree of competition faced and how individual enterprises operate in response to competitive pres-sures. Performance is less likely to be a function of ownership in this context.

## Appendix: Performance Measurement Indicators

Turnover and profit figures used in the calculation of SEFF and VAE were deflated for each company with an appropriate industry/product price index where possible; wherever these figures were unavailable the overall consumer price index (CPI) was taken to be the most appropriate proxy. Since a number of the companies

Table 4A1    Performance Indicators for Non-Financial SOEs

| Indicator | Formula |
|---|---|
| Return on Sales (ROS) | $\dfrac{\text{Profit}}{\text{Turnover}}$ |
| Return on Assets (ROA) | $\dfrac{\text{Profit}}{\text{Total Assets}}$ |
| Sales Efficiency (SEFF) | $\dfrac{\text{Turnover} \div \text{price index}}{\text{Average Number of Employees}}$ |
| Value-Added per Employee Hour (VAE) | $\dfrac{(\text{Wages} + \text{Depreciation} + \text{PBITE}) \div (\text{price index})}{(\text{no. of employees}) \times (\text{average hours worked})}$ |

*Note*: When calculating ROS and ROA, profit before interest, tax and exceptional items (PBITE) is used in order to avoid the distortion caused by changes in accounting practices in relation to exceptional items and interest charges before and after divestiture.

examined had different financial calendars, specific deflators were created for all companies based on the month reported as the financial year-end. The exact deflators used for each company along with the data source for each deflator are provided below.

Figures for average hours worked per week used in the calculation of VAE were sourced from the Central Statistics Office (CSO) and the OECD. Unfortunately, industry-specific data for hours worked was unavailable in most cases and proxies had to be used instead. Figures for the manufacturing industry as a whole were used for the non-financial companies examined, while figures for the business sector were used for the financial companies analysed.

### Irish Sugar deflator

Irish Sugar turnover consisted of revenue from its sugar, food and agribusiness divisions. Separate deflators were used for each category of turnover to calculate real sales. A deflator based on white sugar prices sourced from the CSO was used to deflate sugar turnover, the 'food and non-alcoholic beverages' sub-index of the CPI sourced from the CSO was used to deflate turnover for the food division, and the CPI index excluding food and energy sourced from the CSO was used to deflate turnover for the agribusiness division as no specific deflator could be sourced. Since no breakdown of profit by division was available, the CPI (food and non-alcoholic beverages) index was used as a proxy to deflate profit figures used in the calculation of VAE.

### B&I Line deflator

B&I Line turnover and profit was deflated using a deflator constructed from the 'sea transport' sub-index of the CPI sourced from the CSO. This sub-index was only available from 1990 onwards, consequently, for the years 1986–89 the 'transport' sub-index of the CPI was used as a proxy.

### Irish Steel deflator

It was not possible to source an appropriate industry specific deflator for Irish Steel turnover and profit. Consequently a deflator constructed from the overall CPI was used as a proxy.

### Telecom Éireann/Eircom deflator

Telecom Éireann turnover and profit was deflated using a deflator constructed from the communications sub-index of the CPI sourced from the CSO.

### INPC deflator

INPC turnover and profit was deflated using a deflator constructed from monthly crude oil prices. Prices used were spot oil prices (West Texas Intermediate) in US dollars per barrel sourced from Dow Jones & Company.

### Aer Lingus deflator

Aer Lingus turnover and profit was deflated using the 'transport by air' sub-index of the CPI sourced from the CSO.

### Performance indicators for financial SOEs

Real operating income for each bank was calculated by deflating total operating income for each bank by a deflator constructed from the 'financial services' sub-index of the CPI sourced from the CSO.

**Table 4A2    Performance Indicators for State Banks**

| Indicator | Formula |
|---|---|
| Return on Equity (ROE) | $\dfrac{\text{Profit}}{\text{Shareholder's Equity}}$ |
| Profit Margin | $\dfrac{\text{Profit}}{\text{Total Operating Income}}$ |
| Asset Utilisation | $\dfrac{\text{Gross Income}}{\text{Total Assets}}$ |
| Return on Assets (ROA) | $\dfrac{\text{Profit}}{\text{Total Assets}}$ |
| Cost/Income ratio | $\dfrac{\text{Operating Expenses}}{\text{Total Operating Income}}$ |
| Income Efficiency (IEFF) | $\dfrac{\text{Real Operating Income}}{\text{Average Number of Employees}}$ |

*Note*: (1) Profit before Tax, Provisions and Exceptional items (PBTPE) is used as the numerator for the ROE, ROA and profit margin indicators; (2) Shareholder's equity is simply the difference between total assets and total liabilities on each bank's balance sheet; (3) The Operating Expenses figure used in the calculation of the cost/income ratio excludes provisions for bad debts, liabilities and charges.

**Table 4A3    Performance Indicators for Irish Life**

| Indicator | Formula |
|---|---|
| Return on Investment (ROI) | $\dfrac{\text{Investment Income}}{\text{Total Assets}}$ |
| Claim/Premium Ratio | $\dfrac{\text{Claims Paid}}{\text{Net Premium Income}}$ |
| Income Efficiency (IEFF) | $\dfrac{\text{Real Income}}{\text{Average Number of Employees}}$ |
| Assets per Employee | $\dfrac{\text{Real Total Assets}}{\text{Average Number of Employees}}$ |

*Note*: Real Income = Premium Income + Investment Income.

Real total income and total assets were calculated using a deflator constructed from the 'insurance' sub-index of the CPI sourced from the CSO. This sub-index was not available until 1989, consequently the CPI index excluding food and energy was used as a proxy for the years 1983–88.

# 5
# The Financial Costs of Privatisation

## 5.0   Introduction

Privatisation is often justified on the grounds that that the removal of SOEs from the public sector balance sheet circumvents the need for future capital injections and reduces future pressure on government expenditure and balances. In some cases, the revenues raised from the sale of SOEs have been used to lower the annual borrowing requirement. In the UK, for instance, the Thatcher governments used accounting conventions to deduct the proceeds of privatisation from the public sector borrowing requirement (PSBR).[1] This essentially amounted to a sleight of hand in the accounting sense as privatisation proceeds were financing government expenditure and should therefore have been added to the PSBR. This sleight of hand was recognised by the EC, which disallowed privatisation receipts in the calculation of budget deficits under the Maastricht criteria. Nevertheless, privatisation receipts can be used to reduce government debt, which will indirectly reduce budget deficits via lower interest payments.

From an economic perspective, the key question concerns the precise impact of privatisation on the net worth of the public sector. Vickers and Yarrow (1988: 185–8) describe how it is necessary to distinguish between the short- and long-term effects of privatisation on government accounts in order to determine its real economic position. In the short term, the net effect depends on how much the PSBR is reduced by the sales proceeds, the company's payment of interest and dividends and the capital expenditure programme of the company. However, if the company is profitable (which is a realistic assumption), its profits move out of the public sector accounts, thereby increasing the PSBR.

In the long term, the financial impact depends on whether the assets are correctly priced, and on the magnitude of transaction costs (for example, advertising and professional fees). In essence, an asset is correctly priced if the sale price equals the discounted value of all future income streams to the government. If the government receives this price and does not incur any transaction costs, its net worth does not change. Neither of these circumstances is likely to occur, however. The situation becomes more complicated when one takes into account the impact of privatisation on company behaviour. If the company improves its performance after privatisation, and this is accounted for in the price, then the net worth of the government depends on the direct (for example, advisory fees) and indirect (for example, underpricing) costs incurred in the process of privatisation.

Florio (2004) notes that, at any time, the public sector net worth (PSNW) depends on several variables, including the stock of public capital and debt, the marginal rate of return on public and private capital before tax, and the tax rate. He concludes that in the absence of an appropriate fiscal model, 'we cannot predict the impact of divestitures on the PSNW' (2004: 266). As a result of these methodological difficulties, much of the academic literature on the relationship between privatisation and public finances focuses on aspects such as direct and indirect costs. This chapter adopts a similar approach in examining the exchequer related aspects of privatisation. In particular, it examines the extent to which Irish governments have succeeded in maximising the net proceeds from the divestiture of SOEs. Since cost minimisation represents the corollary of revenue maximisation, we focus on the costs associated with privatisation in Ireland and examine the details and magnitude of these costs in an international comparative context.

## 5.1 The costs of privatisation: Key issues and international experience

### 5.1.1 Direct costs

The direct costs associated with various privatisation programmes include the costs of promotion, professional and advisory fees and underwriting fees. The nature and extent of these costs has received considerable attention in the privatisation literature, with critics of privatisation frequently drawing attention to their excessive magnitude (Martin, 1993), as well as the wider question of the involvement of large accountancy firms and banking interests in both policy formulation and policy implementation in the sphere of public service reform (Shaoul *et al.*, 2007).

Table 5.1   Empirical Evidence on Direct Costs

| Authors | Year | Country | Direct costs as a % of proceeds |
|---|---|---|---|
| Buckland | 1987 | UK | 4.20 |
| Vickers & Yarrow[†] | 1988 | UK | 5.18 |
| Jenkinson & Mayer[†] | 1988 | UK | 3.77 |
| Bel | 1998 | Spain | 4.00 |
| Jones et al.[*] | 1999 | 59 countries | 3.90 |
| Harris & Lye[†] | 2001 | Australia | 3.18 |

[†] Authors' own elaboration of results presented in each study.
[*] Jones *et al.* (1999) only report the cost of underwriting as a percentage of the issue proceeds and do not include other expenses associated with the flotation process.

A selection of the international empirical evidence on the direct costs related to the sale of SOEs is summarised in Table 5.1. The findings in relation to the direct costs incurred as part of the UK's privatisation programme prior to 1988 differ slightly across studies. Both Buckland (1987) and Jenkinson and Mayer (1988) included every privatised SOE in the UK in their analyses, whereas Vickers and Yarrow (1988) only included the sale of major privatised companies. Buckland (1987) argued that costs were higher in the bigger issues as the government used them as a means of widening share ownership, thereby making them more expensive to market. The author claimed that 'the attempt to market abnormally large proportions of large business' equity to a fragmented ownership is inevitably costly and adds to the picture of large-scale, avoidable costs of the policy' (Buckland, 1987: 250).

The fact that Vickers and Yarrow (1988) report higher average direct costs as a percentage of proceeds is thus understandable, since they concentrate solely on large share issue privatisations. The authors noted that in the case of the two most expensive asset sales in their analysis – British Telecom (BT) and British Gas – the two largest components of expenses related to the sales were small shareholder incentives consisting of bill vouchers and bonus shares (totalling GBP£111 million in the case of BT and GBP£185 million in the case of British Gas), and the fees and commissions associated with the underwriting and placing of shares.[2]

Bel (1998) found that the direct costs incurred in Spanish privatisations amounted to 4 per cent of total proceeds, with financial intermediary expenses such as underwriting fees accounting for the majority of direct costs. Harris and Lye (2001) in their study on the fiscal consequences of privatisation in Australia found that the direct costs of

Australian privatisations amounted to just over 3 per cent, suggesting that Australian sales were reasonably cost efficient in comparison to UK divestitures. However, it must be noted that some of the costs presented in their analysis are expected costs sourced from prospectuses and, as such, may be considerably understated.[3] Buckland (1987), Vickers and Yarrow (1988) and Jenkinson and Mayer (1994) all make the point that prospectuses released by companies being privatised tend to significantly underestimate the true costs of the privatisations.

In general, the largest portion of the direct costs incurred as part of privatisation in various countries relates to underwriting fees.[4] Both Mayer and Meadowcroft (1985) and Vickers and Yarrow (1988) argue that there is no overriding reason why governments need to spend large amounts of money on underwriting fees. Governments are far more capable of bearing risk than private firms and, more specifically, underwriters. Moreover, governments do not face the cash flow constraints of a private firm. Private firms often depend critically on selling all of the shares being offered when raising funds or else they face becoming severely indebted. It therefore makes good sense for private firms to underwrite their issues. Governments face no such cash constraint as their borrowing powers can more than make up for any shortfall in share proceeds.

### 5.1.2   Indirect costs

The indirect costs of privatisation include the cost of underpricing, as well as costs related to debt write-offs or indemnities granted as part of a divestiture. By far the largest indirect cost in most privatisations is the cost of underpricing. The vast majority of empirical studies on the costs associated with privatisation concentrate on this particular aspect, rather than direct costs or other less significant costs. Most authors agree that the extent of undervaluation varies according to the method of sale, and to the various underlying political and economic objectives of privatising governments.

Buckland (1987) outlines three methods by which companies can offer shares; they can make:

1) Offers for sale at a *fixed price* – where applicants indicate the number of shares they wish to subscribe to at a pre-announced price;
2) *Tender* offers – where a minimum price is set as a guide and applicants are then invited to bid at or above that price, after which the 'strike price' (sale price) is chosen and the shares allocated. Any applications below the strike price are rejected;

3) *Placements* – where shares are not made available to the general public but are sold to institutional investors and/or large private investors.

Fixed price offers (or offers for sale) generally involve the most uncertainty since, after setting the price, the government must wait one to two weeks to see whether investors accept it. Within that waiting time, movements in other share prices could render the government's price unfeasible. Tender offers, where the forces of supply and demand set the price, are expected to lead to somewhat more accurate pricing and, as a result, the level of underpricing associated with tenders is generally much lower than that of offers for sale (Buckland, 1987; Vickers and Yarrow, 1988; Jenkinson and Mayer, 1994). However, there is a risk that tender offers might be undersubscribed as happened in the cases of Britoil and Enterprise Oil, which were privatised in the UK in the 1980s. Underpricing also depends on whether or not the company is new to the market and if there are similar companies already trading. Where the latter applies, the relevant market price can serve as a benchmark when deciding the issue price for the shares in the privatised company.

In relation to share issue privatisations, whenever a company is new to the market and there are no comparable companies already trading on the stock exchange, underpricing is inevitable as all governments wish to avoid political loss of face, and to minimise the chances that individual investors will incur capital losses. Even when a company is not new to the market, or there are comparable companies listed on the stock exchange, Vickers and Yarrow (1988: 171) claim some degree of underpricing is preferable for governments, since overpricing would leave the government with shares on their hands, applicants for shares would face losses and there would be general embarrassment for the government.

The question of whether share issue privatisations are characterised by excessive underpricing has received some attention in the privatisation literature. Dewenter and Malatesta (1997) explicitly compare privatisation initial public offerings (IPOs) with private company IPOs across 109 divestitures in eight countries. They conclude that there is no general tendency for governments to underprice privatisation IPOs to a greater extent than private issues. The exception to this general finding was the UK where, for larger privatisations, the existence of political objectives was found to have led to discounts far in excess of those in typical private issues in the UK.

Another standout feature of the UK privatisation programme in the 1980s was the decision to sell a number of SOEs in 'one go'. For example, large companies like British Gas and British Airways were sold all in one go, while half of BT was offered at the IPO stage in 1984. Buckland (1987), Vickers and Yarrow (1988) and Jenkinson and Mayer (1994) all argue that the methods of sale chosen by the UK government were seriously flawed and that selling a company's equity in several tranches is far superior to selling all the shares at once.[5] Whilst setting the initial share price remains problematic, 'once the first tranche is sold, a well-established market exists and further tranches can be priced with some accuracy' (Vickers and Yarrow, 1988: 184).

These claims are supported by the findings of Bel (1998), Huang and Levich (1999) and Jones *et al.* (1999) in relation to the level of under-pricing associated with privatisation IPOs and privatisation seasoned public offerings (SPOs). The average underpricing of share issue privat-isations, summarised in Table 5.2, clearly show how the average dis-counts related to the price of IPOs are considerably higher than the discounts related to the prices set for SPOs. For example, Bel (1998) found that the average cost of underpricing for all Spanish share offer-ings was 3.4 per cent. Although the average discount for IPOs was found to be 14.4 per cent, most of the revenues from public offerings accrued from SPOs, where the average discount was found to be just over 2 per cent. The available evidence therefore indicates that selling shares in stages is likely to reduce the extent of underpricing when pri-vatising SOEs.

The international evidence summarised in this section highlights the importance of controlling direct and indirect costs in terms of the objective of maximising the privatisation revenues accruing to the gov-ernment. The following section turns to the Irish case and examines the extent to which proceeds from privatisation have been diminished

Table 5.2   Average Underpricing in Share Issue Privatisations

| Authors | Year | Country | IPO underpricing | SPO underpricing |
|---|---|---|---|---|
| Buckland[†] | 1987 | UK | 15.9 | – |
| Vickers & Yarrow | 1988 | UK | 18.4 | – |
| Jenkinson & Mayer[†] | 1988 | UK/France | 32.8/18.6 | – |
| Dewenter & Malatesta | 1997 | 8 countries | 25.6 | – |
| Bel | 1998 | Spain | 14.4 | 2.1 |
| Huang & Levich | 1999 | 39 countries | 32.1 | 7.17 |
| Jones *et al.* | 1999 | 59 countries | 34.1 | 9.4 |
| Harris & Lye[†] | 2001 | Australia | 13.66 | – |

[†] Authors' own elaboration of results presented in each study.

by direct and indirect costs, as well as other factors such as employee share ownership plans that are pertinent to the Irish case.

## 5.2 Privatisation and exchequer finances in Ireland

Figure 5.1 displays the total proceeds from privatisation accrued by each member of the EU15 between 1977 and 2008. As expected, the four largest countries in the EU15, namely France, Germany, Italy and the UK, have accrued the most revenue with public offerings of shares in their telecommunications and utility companies accounting for a significant amount of the revenue raised. Smaller countries such as Ireland, Denmark and Belgium have generated the least amount of revenue, with Belgium, Denmark and Sweden the only countries to have generated the majority of revenue from private sales rather than public offerings.

A number of different methods have been adopted by the Irish state when divesting of its shareholdings. In the first two sales, those of Irish Life and Irish Sugar/Greencore in 1991, the government floated majority

*Figure 5.1*  Privatisation Revenues by EU15 Country, 1977–2008

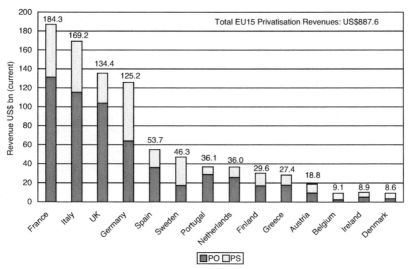

*Source*: Authors' elaboration of data sourced from *Privatization Barometer* database.
*Notes*: (1) PO = public offering, PS = private sale; (2) Luxembourg was not included given the small size of its economy and limited scope for privatisation; (3) The revenues above are expressed in current prices. When expressed in constant prices, the UK privatisation programme is placed first (see Figure 1.3).

shareholdings on the stock exchange by IPO. The remainder of its share-holdings were subsequently sold between 1992 and 1995 in SPOs where shares were placed with institutional investors. Shares were also sold by IPO in the case of Eircom and Aer Lingus. The sale of Eircom was the largest ever flotation on the Irish stock exchange, with the government selling its entire remaining shareholding of 50.1 per cent in July 1999. All other privatisations were executed by trade sale, with the three state-owned banks (ACC, ICC and TSB), B&I Line, Irish Steel and the Irish National Petroleum Corporation (INPC) all sold to going concerns.

### 5.2.1   Direct costs

Table 5.3 displays the actual proceeds that accrued to the exchequer from the ten Irish privatisations to date as well as the direct costs associated with each sale. Direct costs consist of expenses such as advisory, advertising, legal and underwriting fees incurred by the government in order to prepare SOEs for divestiture. Table 5.3 shows that the direct costs incurred for Irish divestitures amounted to an aggregate of 1.43 per cent of gross proceeds. When compared with the international experience, outlined earlier in Table 5.1, the direct costs incurred in

Table 5.3   Exchequer Proceeds and Direct Costs in Ireland

| Company | Year of sale | Proceeds (€'000s) | Expenses (€'000s) | Expenses as a % of proceeds |
|---|---|---|---|---|
| Greencore | 1991 | 210,650.8 | 1,726.84 | 0.82 |
| Irish Life | 1991 | 601,930.8 | 9,404.95 | 1.56 |
| B&I Line | 1992 | 10,792.8 | – | – |
| Irish Steel | 1996 | 0 | 655.68 | – |
| Eircom | 1999 | 6,399,907.9 | 97,642.86 | 1.53 |
| ICC | 2001 | 322,274.8 | 913.49 | 0.28 |
| TSB | 2001 | 408,350.3 | 460.66 | 0.11 |
| INPC | 2001 | 20,000.0 | 1,480.14 | 7.40 |
| ACC | 2002 | 154,603.0 | 1,159.48 | 0.75 |
| Aer Lingus | 2006 | 240,902.3 | 6,000.00 | 2.49 |
| **Total** | | **8,369,412.7** | **119,444.11** | **1.43** |

*Source*: Authors' own calculations from Exchequer Statements, Dáil Éireann reports and information requested from the Department of Finance.
*Notes*: (1) TSB and ACC expenses include advisor fees for proposed TSB/ACC merger incurred between 1999 and 2000. Half of the total fees of €621,346 were allocated to each company; (2) The table above details direct proceeds accruing to the exchequer only. Indirect proceeds that accrued to the privatised company are excluded. For example, when Aer Lingus was floated on the stock exchange in 2006, the government allowed the airline to issue new shares which raised over €530 million for the company.

Ireland are relatively low. However, it must be noted that the direct costs displayed in Table 5.3 exclude the costs incurred by the companies themselves. For instance, Aer Lingus is estimated to have paid some €30 million in commissions, fees and expenses prior to flotation on the stock market in 2006.[6]

As noted earlier, the direct costs associated with share issue privatisations are generally higher than those incurred when other methods of sale are adopted. This difference can be attributed to the significant cost of underwriting large share issues. For example, in their empirical analysis of share issue privatisations internationally, Jones *et al.* (1999) found that the cost of underwriting as a percentage of the issue amount averaged 3.9 per cent. In the Irish case, the most expensive sale was that of Eircom in 1999, with over €74 million of the €97.6 million in direct costs incurred paid to Merrill Lynch/AIB who coordinated and underwrote the IPO. As a percentage of the revenue raised from the IPO, this amounted to approximately 1.77 per cent.[7]

An important question that arises is whether large underwriting fees incurred as part of the Eircom flotation, as well as the other three SOEs floated on the stock market could have been avoided. As noted previously, in comparison to private sector firms, the government's superior capacity to bear risk, and the fact that it faces a considerably lower cash flow constraint, raises the question as to why it does not underwrite any issue itself. The issue of hiring a private sector underwriter becomes even more questionable when one considers the significant underpricing of shares that occurred during the IPOs of the four Irish SOEs floated to date.

## 5.2.2 Underpricing

We calculate the undervaluation of shares in Irish privatisations as the difference between the IPO price and the share price after one day's trading. This avoids the problems that can arise if later prices are used, since they can be affected by events that could not have been taken into account at the time when the shares were originally priced. For example, three days after the flotation of Aer Lingus in 2006, Ryanair launched a surprise hostile takeover bid for the airline that valued shares approximately 27 per cent higher than the initial IPO price.

Table 5.4 demonstrates that the total cost of underpricing in the case of the four Irish public enterprises privatised by IPO amounts to almost €843 million. This figure equates to just over 16 per cent of the proceeds raised from share issue privatisations, and almost 10.1 per cent of the total proceeds from the entire Irish privatisation programme,

Table 5.4    Share Discounts in SOEs Privatised by Flotation in Ireland

| Company | Offer price (€) | Day 1 price (€) | Share discount (%) | Proceeds (€m) | Cost of discount (€m) | Total cost as % gross proceeds |
|---|---|---|---|---|---|---|
| Greencore I | 2.92 | 3.25 | 11.30 | 80.019 | 9.042 | – |
| Greencore II | 3.36 | 3.52 | 4.70 | 41.913 | 1.970 | – |
| Greencore III | 3.49 | 3.75 | 7.27 | 88.719 | 6.450 | – |
| | | | | *210.651* | *17.462* | *8.29* |
| Irish Life I | 2.03 | 2.12 | 4.38 | 343.337 | 15.038 | – |
| Irish Life II | 2.41 | 2.54 | 5.39 | 132.688 | 6.634 | – |
| Irish Life III | 2.73 | 2.73 | 0.00 | 125.906 | 0.00 | – |
| | | | | *601.931* | *21.672* | *3.60* |
| Eircom | 3.90 | 4.62 | 18.46 | 4,212.215 | 777.575 | 18.46 |
| Aer Lingus | 2.20 | 2.44 | 10.91 | 240.902 | 26.282 | 10.91 |
| *Total* | | | | *5,265.699* | *842.991* | *16.01* |

*Source*: Exchequer Statements, Irish Stock Exchange, Davy's Stockbrokers, Goodbody's Stockbrokers.
*Notes*: (1) The Day 1 price quoted above for the second and third placements of shares in both Irish Life and Greencore relate to the closing price on the day *prior* to the placement of shares. (2) The total cost of discount in the case of Greencore and Irish Life excludes the cost of free shares granted to employees as well as the offer of further shares at a discount.[8]

a substantial loss of revenue to the exchequer. The level of discounting ranged from 4.38 per cent in the case of the IPO of Irish Life to 18.46 per cent in the case of Eircom. Although significant, especially in the case of Eircom, the discounts related to Irish IPOs have been relatively low when compared with the international empirical evidence outlined previously in Table 5.2.

The high cost of discounting in the case of Eircom (18.46 per cent) compared to Irish Life (3.6 per cent) and Irish Sugar/Greencore (8.29 per cent) is attributable to the method of sale chosen in each case. Contrary to indications given just months before flotation, the government opted to float its entire 50.1 per cent stake in Eircom in one go. In contrast, both Irish Life and Irish Sugar were sold in three stages with an IPO establishing a market price, which allowed subsequent placements of shares to be priced more accurately, thus reducing the size of discounts. The Irish experience is thus in line with the empirical evidence reviewed in section 5.1.2, where a number of authors argued that this approach to privatisation maximises exchequer proceeds.

In the most recent share issue privatisation, the government opted to retain approximately 28 per cent of its 85.1 per cent shareholding in Aer Lingus at the time of flotation. A valuation range for the airline was set between €2.10 and €2.70, with the government eventually opting to set the IPO price at the lower level of the range at €2.20. This was surprising given that the main objective of the flotation was to raise capital for the airline's future investment requirements. Although the underpricing from the first day's trading amounted to just under 11 per cent, Ryanair's hostile bid for the airline three days after the flotation valued Aer Lingus at €2.80 per share, indicating that the airline had been significantly undervalued.

### 5.2.3   Debt write-offs

Indirect costs incurred as part of the sales of public enterprises can also consist of debt write-offs and other financial undertakings on the part of the exchequer in order to prepare a company for divestiture. The sales of B&I Line, Irish Steel and the INPC all involved significant debt write-offs and the payment of other liabilities outstanding prior to being sold. In the case of B&I Line, all of the company's substantial long-term debt of over €44 million was written off prior to divestiture, with the government claiming it was necessary in order for any bid for the company to be made. The rationale behind such a large write-off in conjunction with the low purchase price ultimately accepted (€10.8 million) was questionable for a number of reasons:

1)   The company had recently begun to turn itself around after implementing significant rationalisation measures and was projecting an operating profit of over €5 million before repayments on debt in the year of privatisation;[9]
2)   An accumulated €127 million in corporation tax losses would be transferred to the new owners, which would enable them to avoid paying any corporation tax for a number of years;[10]
3)   The new owners would have access to the surplus on B&I Line's pension fund which was over-funded by approximately €14 million;[11] and
4)   The government had recently injected some €7.6 million into the company in preparation for privatisation which, in effect, represented an indirect debt write-off.

It was well known that the government had been conducting private negotiations with B&I Line's new owner, ICG, since 1990 and was very much in favour of an ICG takeover of B&I Line, especially given that ICG was an Irish operation. The €7.6 million cash injection into the

company prior to divestiture was seen as a further incentive to facilitate an ICG bid for the company.[12]

While the government's decision to sell B&I Line is understandable
given the substantial capital injections it had made in the company since
1965, the timing of the company's sale makes little sense. Had the government written off B&I Line's debt and then let the company trade
profitably without being hindered by debt repayments for a number of
years, it could have established a solid trading record and would arguably
have attracted a significantly higher bid if sold.[13] Although it is difficult
to estimate the true value of B&I Line, it is worth noting that ICG
was trading at 8.8 times its pre-interest earnings at the end of 1990.[14]
Given that B&I Line had made an operating profit of €3.17 million
in 1991, and was projecting operating profits of over €5 million in
1992 with further increases likely due to the implementation of more
rationalisation measures, the company was arguably worth three to
four times the €10.8 million received using even a conservative earnings
multiplier.[15]

The sale of Irish Steel necessitated the write-off of €21.5 million
in debt, as well as the payment of approximately €25.7 million to the
new owner, ISPAT, to cover various items such as interest charges
on debt, environmental works, provision for expenses, indemnities
and compensation for future restrictions on production.[16] The rationale
for the considerable debt write-off in this case was reasonable given
the large losses incurred by the company and its poor performance
record, despite significant capital investment by the state in the years
prior to privatisation. Although the government only received a nominal sale price of IRP£1,[17] ISPAT took on the remaining debt of almost
€25 million as part of the deal, as well as agreeing to invest approximately €30 million over a five-year period after privatisation.[18] The
sale of Irish Steel to ISPAT was arguably the best deal the government
could have expected to achieve, saving the company from prob-
able liquidation and securing the future of the company for another
five years.

The privatisation of the INPC[19] involved a large debt write-off as
well as a USD$75 million indemnity to cover any future environmental
liabilities the new owners might incur owing to pollution from the
refinery and terminal operations. Prior to the sale of the INPC, the
company had invested some €60 million in upgrading the Whitegate refinery in 1999 in order to meet EU Auto Oil 1 emission standards introduced in 2000. The debt associated with this investment
was written off as part of the sale with the overall costs and write-

offs of the assets and liabilities related to the sale amounting to €76 million. A total consideration of €47 million was received from the sale resulting in a net loss of €28.75 million (INPC, 2002).[20]

Following the sale of the refinery and terminal subsidiaries, the INPC's sole remaining activity was the management of the national strategic stocks which was carried out by its subsidiary, the National Oil Reserve Agency (NORA). It should be noted that following privatisation the INPC was left with its outstanding debts totalling €54.464 million in net terms at the end of 2001 (INPC, 2002). Moreover, the INPC incurred a number of further costs related to various transactions and provisions covered by the terms of the sale agreement with Tosco in subsequent years. These costs amounted to over €8.3 million (net) over the period 2002–05 and the INPC retains responsibility for future environmental liabilities (capped at USD$75 million).[21]

The large write-off and indemnity granted as part of the sale of the INPC represented a very poor deal for the exchequer, particularly given the fact that the company had only recently invested a considerable sum of money in upgrading its refining operations. The failure of the government to secure a better deal was highlighted at the beginning of 2007 when ConocoPhillips announced that it was putting the Whitegate refinery up for sale for approximately €350 million.[22] Although ConocoPhillips had invested in further upgrading of the facility since 2001, and ultimately decided not to sell the refinery, the high value placed on the facility raises questions about the government's decision to sell the refinery for just €116 million, while writing off much of the company's debt, as well as guaranteeing future environmental liabilities.[23]

In the case of the ACC bank, the government also granted an indemnity of €12.7 million to its new owners, Rabobank, to cover them from any potential liability that could have arisen from an ongoing legal case against the ACC.[24] This represented a significant transfer of risk particularly given the low sale price ultimately agreed upon. Rabobank acquired the ACC for €165 million, equivalent to the ACC's book value at the end of 2000 but just 0.9 times the expected book value for the 2001 year-end. Although the bank made a loss in 2000 after being fined €21 million in relation to tax arrears, the ACC had improved its profitability in the years leading up to its sale, and one must question the rationale of the government in selling the bank at a 10 per cent discount when banks are generally sold at a premium. Indeed, the TSB had been sold to IL&P earlier in the year at 1.8 times its book value.[25] Moreover, when one considers that part of the proceeds to the exchequer arising from the sale of the ACC were transferred to employees as part of the ESOP agreement, the deal represents a very poor return for the taxpayer.

The rationale behind privatising companies such as the B&I Line, Irish Steel and the INPC is understandable. However, the government's failure to secure a better return for the exchequer when selling the INPC and B&I Line resulted in significant losses for the exchequer. Had the government allowed the B&I Line some time to operate without its crippling debt burden, the taxpayer would arguably have recouped some of the investment that went into the company in the preceding 25 years. Similarly, in the case of the INPC, the failure of the government to negotiate a better deal, particularly given the substantial capital injections into the Whitegate refinery prior to divestiture, resulted in the loss of significant revenues to the exchequer.

### 5.2.4 Employee share ownership plans

Chapter 3 described how the transfer of significant shareholdings to employees has been a distinguishing feature of the privatisation process in Ireland. These schemes are commonly referred to as Employee Share Ownership Plans (ESOPs), and are generally granted in return for a restructuring and rationalisation deal. The details in relation to the creation of ESOPs and their impact in terms of the transfer of financial benefits and organisational power are discussed in Chapter 6. With regard to exchequer finances however, the key point is that the conditions

Table 5.5   Cost of Employee Share Ownership Plans in Irish Privatisations

| Company | 14.9% sold for (€'000s) | 14.9% value (€'000s) | Cost of ESOP (€'000s) |
|---|---|---|---|
| Eircom | 241,250 | 1,252,735 | 1,011,484 |
| ICC | 25,141 | 52,028 | 26,887 |
| TSB | 25,141 | 64,136 | 38,995 |
| ACC | 12,189 | 24,585 | 12,385 |
| INPC | n/a | 8,870 | n/a |
| Aer Lingus | n/a | 173,730 | n/a |
| *Total* | | | *1,089,751* |

*Source*: Authors' own calculations from government publications.
*Notes*: (1) in the case of the INPC, the company contributed €8.87 million to fund an ESOP for employees transferred to the purchaser. The cost of this was charged to the P&L account of the INPC and was not directly incurred by the exchequer; (2) the Aer Lingus ESOP had been in existence for a number of years prior to privatisation and it was not possible to estimate the cost to the exchequer.

attached to ESOPs have involved the allocation of shares to employees at less than their market value. ESOPs have therefore had the effect of significantly reducing the privatisation revenues accruing to the Irish exchequer.

In most cases, ESOPs have involved employees receiving 14.9 per cent of the company in exchange for the acceptance of a transformation agreement. The structure and details of the Eircom ESOP created a template that was largely followed in later divestitures. In the case of Eircom, 5 per cent of shares were granted in return for employees' acceptance of a rationalisation plan[26] with a further 9.9 per cent of shares purchased by the ESOP at a preferential rate of €241 million, which was determined by an independent valuation of the firm. As part of a partnership agreement, Eircom agreed to contribute €127 million[27] towards the cost of acquiring these shares, with the remaining €114 million funded by the ESOP through a loan.

Based on the proceeds from the sale of the government's 50.1 per cent shareholding (which raised €4.2 billion), the 14.9 per cent stake transferred to the ESOP was worth some €1.25 billion. The difference between the price paid by the ESOP and the actual value of its shareholding, amounted to over €1.01 billion. Table 5.5 provides the calculations of exchequer revenues foregone as a result of the establishment of ESOPs in other privatised companies. We estimate that the aggregate cost of ESOPs to the exchequer amounts to almost €1.1 billion, which represents over 13 per cent of total privatisation proceeds.

## 5.3   Conclusion

The privatisation of SOEs offers an attractive opportunity for governments to raise significant revenues for the exchequer. This chapter quantifies both the direct and indirect costs incurred in the execution of the ten divestitures in Ireland to date. Table 5.6 illustrates that these costs have amounted to over €2.14 billion, or 25.6 per cent of total exchequer proceeds. We find that, with the exception of Eircom, the level of underpricing and direct costs incurred have been modest compared to those in other industrialised countries. However, in the case of Eircom, which accounts for approximately 88 per cent of aggregate privatisation costs to date, these costs have been considerable.

We argue that the relatively high cost of underpricing in the case of Eircom can be largely attributed to the government's decision to sell its entire stake in Eircom in one go. In this regard, the case of Eircom is an outlier in European comparative terms. In most other EU15 countries,

Table 5.6    Gross Proceeds and Total Costs (€ millions)

| Company | Gross proceeds | Direct costs (1) | Indirect costs (2) | ESOPs (3) | Total 1+2+3 |
|---|---|---|---|---|---|
| Greencore | 210.651 | 1.727 | 17.462 | – | 19.189 |
| Irish Life | 601.931 | 9.405 | 21.673 | – | 31.078 |
| B&I Line | 10.793 | – | 44.441 | – | 44.441 |
| Irish Steel | 0 | 0.656 | 47.328 | – | 47.984 |
| Eircom | 6,399.908 | 97.643 | 777.575 | 1,011.484 | 1,886.702 |
| ICC | 322.275 | 0.913 | – | 26.887 | 27.800 |
| TSB | 408.350 | 0.461 | – | 38.995 | 39.456 |
| INPC | 20.000 | 1.480 | – | – | 1.480 |
| ACC | 154.603 | 1.159 | – | 12.385 | 13.544 |
| Aer Lingus | 240.902 | 6.000 | 26.282 | – | 32.282 |
| Total | 8,369.413 | 119.444 | 934.761 | 1,089.751 | 2,143.956 |

*Note*: Indirect costs include the cost of underpricing and debt write-offs.

national telecommunications companies have been sold by floating partial stakes on the stock market followed by the sales of further tranches.[28] As the majority of these sales preceded the flotation of Eircom, the Irish government's decision to eschew the option of a staggered divestiture is particularly questionable.[29]

The transfer of sizeable shareholdings to employees at considerable discounts has cost the Irish exchequer over €1 billion in terms of revenues foregone, and ESOPs account for the most significant proportion of costs in sales to date. It is worth noting that this calculation does not account for the fact that shares were allocated to employees on a tax-free basis. The capital gains tax revenue foregone serves to compound the overall loss to the exchequer. It is striking that there was no international precedent for either establishing a structured ESOP as part of the privatisation process or for the transfer of a shareholding of such magnitude to employees. The establishment of ESOPs has now become the norm for Irish SOEs slated for privatisation. In Chapter 6, we examine ESOPs in terms of their structure and outcomes to date.

Once the decision is made to privatise a company, a number of important subsequent decisions arise in relation to the privatisation process. These include decisions in relation to the timing of the sale, the amount of shares to be sold, the pricing of shares, and distributional issues such as preferential share allocations. This chapter highlights a number of suboptimal decisions concerning these issues in individual cases of privatisation in Ireland. Whereas the precedent-setting Eircom ESOP, as well as the decision to sell the government's entire stake at the IPO stage, dominate the aggregate costs incurred, the analysis also draws attention to debatable decisions in relation to debt write-offs (B&I Line and INPC), indemnities granted (INPC and ACC) and the valuation of companies (B&I Line, ACC and INPC).

Looking forward, it is important to note that the Irish state continues to hold majority shareholdings in enterprises operating in important sectors such as energy, transport and communications. The recent deterioration in the Irish public finances has prompted a number of calls for the privatisation of some of these enterprises. Although privatisation can raise useful revenues for the exchequer in the short- to medium-term, it cannot be justified on this basis alone. The analysis provided in this chapter shows that the revenues from such sales are rarely maximised as policymakers face a number of trade-offs when implementing privatisation policies. Balancing these trade-offs poses significant challenges and the findings presented in this chapter shows that Irish policymakers have much to learn from the privatisation programme to date.

# 6
# Employee Share Ownership Plans

## 6.0  Introduction

A unique feature of Ireland's privatisation experience has been the size of the shareholdings accrued by employees as part of all sales since the privatisation of Eircom in 1999. As discussed in earlier chapters, the Eircom privatisation set a precedent whereby employees secured a shareholding of 14.9 per cent of equity in privatised firms. This is far in excess of the size of shareholdings granted to employees as part of the divestiture of SOEs in other countries. The employee share ownership plans (ESOPs) granted in the Irish case have had significant impacts. In distributional terms, ESOPs have resulted in non-trivial losses of revenue to the exchequer while employees have made handsome gains. ESOPs have also had important consequences in terms of corporate governance with employees exercising considerable influence in the context of key strategic decisions. In this chapter, we examine the origins of ESOPs in the case of the Irish privatisation programme. We move on to describe the precise nature of the ESOPs and discuss the financial benefits accrued by employees as a consequence of significant share ownerships. We then turn to the role of the ESOP in strategic decisions in relation to Eircom and Aer Lingus, and ask whether these ESOPs have fulfilled the objectives normally ascribed to such schemes.

## 6.1  Employee share ownership plans: Objectives and evidence

The origins of employee share ownership can be traced back to US lawyer, Louis Kelso. According to Allen (2007), Kelso developed the concept of ESOPs as a means of reducing industrial conflict. The underlying rationale was that that if employees were given tax breaks to purchase shares in their own company, this would create a sense of identification with the company, and incentivise employee share owners to work in the interests of improving company performance and profits. Since Kelso first promoted his ideas in the 1950s, the level of employee share ownership in the USA has grown considerably, particularly after the introduction of legislation granting tax concessions on such schemes in 1974. Kim and Ouimet (2009) cite a survey by the *National Center for Employee Ownership* in the USA which reported that in 2007 nearly 14 million employees participated in 9,650 ESOPs with combined assets of over $925 billion in public and private firms.

The objectives of ESOPs are relatively straightforward, although they can vary from country to country. One of the principal reasons for the establishment of ESOPs in the USA is to provide retirement income for employees. The origins of ESOPs in the USA can be attributed to the fact that:

> ...there is no mandatory requirement that a [...] private sector employer provide retirement savings plans for employees. Employees participating in an ESOP [...] do not own the company stock directly, but receive the stock, generally when they retire, die, become disabled, or leave the company to work elsewhere.[1]

In addition to the objective of providing post-retirement income, ESOPs are also commonly established in order to align employee interests with those of other shareholders, and to provide employee compensation for firm restructuring in the form of a share of enterprise profits. In discussing the objectives of ESOPs, Irish trade unionist Paul Sweeney (2004) goes beyond financial considerations and emphasises goals such as providing employees with a collective influence on the operation of enterprise, and ensuring that shareholder interests do not dominate those of wider stakeholders (for example, consumers, employees and suppliers).

Cahill (2000) conducted a comprehensive review of international studies concerning the extent to which ESOPs have succeeded in the achievement of various objectives. The findings in relation to share ownership and employee satisfaction tended to be mixed, with some studies showing a positive relationship and others failing to establish a relationship between the two variables. It was, however, noteworthy that that in several of the studies covered there was evidence of a higher level of satisfaction only for those employee owners who perceived greater influence or participation in the enterprise. There was stronger evidence in relation

to organisational commitment and identity, with most studies finding a positive relationship, but in some studies this was conditional on
employee workplace participation. On the question of the relationship
between share ownership and employee behaviour, Cahill (2000) failed
to conclude that there was an automatic impact, but again some studies
found evidence that a combination of ownership and workplace participation had a positive effect. Cahill (2000) also reviewed the empirical
literature on employee share ownership and company performance. The
US-based experience, which has been the most comprehensively researched,
provides somewhat weak evidence that employee ownership alone may
improve corporate performance, but stronger evidence that a combination of employee ownership and employee participation may contribute
to improved performance.[2]

## 6.2   Privatisation and employee share ownership

Employee share ownership has been a feature of privatisation programmes
around the world as governments have used preferential allocation of
shares to employees in order to build support for privatisation. Shares are
generally offered to employees for free or at a discounted price in order to
ensure their consent to company restructuring and avoid opposition to
privatisation (Jones *et al.*, 1999). In a review of the impact of privatisation
on labour published by the World Bank, Kikeri (1998) notes how ESOPs
have been used in a wide range of sectors across countries including
Argentina, Bangladesh, Chile, Ghana, Mexico, Mozambique, Pakistan,
Turkey and others. In general, governments reserve anything between
3 and 10 per cent of shares for employees, depending on the size of the
transaction. Kikeri (1998) asserts that employee share ownership helps
improve labour relations and increase productivity as employees are given
a direct stake in the performance of the company. These improvements
are more likely when share ownership is combined with a system of workplace participation that includes initiatives such as the establishment of
quality work circles and continuous improvement programmes.

There is little in the line of detailed empirical research into the impact
of employee share ownership in the context of privatisation *per se*. The
extant research focuses mainly on financial rewards accrued by employees in the context of ESOPs. For example, Kikeri (1998) draws on examples such as the privatisation of telecommunications in Argentina and
electricity generation in Chile, and asserts that they produced large
financial gains for employees. She cites Shirley (1994) who details how
employees in Entel, Argentina's privatised telecommunications company,

received shares at one-sixth of the price paid by the winning consortium, and how the average employee realised capital gains of USD$25,000 due to the appreciation in share price. These studies do not address the impact of ESOPs in terms of other objectives such as employee commitment and behaviour, or corporate performance.

## 6.3 Privatisation and ESOPs in Ireland

### 6.3.1 Social partnership and the origins of ESOPs

There was little encouragement of employee share ownership in the first two cases of privatisation in Ireland (Irish Sugar and Irish Life). Although the Irish government followed the international trend of allocating shares at discounted prices to employees at the time of flotation, the size of the allocations was small. For example, when Irish Sugar was floated in 1991 the amount of shares allocated to employees was confined to 0.025 per cent free of charge and a further 2.1 per cent sold at a discount.[3]

The first sizeable share-ownership scheme in an Irish SOE was established at the national airline, Aer Lingus. Following the company's near collapse after the first Gulf War, a major rationalisation plan was agreed between management and trade unions. In return for accepting large-scale redundancies and changes to work practices, employees were granted 5 per cent of company equity as part of an Employee Share Participation Scheme (ESPS) in 1996. While representation at board level was in place in a number of SOEs, the share ownership scheme established at Aer Lingus marked a new departure in terms of employee participation.

The Aer Lingus scheme set a precedent for employee share ownership that the Irish trade union movement was keen to embrace. Although the trade union movement traditionally held a sceptical view of employee share ownership, this stance was modified in the mid-1990s. Allen (2007) describes how the Irish Congress of Trade Unions 'embraced the idea of the "social market" economy claiming it was not opposed to the declared aim of a shareholding democracy' (2007: 218). The same author attributes this change in approach to the deepening of the social partnership model, which brought about important changes with the unions shifting 'from believing there was a conflict of interest between capital and labour to viewing business as its actual partner' (2007: 218).

Social partnership is the short-hand term for the institutional arrangements that have, since 1987, brought together government, employers, unions, and (since 1996) non-government organisations to negotiate a strategic consensus on economic and social policy. These negotiations have manifested in a series of agreements that started with the *Programme for National Recovery* (PNR) for 1987–90 and culminated with *Towards 2016* for 2006–16. The origins of social partnership can be traced back to the 'deep economic, social, and cultural crisis' that gripped the country in the mid-1980s (O'Donnell, 2008). The agreements were largely framed in terms of a trade-off between wage restraint on the one hand, and social benefit and improvement and income tax reduction on the other (Smith, 2005).

Social partnership is often characterised as a form of neo-corporatism, the approach to political and economic management adopted in Europe, especially Austria and the Scandinavian countries after the Second World War (O'Donnell, 2008). Teague (1995), however, has observed that the Irish model was initially much more weakly developed than classical neo-corporatist models, especially at enterprise level, although this has changed over time. Smith (2005) noted how new institutional agreements included the establishment of a National Centre for Partnership in 1997 for the purpose of fostering partnership at an enterprise level.[4] This encouraged different forms of employee participation in line with a number of EU recommendations to this effect (Pendleton *et al.*, 2003), and provided a suitable institutional framework for the establishment of ESOPs in the context of privatisation.

### 6.3.2   Background to the first ESOP: Eircom

The ESPS at Aer Lingus established the principle of share ownership in the Irish SOE sector. However, the size of this shareholding was limited to 5 per cent of ordinary share capital. It was not until the establishment of an ESOP at Eircom that large-scale ESOPs became the norm, and therefore a unique feature of the Irish privatisation programme. Social partnership provided the wider context for the establishment of the Eircom ESOP. Although trade unions secured an effective veto on the privatisation of SOEs as part of the first social partnership agreement, the *PNR (1987–1990)*, this veto did not carry over into subsequent agreements. As previously discussed, Allen (2007) asserts that unions dropped their ideological opposition to privatisation as part of embracing employee share ownership in the 1990s. He quotes the then General Secretary of the Communications Workers Union (CWU), David Begg, who in 1996 advocated employee share ownership on the grounds that it 'would transform the relationship within companies between management and workers to one of cooperation and consensus' (quoted in Allen, 2007: 218).

In this context, the CWU supported Eircom's pursuit of a strategic alliance in exchange for employee participation and employee share ownership. In the run-up to the strategic alliance, the then Minister for Transport, Energy and Telecommunications, Alan Dukes, agreed the principle of employee share ownership in Eircom and offered a 5 per cent stake in exchange for significant restructuring. However, a coalition of the main unions in the company rejected this offer and sought a more significant stake in the company (McCarthy, 2007). Following the establishment of the strategic alliance in late 1996, trade unions and management formally agreed the *Telecom Partnership*, an enterprise-level agreement between trade unions and the company that centred on the introduction of a new partnership structure and significant changes to levels of employment and work practices. The *Telecom Partnership* provided the mechanism for agreeing that employees would obtain a 14.9 per cent stake of the company as part of the privatisation process. Sweeney (2004) explains that this percentage was based on the then government's decision to retain 50.1 per cent shareholding in Eircom (and all other SOEs). Since KPN/Telia owned 20 per cent and had an option to increase this to 35 per cent, the size of the ESOP was effectively the residual 14.9 per cent. Following a change of government in 1997, the new Fianna Fáil/Progressive Democrat coalition imposed a cap of 14.9 per cent on employee shareholdings in any Irish SOE (Sweeney, 2004).

In the case of Eircom, employees were not required to pay cash for the first 5 per cent stake in the company. This was granted on the basis of an agreement to accept significant changes in work practices, reduced employee numbers, increased employee pension contributions and the disbandment of existing employee benefit schemes. In exchange for accepting these measures, employees received a shareholding in the firm through the establishment of the Eircom ESOP. The remaining 9.9 per cent was made available in return for a discounted cash payment which could be paid from future profits. This provided a template for ESOPs in the case of later privatisations.

## 6.4 Eircom ESOP: Structure and financial gains for employees

### 6.4.1 ESOP structure

The Eircom ESOP is structured around a limited liability trust known as the Eircom ESOP Trustee Ltd (the Trustee). The Trustee consists of seven directors, four of whom are nominated by the union coalition, two of whom are nominated by the company and one of whom is independent. The Trustee retains and exercises ownership rights over the ESOP's shareholding on behalf of its participants. It is also responsible for the appointment of the ESOP's representatives to the company's board of directors. In addition, the Trustee administers its two constituent bodies, the Employee Share Ownership Trust (ESOT) and the Approved Profit Sharing Scheme (APSS). The precise architecture of these bodies is based on the purpose of acquiring shares in Eircom and distributing them to ESOP members.

The main functions of the ESOT are to acquire and hold shares on behalf of participants. The full 14.9 per cent of Eircom's ordinary share capital was acquired by the ESOT in December 1999. Five per cent was received on a phased basis as a *quid pro quo* for the implementation of restructuring measures, and the remaining 9.9 per cent was purchased by the ESOT at a significant discount. Participation in the scheme is based on length of service, with eligibility to membership initially based on the requirement of one year of continuous service prior to the establishment of the ESOP in November 1998.[5] Employees recruited between November 1998 and November 2002 became eligible for membership after one year of continuous service, but employees recruited after November 2002 did not qualify. While shares are held by the ESOT, the participants do not hold ownership rights. The ESOT holds voting rights in block, which it exercises on the basis of the wishes of participants expressed by way of ballot, with each member receiving one vote (McCarthy, 2007).

The ESOT distributes shares on a tax-efficient basis via a separate body, the APSS. Under tax legislation, once the shares have been retained (by the ESOT) for a period of three years, it is at the discretion of the ESOT to make annual tax-free distributions of up to €12,700 to each participant. Shares are appropriated by the APSS on behalf of participants and, in most cases, are distributed to participants immediately after apportionment.[6] Once distributed, participants can instruct the APSS to distribute the shares to them or a third party, to sell the shares on their behalf, or to retain the shares on their behalf.

### 6.4.2   Value to participants

To date, the Eircom ESOP has made twelve separate distributions to its participants (see Table 6.1). The first distribution followed the de-merger of the company's mobile phone operation, Eircell, which was sold to Vodafone in 2001. Following the de-merger, the ESOP held a large number of Vodafone shares which were distributed in May 2002 and December 2005. After separate takeovers by the Valentia consortium in 2001 and Babcock and Brown in 2006, the firm was de-listed from the stock exchange and ESOP participants were thus unable to

Table 6.1   Eircom ESOP Distributions, 2002–09

| Date | Type of shares | No. of shares* | Cash value (€) |
|------|----------------|----------------|----------------|
| May 2002 | Vodafone ordinary shares | 7,270 | 11,904 |
| Dec 2003 | Redeemable preference shares | 6,872 | 6,872 |
| April 2004 | Redeemable preference shares | 6,872 | 6,872 |
| Dec 2004 | Eircom ordinary shares | 3,307 | 5,556† |
| Mar 2005 | Eircom ordinary shares | 3,307 | 6,614† |
| Dec 2005 | Vodafone ordinary shares | 2,688 | 4,781 |
| Nov 2006 | Redeemable preference shares | 13,701 | 8,073 |
| June 2007 | Redeemable preference shares | 13,714 | 8,080 |
| Nov 2007 | Redeemable preference shares | 4,619 | 4,619 |
| June 2008 | Redeemable preference shares | 13,748 | 7,022 |
| Nov 2008 | Redeemable preference shares | 5,065 | 5,065 |
| June 2009 | Redeemable preference shares | 3,916 | 2,000 |
| Total | | – | 77,458 |

*Source*: www.esop.eircom.ie
* Figures represent distributions per employee with a full allocation.
† Value based on share price on day of distribution

realise the value of Eircom ordinary shares. As a consequence, the ESOP used the proceeds from redeemable preference shares to distribute cash benefits to participants.

In total, the Eircom ESOP has distributed over €770 million to its members since 2002. Table 6.1 shows that the value of distributions to employees entitled to a full allocation to date has amounted to over €77,000, although the full value of the ESOP to employees cannot be calculated until it has been wound up. Legislation dictates that the Trustee must distribute all of its shares by May 2019. In addition, under a provision of the *Taxes Consolidation Act 1997* known as the '15 year rule', the ESOP can only appropriate shares to former employees in a tax-efficient manner until May 2014. Given that the majority of ESOP members are no longer employees of the firm, it is likely that the ESOP will finalise distributions by that date.

## 6.5   Other ESOPs: Structure and employee gains

With the Eircom ESOP in place, a template was set for the establishment of similar programmes in other SOEs. In the three years after the full divestiture of Eircom, four other SOEs were privatised and ESOPs were granted in all cases. The three state-owned banks – the ACC, ICC and TSB – were all sold to larger banks between 2001 and 2002 and, in each case, ESOPs of 14.9 per cent were granted to employees. The INPC was sold in 2001 and also included an ESOP, however in this case employees did not receive a 14.9 per cent stake, instead receiving the approximate equivalent of a 7.6 per cent stake in the company. The most recent privatisation, that of the national airline, Aer Lingus, in 2006 also included an ESOP. However, the Aer Lingus ESOP is different to the others, in that a separate share-ownership scheme had been in existence at the airline for a number of years prior to divestiture.

The structure of the ESOPs established in the case of the three state banks is very similar to that of Eircom. In each bank, employees were granted a 5 per cent shareholding in return for the acceptance of a major transformation and flexibility agreement, whereby employees agreed to cooperate with the change of ownership process and subsequent changes in working practices and staff conditions. A further 9.9 per cent stake was then purchased by each bank on favourable terms, with the share purchase generally funded through contributions from each bank and borrowings. The structure of the INPC and Aer Lingus ESOPs differed from those established for the banks and a short summary of the ESOP established in each company is outlined below.

### 6.5.1    ACC ESOP[7]

The ACC was sold to the Dutch co-operative bank, Rabobank, for €165 million in February 2002. Employees received a 5 per cent shareholding in return for entering into a transformation agreement, and purchased a further 9.9 per cent shareholding for €12.2 million (the 9.9 per cent stake was actually worth €16.4 million based on the sale price). The purchase of shares was funded through ESOP borrowings and a contribution from the ACC, which bought out part of the staff's bonus scheme. The ESOP's 14.9 per cent shareholding was then sold to Rabobank in return for a Rabobank bond. The reason for this was the co-operative ownership structure of Rabobank, which did not allow for shares to be held in the bank. The Rabobank bond was held by the ESOP Trustee in the same way that shares would otherwise be held and distributed by other ESOPs such as that of Eircom. The amount borrowed by the ESOP to purchase the 9.9 per cent stake would be repaid partly through a 5 per cent profit sharing arrangement (subject to a cumulative limit of €6.35 million) and partly from interest income on the bond. Based on the sale price of the firm, the 14.9 per cent ESOP stake was worth €24.6 million, or approximately €50,000 per employee.

### 6.5.2   ICC ESOP[8]

The ICC was sold to Bank of Scotland (Ireland) for €349.18 million in February 2001. Prior to the sale of the bank, employees were granted a 5 per cent stake in the ICC in return for accepting the terms of a transformation and flexibility agreement, where employees agreed to considerable changes to work practices, including increased working hours and pension contributions. A further 9.9 per cent stake was purchased for €25.14 million (though this stake was in fact worth €34.57 million based on the sale price).[9] The purchase of the stake was funded through a contribution from the ICC and borrowings which would be largely repaid from dividends and a 5 per cent profit sharing arrangement (subject to a cumulative limit of €7.62 million). Based on the sale price of the ICC, the ESOP's 14.9 per cent stake was worth €52.03 million, or approximately €145,328 per employee.[10] Once the sale of the ICC went ahead, the ESOP's 14.9 per cent stake was swapped for shares in the Bank of Scotland. As in the case of Eircom and other ESOPs, the ESOP Trustee then managed these shares on behalf of employees, appropriating shares and making distributions to employees in a tax efficient manner.

### 6.5.3   TSB ESOP[11]

The TSB was sold to Irish Life & Permanent (IL&P) for €430.44 million in April 2001. As with the other state banks, employees received a 5 per cent stake in return for accepting a transformation agreement, and purchased a further 9.9 per cent stake for €25.15 million (this stake was in fact worth €42.61 million based on the sale price).[12] Since the TSB was not a company and was run by trustees, the bank had no shares and it was not possible to establish an ESOP. It was also not possible to establish an ESOP for TSB employees after the merger of the TSB's business with IL&P, since it was not possible to establish an ESOP for a particular group of employees within one company. It was therefore necessary to create a new subsidiary company of IL&P, Kencarol Ltd, and transfer all of the TSB's assets and liabilities to the new subsidiary company. TSB employees then acquired a 14.9 per cent stake in Kencarol which was transferred on, with the ESOP in place, to IL&P. Based on the sale price of the firm, the 14.9 per cent stake acquired by the TSB ESOP was worth €64.14 million, or approximately €53,446 per employee.[13]

### 6.5.4   INPC ESOP

The refinery and terminal operations of the INPC, which accounted for all of the INPC's trading activities, were sold to Tosco Corporation in

July 2001 for €116 million.[14] Unlike the three state banks and Eircom, employees of the INPC who transferred to Tosco were not granted the equivalent of a 14.9 per cent stake in the INPC. Instead, the ESOP established was provided with €8.87 million from the INPC to fund the purchase of shares in Tosco. The amount transferred to the ESOP thus represented the equivalent of approximately 7.6 per cent of the sale price and amounted to €38,734 per employee.[15]

### 6.5.5   Aer Lingus ESOP[16]

Prior to the establishment of the Aer Lingus ESOP, a separate employee share ownership scheme existed within the firm. In return for accepting the terms of a 1993 survival plan for the airline, an Employee Share Participation Scheme (ESPS) was established in March 1996. Under the terms of the scheme, employees could receive 10 per cent of the firm's profits before tax and exceptional items in the form of shares and/or cash. The scheme placed a limit of 5 per cent of issued share capital on the number of shares that could be made available. The scheme also placed a cumulative limit of €15.5 million on the amount of cash that could be paid out. The ESPS reached the maximum limit of shares in 1999 and the maximum limit of cash in December 2002.

The Aer Lingus ESOP was established in 2003, again in return for employees accepting a restructuring plan (the 2001 'Survival Plan' which was drawn up following the crisis that arose from the September 11th terrorist attacks in the USA). As part of the agreement, employees were allowed to increase their stake in the firm to 14.9 per cent in exchange for a pay freeze, staff reductions and changes in conditions of employment aimed at improving labour productivity. The 14.9 per cent stake that employees received consisted of the remaining shares held by the ESPS (4.26 per cent), shares received in exchange for the transformation of work conditions (0.74 per cent), and shares in lieu of pay forgone under the pay freeze (9.9 per cent). Under the terms of the ESOP, the ESPS was amended to become the Aer Lingus APSS. When the decision was made to privatise the airline by flotation on the stock market in 2006, the Aer Lingus ESOP acquired a 12.6 per cent stake in the firm (with the residual of the 14.9 per cent stake held by the APSS). Based on the €1.166 billion value of the airline on the date of flotation, the 12.6 per cent stake was worth €146.92 million, or approximately €31,493 per employee.[17] Employees who were also members of the ESPS established in 1996 would have received benefits in addition to those provided by the ESOP.

The details provided above offer some indication of the extent to which employees accrued financial gains from participation in ESOPs. Although an accurate quantification of gains is only possible after all distributions of shares to participants are complete, the *ex ante* estimates given above show that the value of ESOPs to employees ranged from €31,493 to €145,328. These amounts constitute considerable boons, although it is important to note that they are given in return for cooperation with measures such as reductions in the size of the labour force and considerable changes in working conditions.

### 6.5.6   Ex post analysis of financial gains in other ESOPs

The actual gains realised by ESOP participants only materialise over time, and depend on the timing of distributions and the value of shares at that time. Moreover, as in the case of Eircom, the gains made by employees can be affected by factors such as further changes in ownership as a result of company takeovers or mergers.

While information on the appropriation of shares and the distributions made to members of the Eircom ESOP are readily available from the Eircom ESOP website, there is very little publicly available information on the amounts that have been distributed to members of the other ESOPs established in privatised SOEs. From the information that is available, it appears that the ICC and TSB ESOPs became active investors in the shares of their new parent companies. Both ESOPs used the dividends received on the shares held by the Trustee to invest in further shares for the ESOP (once the borrowings for the 9.9 per cent stakes purchased had been paid off). The reason for this was that dividends did not qualify under the ESOP tax exemptions and any dividends distributed to members would have been heavily taxed.[18]

ESOPs in the ICC, TSB and the INPC benefited significantly from increases in their parent company's share prices post-privatisation. When Halifax took over Bank of Scotland in the summer of 2001, the ICC ESOP received shares in the newly merged HBOS. The ESOP then benefited from a sustained increase in the HBOS share price prior to the UK banking crisis in 2008. The ICC ESOP has made a total of seven appropriations to its members since 2003. Assuming employees received a full tax-free allocation of shares each time, this totals approximately €88,900 per employee.

The ESOP also borrowed money to purchase shares during a number of rights issues over the years so as to avoid a dilution of its shareholding, with borrowings to be repaid through share dividends. However, since the onset of the UK banking crisis in 2008, HBOS has been taken over by Lloyds TSB. The ICC ESOP subsequently received shares in Lloyds which are now trading at a fraction of their pre-crisis value. Moreover, in return for a bailout from the UK government, Lloyds agreed not to issue any dividends to investors until 2012. This has put the ICC ESOP in a particularly difficult situation as it has borrowings which need to be repaid. Since it will not receive any dividends until 2012, and it is unfeasible to sell any of its remaining shares to pay off debt given the low Lloyds TSB share price, the ESOP is currently in the position where it must retain its remaining shares and use the future dividends from these shares to pay back its borrowings. ESOP members are thus unlikely to receive an appropriation of shares for a number of years and, while it is impossible to predict the final amount received by employees, it is likely to be considerably less than our *ex ante* estimation earlier.[19]

The INPC ESOP benefited from two separate changes in the ownership of its parent company Tosco. While Tosco was in the process of purchasing the INPC in 2001, Tosco itself was purchased by Phillips Oil Corporation who, in turn, were in the process of merging with Conoco Oil Corporation. The INPC ESOP therefore ended up with shares in ConocoPhillips and benefited from increases in its share price. By December 2007, the INPC ESOP had already made three annual appropriations to its members totalling USD$6.78 million, with a further USD$12.77 million worth of shares still held by the ESOP for future distribution.[20] This indicates that, in total, former employees of the INPC could receive approximately USD$83,000 each.[21] Even allowing for the depreciation of the US dollar against the euro between 2001 and 2008, this amounts to far more than our *ex ante* estimation earlier.

In relation to the TSB ESOP, the shares held by the Trustee benefited enormously from large increases in the IL&P share price between 2003 and 2007. Table 6.2 details the evolution of the TSB ESOP's shareholding and shows how significant amounts of new IL&P shares were purchased by the ESOP over the years (a total of 981,584 shares were purchased between 2001 and 2009, an 18.2 per cent increase in the amount of shares initially allocated to the ESOP). Table 6.2 also shows that there was a transfer of shares from the ESOT to the APSS every year from 2004 to 2009. Although it is not possible to determine exactly how much was allocated to each member, assuming that the maximum tax-free amount of €12,700 was appropriated to members who qualified for a full allocation on each occasion, such members would have received approximately €76,000 each, substantially more than the estimated benefits per employee based on the initial value of the ESOP.

Table 6.2   Development of TSB ESOP Shareholding 2001–09

| Date | Change in shares | Price per share | Total ESOP shares | Total transaction value (€'000) | Description of transaction |
|---|---|---|---|---|---|
| Apr. 2001 | – | – | 5,369,250 | 66,900.00 | Initial ESOP shares |
| 2001 | 62,237 | – | 5,431,487 | – | Purchase of shares |
| 2002 | 52,117 | – | 5,483,604 | – | Purchase of shares |
| Feb. 2003 | 96,119 | 10.274 | 5,579,723 | 987.53 | Purchase of shares |
| Dec. 2003 | 58,879 | 12.45 | 5,639,052 | 733.04 | Purchase of shares |
| Dec. 2003 | 95,368 | – | 5,734,420 | – | Purchase of shares |
| Apr. 2004 | (1,030,706) | – | 4,703,714 | – | Transfer to APSS |
| Dec. 2004 | 62,960 | 13.65 | 4,766,674 | 859.40 | Purchase of shares |
| Apr. 2005 | (1,084,532) | 13.3 | 3,682,142 | (14,424.28) | Transfer to APSS |
| Jun. 2005 | 31,902 | 14.55 | 3,714,044 | 464.17 | Purchase of shares |
| Nov. 2005 | 41,550 | 15.45 | 3,755,594 | 641.95 | Purchase of shares |
| Apr. 2006 | (648,737) | 20.625 | 3,106,857 | (13,380.20) | Transfer to APSS |
| May 2006 | (10,029) | 18.78 | 3,096,828 | (188.35) | Transfer of shares |
| Nov. 2006 | 56,000 | 19.6 | 3,152,828 | 1,097.60 | Purchase of shares |
| Apr. 2007 | (622,656) | 20.8 | 2,530,172 | (12,951.25) | Transfer to APSS |
| May 2007 | 60,778 | 20.8 | 2,590,950 | 1,264.18 | Purchase of shares |
| Nov. 2007 | 50,562 | 11.72 | 2,641,512 | 592.59 | Purchase of shares |
| May 2008† | (938,552) | 10.285 | 1,702,960 | (9,653.01) | Transfer to APSS |
| Jun. 2008 | 90,309 | 9.2956 | 1,793,269 | 839.48 | Purchase of shares |
| Nov. 2008 | 222,803 | 1.525 | 2,016,072 | 339.78 | Purchase of shares |
| Apr. 2009† | (2,013,172) | 1.64 | 2,900 | (3,301.60) | Transfer to APSS |

*Source*: Authors' calculations from IL&P regulatory information (Notification of Interests of Directors and Connected Persons) supplied to London Stock Exchange, and IL&P Annual Reports.
*Note*: for some of the transactions it was not possible to establish the exact date of the transaction or the corresponding share price.
† The price of shares that were transferred to the APSS was not included in regulatory information for this transaction. Total transaction value therefore based on closing share price on day of transfer to APSS sourced from the Irish Stock Exchange.

There is little information available in relation to the ACC ESOP. Following a takeover by Rabobank the new owners issued the ESOP with a Rabobank bond. It is reasonable to assume, therefore, that ACC employees have accrued gains in accordance with our *ex ante* estimate. Members of the Aer Lingus ESOP have not fared as well. In this case, the ESOP borrowed heavily to purchase shares as part of the effort to fend off Ryanair's unwelcome takeover bid in 2006. This coincided with the global economic recession that has seen share prices plummet. Aer Lingus shares, which were originally floated at €2.20, were trading below €0.80 in June 2010. In these circumstances it is unlikely that employees will accrue gains in accordance with our *ex ante* estimates.

Overall, a number of the ESOPs established experienced significant increases in the value of their shareholdings, resulting in benefits for their members far in excess of those envisaged at the time of privatisation.

However, it is important to take account of the fact that the preceding estimations assume that employees who received their annual appropriations of shares divested of them immediately. Had members of the ICC or TSB ESOPs instead opted to hold on to their shares for a number of years, the value of their retained shares would currently be drastically lower given the collapse in the share price of their parent companies since the banking crisis began in 2008. In addition, members of the Aer Lingus ESOP have yet to realise significant gains since privatisation.

The major difference between the ESOPs established at the former state banks and the INPC compared to those established at Eircom and Aer Lingus relates to the size of the ESOP's shareholding as a percentage of the total issued share capital of the post-privatised company. The three banks and the INPC were all subsumed into much larger corporations where the shares allocated to the ESOPs amounted to mere fractions of the issued share capital of their new owners. These ESOPs thus had no influence within their new companies and their roles were mainly administrative. Conversely, the Eircom and Aer Lingus ESOPs gained considerable influence in the newly privatised companies by virtue of their 14.9 per cent shareholdings and the associated voting rights. The significant power handed over to these ESOPs and the decisions both have made since privatisation are examined in subsequent sections.

## 6.6   The ESOP and the post-privatisation direction of Eircom

In addition to conferring considerable financial gains, the establishment of an ESOP in Eircom also allocated significant power to employees and trade unions by virtue of the size of the shareholding. Chapter 7 describes how the break-up of Eircom following the de-merger of its mobile operation and later changes in ownership contributed to a deterioration in company performance, serious underinvestment in telecommunications infrastructure and negative implications for the wider economy. The ESOP played a pivotal role in determining the post-privatisation direction of Eircom and serious questions have arisen about the precise objectives of ESOPs, and the balance that ought to be struck between protecting the narrow financial interests of ESOP members and the role of organised labour in protecting the wider public interest. The following sections detail the changes in ownership of Eircom following privatisation and the role of the ESOP in shaping these changes.

### 6.6.1 The Eircell de-merger

The first major change in the structure and direction of Eircom after privatisation was the de-merger of its mobile communications subsidiary, Eircell. Originally established in 1985, Eircell was the most profitable and fastest growing division of Eircom, accounting for approximately 70 per cent of Eircom's market value with over 1.9 million subscribers at the time of the de-merger. In October 2000, it became known that Eircell was a potential takeover target of the British mobile operator, Vodafone.

Given the fall in the Eircom share price in the months following flotation, the Vodafone offer provided an opportunity to placate shareholders nursing significant losses. After months of negotiation, an agreement on the sale of Eircell for €4.5 billion to Vodafone was made just before Christmas 2000. Under the terms of the deal, Eircom shareholders would get 0.9478 of a Vodafone share for every two Eircell shares they held following the de-merger.[22] The actual cash value of the deal would depend on the Vodafone share price on the day the deal was closed. The deal was structured to allow Eircom to cancel the sale if Vodafone shares fell below GBP£2.20 at any stage before the deal went through. Since the average Vodafone share price throughout the course of the talks on the deal was GBP£2.60, this was deemed to be highly unlikely.[23] A non-competition agreement between Eircom and Vodafone was also entered into as part of the deal. Under the agreement, Eircom would not be allowed to re-enter the mobile market and compete with Vodafone for a period of three years.

The final decision on the de-merger of Eircell and its sale to Vodafone took place at an Eircom extraordinary general meeting (EGM) in May 2001. Given that the share price of Vodafone had fallen well below the GBP£2.20 threshold agreed, and was trading at GBP£2.03 on the day of the EGM, it is hard to understand why the board of Eircom was still so keen to sell off Eircell. The low value of Vodafone shares meant that the all-paper deal for Eircell was now only worth approximately €3.3 billion rather than the €4.5 billion it was worth when first agreed in December 2000. Many shareholders questioned the failure of the board to negotiate a cash alternative for the all-share deal. If cash had been offered when the initial agreement was made, Vodafone would have been locked in at approximately €4.2 billion.[24] Although the de-merger vote failed on a show of hands at the EGM, it was carried by proxy when over 99.5 per cent of shareholders who took part in the ballot cast their votes in favour.

While the ESOP was not in a position to block the deal, Vodafone was keen to gain its support as it represented the firm's workforce and could influence other shareholders (Eircom ESOP Trustee, 2001a). Following a ballot, 57 per cent of ESOP participants voted in favour of the de-merger, which offered important advantages compared to any kind of cash deal as any cash distributions would have been taxable. By using its 14.9 per cent stake at the EGM to support a de-merger, the ESOP effectively cashed in some of its share of company value. By supporting the divestiture of the fastest growing element of Eircom's business, the ESOP also signalled a short-term perspective that became increasingly evident over the following years. Not surprisingly the company sought to reverse its hasty exit from the mobile communications market as soon as the no-competition clause expired in 2004.

### 6.6.2 The first takeover: The Valentia Consortium

While negotiations on the sale of Eircell were ongoing, a number of groups expressed an interest in acquiring the remaining Eircom fixed-line business. Once the sale of Eircell was formally completed on 14 May 2001, a deadline was set for the receipt of bids for what was left of Eircom. Although there were a number of contenders, two different consortia emerged as the most likely buyers: the Valentia consortium, headed by Irish investor Anthony O'Reilly, and the eIsland consortium, headed by another Irish businessman, Denis O'Brien.

The ESOP held significant power throughout the bidding process, since any takeover would require the support of more than 80 per cent of shareholders, a practically impossible hurdle for any bid to clear if it did not get the support of the ESOP's 14.9 per cent shareholding. Although the final eIsland offer was higher than that of Valentia, the board of Eircom controversially accepted the Valentia offer on the basis of some debatable calculations concerning warrants offered by both consortia.[25]

The fact that the ESOP openly favoured the Valentia bid, which allowed them to build up a bigger stake in the firm, was what ultimately led to the success of the Valentia bid. The final deal resulted in the ESOP taking a 29.9 per cent stake in Eircom. In addition, the ESOP secured two of the 11 seats on the board of directors, one of which was the vice-chair. The Valentia consortium was made up of two US-based private equity groups (Providence Equity Partners and Soros Private Equity Partners), US bank Goldman Sachs and Irish investor Anthony O'Reilly. It formally completed the takeover of Eircom on 10 December 2001 for €2.8 billion through a highly leveraged buyout.

There were a number of risks associated with selling to a consortium of private equity investors. The objectives and strategy commonly adopted by private equity investors executing leveraged buyouts (LBOs) create risks that can have serious implications for the long-term future of the relevant company. According to Melody (2008), the principal objective of such new owners is to maximise short-term profits rather than invest in the long-term growth of the target firm. Such private equity LBOs generally involve a small group of investors that provide approximately 20 per cent of the equity required to purchase the target firm, with the remaining funds made up of debt capital secured on the assets of the target firm. The new owners then generally recoup their equity investment by restructuring the target firm, extracting cash from the business and reselling the firm, typically within 3–5 years.

After the LBO, the target firm is generally in a position where its debt ratio has increased significantly. It also faces considerable cash requirements to pay interest on its new debt and pay out high returns to its new investors, absorbing most of the internally generated funds that might otherwise have been allocated to long-term investment. Where private equity groups take complete control, the target firm is de-listed from stock exchanges and therefore avoids securities and public accountability regulations, thereby dramatically reducing transparency (Melody, 2008). Financial and operating policies that would not have been acceptable or appropriate when listed on the stock market can then be pursued by the new owners. This information advantage for the new owners allows them to raise debt financing levels, reduce the levels of operational expenses, and reduce capital investment levels to a minimum, all of which allow for the maximising of short-term cash flow for payouts to investors (Melody, 2008).

In addition, private equity group managers tend to maximise the cash available for dividend payments to investors by significantly reducing operating expenses in order to increase EBITDA cash flow.[26] This increases debt to the point where the corporation tax deductibility of the interest expenses reduces taxes to a minimum, and reduces capital investment to the minimum level required for continued operation. The change in the target firm's planning horizon to a short-term focus on debt management and short-term cash generation for payouts to investors has significant implications for the long-term growth of the firm.

In the case of Eircom, the risks associated with the LBO were explicitly identified by the ESOP Trustee when they recommended the Valentia takeover to participants. With Eircom's debt level increasing from just €105 million to over €2.2 billion the Trustee recognised the substantial:

> ...financial risk to which holders of shares in Valentia (including the ESOP) are exposed (in that Valentia will be obliged to pay interest

on the debt and, over time, repay the borrowings, irrespective of the financial performance of the business). The future value of Valentia's ordinary and 11.5 per cent preference shares is highly dependent on the eircom business generating sufficient cashflows to meet the obligations on the debt. Eircom currently has little debt; it generated net cashflow from operations of €575 million in the year ended 31 March 2001.

(Eircom ESOP Trustee, 2001b: 15)

Despite these risks, the LBO was justified on the grounds that it was in accordance with what the Trustee described as the ESOP's 'primary purpose' of encouraging and facilitating the acquisition and holding of shares in Eircom (Eircom ESOP Trustee, 2001b: 6). The lesser priority given to the long-run sustainability of the company or national economic interests became all the more evident 20 months later when the new owners, with the approval of the ESOP Trustee, implemented a significant restructuring of the company's debt, which resulted in the extraction of a high level of company value in the form of dividends.

The debt restructuring implemented by Valentia was rationalised in terms of taking advantage of lower interest rates that prevailed over the summer of 2003. By raising a new bank loan of €1.4 billion and issuing bonds for €1.05 billion, the company paid off existing bank debt. This facilitated the payment of a dividend of €446 million to shareholders, of which €280 million went to the private equity investors. The ESOP received a total of €230 million (as holder of ordinary and preference shares), which allowed it to recoup over half its original investment in Valentia, as well as make a distribution of cash benefits to participants.

The benefits accrued by the ESOP can be weighed against the implications for the company. The dividend paid to the ESOP and private equity investors constituted a significant extraction of value from the company. It also added to the company's growing indebtedness. The initial takeover by Valentia increased Eircom's long-term debt from €599 million in March 2001 to €2.125 billion in March 2003, with this figure increasing to €2.253 billion following the debt restructuring. This latter also resulted in shareholder funds being significantly reduced from €757 million to €279 million, increasing the ratio of debt to debt plus equity from 75 per cent to 89 per cent (McCarthy, 2007). As Chapter 7 describes, Eircom's debt burden has had significantly negative implications for investment in Ireland's telecommunications infrastructure, and served to undermine the competitiveness of the export-dependent Irish economy. This development owes much to the objectives of private equity holders and their co-owners, the ESOP, whose focus was on seeking to maximise short-term profits (and the size of its ownership stake in the case of the ESOP), rather than safeguarding the long-run sustainability of the company.

### 6.6.3   The second takeover: Babcock and Brown

Having realised sizeable gains already from its acquisition of Eircom, the next step for the Valentia consortium was to execute a successful exit from its investment. In March 2004, less than a year after finalising the debt restructure and value extraction exercise, Eircom was refloated on the stock exchange with investors accruing a capital gain of over 20 per cent.[27] As part of the return to the stock market, the ESOP secured a third seat on the board of directors.

In the brief period that Eircom was listed on the stock exchange, it re-entered the mobile telephony business through the purchase of Meteor Mobile Communications, Ireland's third mobile operator. Shortly after, Eircom became the target of a takeover approach from Swisscom AG. Although the Swiss government blocked any potential purchase of Eircom, the company remained the focus of takeover speculation. This materialised in April 2006, when Babcock and Brown Capital Limited (BCM) and the ESOP agreed the basis for a joint purchase of Eircom. Since the company had been refloated on the stock exchange, BCM had accumulated approximately 28 per cent of the ordinary share capital of Eircom, while the ESOP's share had diluted to 21.4 per cent. The purchase of Eircom, which was completed in September 2006, resulted in an increase in the ESOP's share of ordinary share capital to 35 per cent and the retention of three seats on the board of directors. Once again, the ESOP successfully pursued its key objectives of increasing the size of its shareholding and maximising returns to participants. However, as in the case of the Valentia takeover, this buyout was highly leveraged and resulted in an enormous increase in the level of Eircom's total borrowings, from €2.467 billion in March 2006, to €4.268 billion by March 2007.[28]

Although BCM initially stated that it planned to be a long-term investor in Eircom and that its aims included continued investment in Eircom's network infrastructure, financial difficulties at its parent company prompted its withdrawal from Eircom and a fourth change of ownership since full privatisation in 1999. Singapore Technologies Telemedia (STT) which is owned by the Singapore state investment company, Temasek, launched a bid for Eircom in June 2009. In supporting the bid by STT, the ESOP and trade unions displayed a complete change of heart in terms of the considerations it asserted should guide participants when they cast their votes. The CWU, which is the biggest member of the union coalition, urged members to vote in favour of the STT bid on the grounds that it is an 'industry player with a significant global footprint' and a rejection of the bid 'may open the door [for] less welcome suitors (private equity groups) for the business'.[29] The considerable influence of the ESOP was again made evident as its support for STT's proposed bid effectively knocked all other interested parties out of the bidding contest.

## 6.7   The ESOP and post-privatisation events in Aer Lingus

Whereas the Eircom ESOP has largely operated on the basis of increasing the value of the ESOP's investment and maximising returns to participants, the post-privatisation role of the Aer Lingus ESOP has largely centred on thwarting an unwelcome takeover bid from rival airline, Ryanair. Three days after the flotation of shares in Aer Lingus, Ryanair, the Irish low-cost carrier and Europe's largest airline, announced its intention to purchase a majority shareholding in the company. Ryanair had already swept up approximately 16 per cent of shares in Aer Lingus when it announced a takeover offer of €2.80 per share (a premium of 27 per cent over the flotation price), thus valuing the airline at €1.481 billion. Acquiring a majority shareholding would have been almost impossible without the support of the ESOP, a point that was acknowledged by Ryanair chief executive, Michael O'Leary. In addition, the offer was conditional on approval from the European Commission and other regulators.

In the weeks following Ryanair's announcement, a number of interested parties, including the ESOP, took measures to fend off the takeover bid. The purchase of ownership stakes by Aer Lingus pilots (2.2 per cent) and businessman Denis O'Brien (2.1 per cent), in addition to the stakes held by the government (25 per cent) and the ESOP (14.9 per cent), created a 45 per cent block that opposed the deal. The ESOP was always likely to oppose the Ryanair bid on the basis of Ryanair's well-known antipathy towards trade unions. In addition, it rejected an assertion by Ryanair that the offer was worth €60,000 to each employee. The ESOP claimed that this ignored the €35 million it borrowed to purchase shares in Aer Lingus, and that there was uncertainty about how a takeover might affect the profit sharing deal it had with the company.[30] Another concern for the ESOP related to the fact that Ryanair's cash-offer would be less tax-efficient than a paper deal.

Although the ESOP was initially careful to avoid outright rejection of the bid, an overwhelming majority of members voted against acceptance of the bid when a ballot was conducted in November 2006. In June 2007, the EC published its decision to prohibit the takeover on the grounds of competition concerns on 35 routes operated by both companies. Whether the ESOP acted in the interest of participants or the wider interests of the company is open to speculation. Nevertheless, the episode gave a clear demonstration of the significant power conferred on employees by virtue of a sizeable ESOP, and the pivotal role that employees played in determining the post-privatisation structure and direction of the company.

## 6.8    Conclusion

The allocation of 14.9 per cent of ordinary share capital to employees in privatised companies is a unique feature of the Irish privatisation programme. This has had a considerable influence on the distributional impact of the Irish privatisation programme, with employees accruing appreciable financial benefits and, in some cases, significant influence on the operation of privatised companies.

Although the precise objectives of the ESOPs established in former SOEs in Ireland have never been stated on a clear and consistent basis, it is reasonable to infer that they were established to achieve objectives including *inter alia*: the cooperation of employees and trade unions with privatisation, the alignment of employee interests with those of other shareholders, the provision of employee compensation in the form of shares and dividends, and the granting of a collective influence on the operation of the enterprise.

The evidence presented in this chapter demonstrates that employees have been handsomely compensated for cooperation with the change to private ownership. We have estimated that the *ex ante* gains to employees have ranged from approximately €30,000 to €145,000. In most cases, the exchequer has indirectly financed the allocation of shareholdings by foregoing a substantial amount of the revenues it would have accrued in the absence of ESOPs. In addition, the exchequer has foregone significant tax revenues as all ESOPs have been structured in order to distribute shares on a tax-free basis. Gains have not been confined to employees. Sweeney (2004) highlights how, in the case of Eircom, the directors of the ESOP received substantial remuneration in the form of salaries, free shares, share options and pension entitlements. The deputy chair (also the general secretary of the CWU) received a package of €1.8 million (including pension entitlements).

There is a paucity of evidence concerning privatisation ESOPs and their impact on employee attitudes and motivation. However, recent research by McCarthy *et al.* (2010a, 2010b) suggests that the impact is not as strong as advocates of ESOPs might expect. A survey of over 700 employees in Eircom was conducted to examine the relationship between the ESOP and employee perceptions of changes in commitment and behaviour. It was concluded that the ESOP had failed to substantially impact on employee attitudes and behaviour, and failed to create a greater sense of ownership or control among employees. The authors reported that their findings are consistent with those from international studies on employee share-ownership.

When considering the issue of ESOPs in the Irish case, it is important to distinguish between those that are mainly mechanisms for compensating workers (for example, the former state-owned banks and INPC) and those that confer influence by allocating large-scale shareholdings and directorships (for example, Eircom and Aer Lingus). The Irish experience demonstrates how ESOPs that control large shareholdings can have a pivotal influence on the strategic direction of newly privatised companies. A key issue that has arisen in the case of Eircom concerns the precise objectives of ESOPs, and whether their purpose is to advance the interests of insiders (that is to say the participants) or to safeguard the long-term sustainability of the enterprise and the wider public interest. This is a major issue for trade unions and employees that will require serious consideration in future sales.

# 7
# Telecommunications: A Tale of Privatisation Failure

## 7.0   Introduction

The privatisation of Eircom in 1999 has proved to be one of the most controversial episodes in Irish business history. The divestiture of the firm has been associated with enormous dissatisfaction on the part of most stakeholders, including small shareholders who incurred considerable losses, customers who have failed to receive a modern and reliable service and competitors who have struggled to gain a foothold in relevant markets. From a national perspective, the privatisation of Eircom has had negative consequences for a regional economy that relies heavily on its telecommunications infrastructure and services to create the conditions necessary for the creation of a modern knowledge economy.

This chapter examines the factors that have contributed to these outcomes. It highlights how Eircom stymied the growth of competition in the fixed-line market and failed to make adequate investment in telecommunications infrastructure. This has had particularly grave consequences for the rollout of high-speed broadband services, with Ireland perennially ranked among the worst performers in the EU across most broadband development indicators. As a consequence, the Irish state has had to re-enter the telecommunications sector and seek to address the market failures that have arisen since the national telecommunications operator was transferred to full private ownership. Before focusing on the post-privatisation experience in the Irish telecommunications sector, the chapter puts these developments in context by outlining the major changes in the European telecommunications industry over the past two decades and the evolution of the sector in the Irish case.

## 7.1   Telecoms liberalisation and privatisation in Europe

A significant proportion of the privatisations that have taken place in Europe in the past three decades have involved utility companies that were originally nationalised because of their natural monopoly characteristics. Prior to the 1980s, it was generally accepted in Europe that the efficient operation of utility industries such as telecommunications, electricity and gas could only be achieved under state ownership. It was believed that private ownership of such natural monopolies would only lead to abuse of market power and, consequently, most countries in Europe created national telecommunications, electricity and gas operators during the twentieth century. In the case of telecommunications in Western Europe, there have been a number of structural changes over the past 30 years which have undermined traditional arguments in favour of a heavily protected and politicised framework of public ownership and universal access. Hulsink (1999: 308) outlines the main structural forces as:

1) The impact of technological developments;
2) The emergence of global and differentiated communications markets;
3) Increasing international deregulation; and
4) European integration.

These structural forces have led to a new European model of telecommunications provision whereby the EU has applied pressure on member states to open up telecommunications markets to competition. Telecommunications markets in all EU member states were gradually deregulated prior to full liberalisation, which came into effect on January 1st 1998. The development of new technologies necessitating large-scale investment, coupled with EC directives on liberalisation and state aid, in effect led to the decision by many countries to partly or fully privatise their national operators, although the EC stopped short of taking an explicit stance on the question of ownership (Parker, 1998).

Developments in the EU, particularly in the case of telecommunications and other utilities, have mirrored worldwide trends where there has been a wave of privatisation activity. State ownership of network utilities is no longer seen to be efficient. Instead, policy has shifted towards restructuring such industries by separating the core network – the main natural monopoly element – from the other potentially contestable activities that such firms engage in. Advocates of utility privatisation argue that once separated, only the network activity of the firm requires regulation while the introduction of competition in contestable activities will lead to significant gains in economic efficiency (Saal, 2003).

The privatisation of national telecommunications companies is invariably controversial given their size and strategic importance. Furthermore, they are often the biggest single divestiture in terms of their financial impact on the privatisation programmes of most countries. Between 1981 and 2008, the proceeds generated from the privatisation of telecommunications firms in the EU15 alone has amounted to over USD$219 billion, or almost 25 per cent of all privatisation revenues.[1] The vast majority of this revenue (over USD$211 billion) has been generated from 1991 onwards, with the sale of just over 50 per cent of British Telecom in 1984 the only significant privatisation that took place during the 1980s.

As Figure 7.1 illustrates, the late 1990s was the busiest in terms of telecommunications privatisation activity, with almost every EU member state divesting partial or full stakes in their national operators during this

*Figure 7.1*  Telecommunications Privatisation Revenues in the EU15, 1991–2008

*Source*: (1) Authors' own elaboration of data sourced from *Privatization Barometer* database used for privatisation revenues; (2) Telecommunications price index used was the Dow Jones STOXX 600 Telecommunications Price Index (Symbol: SXKP). While the companies used to create the index have changed over time, the majority of the former national telecommunications operators in each EU15 country which have been privatised by public offering have been included in the index since their respective flotations.

period. These sales coincided with the full liberalisation of the EU telecommunications market in most member states by 1998. The surge in demand for telecommunications stocks during the late 1990s is evident from the telecommunications share price index in Figure 7.1. The flotation of shares in almost every EU15 national telecommunications operator contributed to the unprecedented increase in the share price index prior to 2000, as well as a wave of merger and acquisition activity within the industry and significant demand for high-tech stocks in the run up to the burst of the dot-com bubble in 2000.

In addition to the influence of the structural changes in the European telecommunications sector, the decision to privatise national telecommunications operators was driven by the inflated value placed by the markets on telecommunications companies during the latter half of the 1990s. This provided European governments with a major incentive to raise exchequer revenues by floating partial stakes in their national telecommunications operators on the stock market, particularly in the context of the requirement to meet the January 1999 convergence deadline for the Maastricht criteria in relation to budget deficits and national debt for EMU entry (see Chapter 1).

Similar factors influenced the decision of the Irish government to join the European trend towards the privatisation of national telecommunications operators. The following section briefly outlines the evolution of the Irish telecommunications industry from its inception to the stage where liberalisation and privatisation became key features of government policy. This sets the stage for an analysis of the sector under private ownership.

## 7.2   Evolution of the telecommunications sector in Ireland

Prior to 2001, the experience of Ireland in relation to developments in the telecommunications sector was very much in line with that of Western Europe. Up until the 1990s, the telecommunications and postal sectors in most Western European countries were characterised by a high degree of government intervention, with the operation and control of these strategic sectors generally entrusted to a monopolistic government department or SOE.

The evolution of the ownership and control of Ireland's national telecommunications network is summarised in Table 7.1. Up until 1983, Ireland's telecommunications service was run by the civil service which

Table 7.1  Historical Development of Irish National Telecoms Operator

| Year | Main provider of telecoms services & milestones | Details |
|---|---|---|
| 1880 | United Telephone Company | First telephone exchange in Ireland opened in Dublin with five subscribers. |
| 1882 | Telephone Company of Ireland | The Telephone Company of Ireland took over from the United Telephone Company. |
| 1893 | National Telephone Company | The National Telephone Company took over from the Telephone Company of Ireland, at which time the service was only available in seven cities and towns in Ireland. |
| 1912 | Post Office | The Post Office took over the whole telephone system from the National Telephone Company once the company's licence to operate expired in 1911. |
| 1923 | Department of Posts and Telegraphs | Following the War of Independence, the control of the post and telephone system was transferred to the Department of Posts and Telegraphs after the establishment of the Irish Free State in 1922. |
| 1984 | Telecom Éireann | The telecommunications and postal services were corporatised from the civil service with the creation of two separate commercial SOEs. An Post took over the operation of postal services while Telecom Éireann took over the operation of telecommunications services. |
| 1996 | Part-privatisation of Telecom Éireann | A 20 per cent stake in Telecom Éireann was sold to the Comsource consortium as part of a strategic alliance. |
| 1998 | Full market liberalisation | The Irish telecommunications market was fully liberalised on the 1st December 1998. |
| 1999 | IPO and full privatisation of Telecom Éireann | Telecom Éireann was floated on the stock market in July 1999 under the new name Eircom. The government sold its entire 50.1 per cent stake as part of the IPO. The remaining shares floated were held by Comsource (who acquired a further 15 per cent of the company) and an ESOP (which was granted a 14.9 per cent stake). |
| 2001 | Break-up of Eircom | The mobile division of Eircom, Eircell, was sold to Vodafone in May 2001. The remaining fixed-line business of Eircom was sold to a consortium of private equity investors, Valentia, in December 2001 and the company's shares were delisted from the stock market. |
| 2004 | Reflotation of Eircom | The Valentia consortium decided to wind up their investment in Eircom and refloated the company on the stock market in March 2004. |
| 2006 | Babcock & Brown takeover of Eircom | The Australian investment company, Babcock & Brown, made a successful bid for Eircom as part of a leveraged buyout deal in August 2006 and the company's shares were again delisted from the stock market. |
| 2010 | STT takeover of Eircom | Singapore Technologies Telemedia (a subsidiary of the Singaporean sovereign wealth fund, Temasek) purchased Eircom in January 2010. |

*Note*: Details for years 1880–1912 sourced from Litton (1962).

had operated the telegraph/telecommunications infrastructure since the founding of the Irish Free State in 1922. After incurring increasing losses during the 1970s, mainly due to low levels of capital investment and a lack of commercial management, a review of the telecommunications service carried out in 1979 recommended that the operation of the telecommunications service be transferred to a state company run on commercial lines. This recommendation was implemented in 1984 when the operation of the telecommunications service was corporatised from the civil service and transferred to a commercial SOE, Telecom Éireann, which went through a period of rapid commercialisation in the late 1980s and early 1990s.

In 1996, 20 per cent of the company was sold to the *Comsource* consortium – consisting of Sweden's national operator, Telia, and the Netherland's national operator, PTT Telecom (later KPN) – as part of a strategic alliance. An agreement in March 1998 on an ESOP with Telecom Éireann employees, whereby employees received 14.9 per cent of shares in the company, paved the way for the eventual full privatisation of the company in July 1999, when the Irish government floated its entire remaining stake of 50.1 per cent on the stock market.[2] These events were described in detail in Chapter 3 and, apart from the granting of a sizable block shareholding to employees, are generally in line with developments in other European member states where national telecommunications operators were gradually privatised during the 1990s.

One unique aspect of the privatisation of telecommunications in Ireland was the decision by the government to sell its entire stake in one go. Every other EU15 government opted to sell partial stakes in their national operators, which were generally followed by the sales of further minor stakes as part of a gradual reduction in ownership. In countries where the state's shareholding in the national operator was eventually reduced to a minority stake or even reduced to zero, governments generally retained a 'golden share' granting them certain veto rights over decisions in relation to changes in company ownership.[3] The Irish government's decision not to retain a minor stake or golden share in Telecom Éireann was surprising, especially given the strategic importance of the telecommunications sector and the precedent set by other European countries.

Prior to the privatisation of Telecom Éireann, the Irish government had recognised that, despite a vast increase in investment in telecommunications infrastructure during the 1990s, this growth had taken place in the context of a rapidly expanding gap between Irish infrastructure and that of its EU and OECD counterparts. The government was also aware that it was crucial that Ireland:

> should not fall behind in the provision of advanced communications and e-commerce facilities and in the provision of the basic infrastructure capacity necessary to support the development of the Information Society [... and ...] that a competitive market alone will not ensure the provision of advanced communications networks and services to the extent required to contribute to national competitiveness and attract inward investment.
>
> (NDP, 1999: 67–8)

Given the Irish government's stated goal of creating an Information Society, the decision not to retain some control over the national telecommunications network, a key component of potential economic development which would be dependent on the availability of advanced information and communications infrastructure, is difficult to understand. When debating the legislation to allow for the flotation of Eircom, the Minister for Public Enterprise indicated that a minimum of 20 per cent of the government's stake would be sold in the IPO. However, the government indicated that it planned to offer more than this with 'market conditions and the level of demand for the shares' the critical factors in the determination of how much would be sold.[4] The subsequent decision to sell the government's entire stake at the IPO stage would thus appear to have been largely driven by the market overvaluation of Eircom and the attraction of significant exchequer revenues.

## 7.3 The fixed-line telecommunications sector since privatisation

The Irish government viewed privatisation as a key part of plans to develop a competitive telecommunications market in Ireland. The benefits anticipated at the time of privatisation have, however, failed to materialise as Eircom has continued to dominate the fixed-line market, stymied competition and underinvested in modern technologies, such as high-speed broadband, that are vital in terms of the interests of the Irish economy and society. The leveraged buyouts (LBOs) of Eircom by two separate private equity groups have been particularly inimical to the development of the competitive and innovative telecommunications sector envisaged at the time of privatisation. Both LBOs resulted in enormous increases in the company's level of debt (see Chapter 6), which have imposed binding constraints on the scope for investment in telecommunications infrastructure. As a consequence, the state has re-entered the sector to address the market failures that have arisen since privatisation.

One of the main obstacles to achieving the proposed benefits of privatisation and liberalisation has been the dominance of Eircom in the fixed-line market. Eircom has used this dominance to ensure that the pace of increased competition in this market has been tortuously slow in the post-privatisation period. Figure 7.2 shows that Eircom maintained an approximate 80 per cent market share from 2001 until 2005. Despite increased competition in fixed-line voice telephony since 2005, it still maintains almost 70 per cent of market share.[5] This dominance has been protected by Eircom's sluggishness in allowing other firms access to its local loop.[6] Under EC regulations, Eircom has been obliged to fully unbundle its local loop since the beginning of 2001, though the company has repeatedly resisted attempts to open its network to competitors, and only reached an agreement with the regulator on plans to accelerate local loop unbundling (LLU) in early 2010.

This market dominance and lack of progress on LLU has had a particularly negative impact on the development of broadband services in Ireland. The following sections detail the development of the Irish

*Figure 7.2*   Eircom Market Share of Fixed-Line Revenue, 2000–09

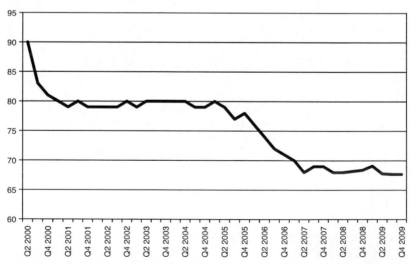

*Source*: ComReg Quarterly Key Data Reports (various years).

broadband market since 2001 and government interventions in the market to date.

## 7.4 The evolution of broadband services since privatisation

The availability and quality of broadband services is of significant strategic importance to any country, but especially to a peripheral small open economy such as Ireland, where improving productivity is a key determinant of economic growth.[7] High-speed telecommunications services are critical for the attraction of foreign direct investment, the development of indigenous industry (particularly SMEs), and the development of a knowledge economy. The increasing importance of the services industry in Ireland only serves to increase the importance of developing an efficient and reliable high-speed communications service.

Quality broadband services also bring numerous societal benefits. Broadband can enable the development of e-government services, thereby improving the efficiency and availability of public services such as health and education. In addition, broadband can enhance the quality of life for

*Figure 7.3*    Historical Broadband Penetration Rates in EU15, 2000–09

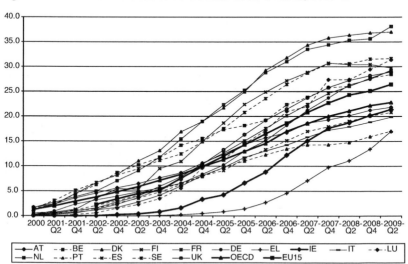

*Source*: Compiled from OECD Broadband Statistics. Data for EU15 average sourced from Eurostat. Broadband penetration is measured as the number of broadband access lines per 100 inhabitants.[8]

consumers through economic, social and cultural development as well as by enabling economic and social inclusion for small rural communities (Forfás, 2006).

Ireland has persistently ranked next to last in the EU15 in terms of broadband penetration per capita with one of the lowest penetration rates in the OECD. As of September 2009, Ireland had a broadband penetration rate of 22.6 per cent, while countries such as the UK, France, Denmark, Finland, the Netherlands and Sweden all recorded penetration levels in excess of 30 per cent.[9] As illustrated in Figure 7.3, Ireland has lagged significantly behind all other EU member states with the exception of Greece. Despite recent progress in seeking to catch up with other industrialised countries, Ireland still remains below the EU15 and OECD averages in this regard.

Ireland's track record as one of the laggards of Europe in terms of broadband penetration can be attributed to a number of factors, and principal among these are: (1) slow and costly LLU; (2) low levels of investment in the network by the privately-owned Eircom; and (3) low levels of competition on competing platforms.

Until recently, the monthly cost for other operators providing services over unbundled or shared access lines in Ireland were the highest in the EU.[10] ComReg has consistently criticised 'the lack of robust and efficient LLU processes from Eircom' which 'continues to hamper investment in what has in other markets been a key driver of innovation and broadband take-up' (ComReg, 2007: 19). Despite repeated ComReg pressure to speed up Eircom's implementation of local loop unbundling (LLU), by September 2009 there were just 16,820 fully unbundled lines and 6,799 shared access lines out of a total of almost 700,000 DSL lines (ECTA, 2009).[11] The number of unbundled lines as a percentage of total DSL lines in Ireland amounts to just 3.4 per cent compared to an average of almost 34 per cent for the EU15.[12]

Although Ireland is not the only European country with low levels of unbundling, it nevertheless has the lowest rate of LLU as a percentage of DSL lines in the EU15. The success of many of the highest ranking countries in terms of broadband penetration in the EU15 can to some extent be attributed to higher levels of LLU which facilitated greater competition in the market and, consequently, accelerated the rollout of broadband services. As illustrated in Figure 7.4, there has been a steady increase in the number of unbundled local loops in the EU15 since 2004, in stark contrast to the situation in Ireland where LLU as a percentage of DSL lines has remained consistently low.

*Figure 7.4*    LLU as a % of Total DSL Lines in the EU15

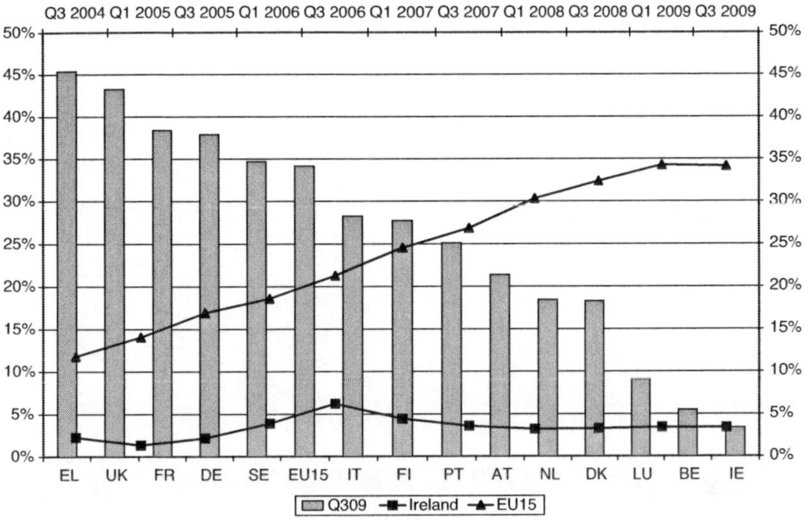

Source: ECTA Broadband Scorecards (2004–2009).
Note: Columns for each country represent LLU as a % of total DSL lines in September 2009.
The lines representing Ireland and the EU15 illustrate the evolution of this measure over
time (as measured on the secondary x-axis from Q3 2004 to Q3 2009).

In addition to slow progress on LLU, Eircom has been slow to invest in
its network. After spending €1.8 billion in acquiring tangible fixed assets
in the three years between 1999 and 2001, Eircom only spent €1.18 billion in capital investment in the five years between 2002 and 2006.[13]
The reduction in investment post-2001 is largely a result of the highly
leveraged buyouts of Eircom's fixed-line business by the Valentia consortium (in 2001) and Babcock and Brown (in 2006). The new private
equity owners implemented substantial cuts in capital expenditure and
a significant amount of labour shedding during their years in ownership
(see Chapter 6 for a detailed description of the Valentia and Babcock LBOs
and their implications in terms of Eircom's debt and capacity to invest).

Figure 7.5 shows that capital expenditure since 2001 has been consistently below depreciation allowances in each year, indicating that the
company did not invest enough even to replenish its asset depreciation.
Whereas Eircom had invested almost €480 million more than its depreciation allowances between 2000 and 2001, capital investment was just
over €400 million less than depreciation allowances between 2002 and
2004.

*Figure 7.5*   Eircom Capital Expenditure and Depreciation Allowances, 1999–2009

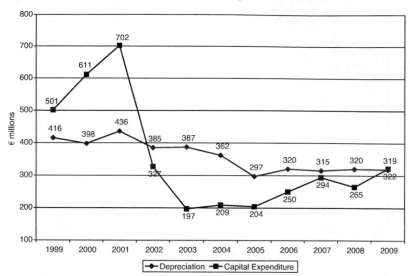

*Source*: Authors' calculations from Eircom financial reports. Results are for the 12 months to the 31 March in each year.

Slow LLU and low levels of capital investment have contributed to a historically low level of availability of broadband services in Ireland up until recently. While most other European countries had launched full-scale broadband services in 2001, Ireland was a full 18–24 months behind. For years, national DSL coverage by population in Ireland was among the lowest of the EU15, with this largely explained by low levels of coverage in rural areas. While DSL coverage in urban and sub-urban areas in Ireland has effectively been at 99 per cent since the end of 2005, the expansion of DSL coverage in rural areas in Ireland has been extremely slow in comparison to other European countries.

Figure 7.6 highlights the fact that Ireland has consistently ranked next to last in the EU15 in terms of rural DSL coverage. This is of considerable concern given that Ireland has one of the highest rural populations in the EU, with almost 40 per cent of the population living in rural areas. While relatively lower DSL coverage is to be expected in countries with a higher proportion of rural populations or lower population densities, it should be noted that countries such as Austria and Finland, who also have a high proportion of their population living in rural areas, have recorded superior rural DSL coverage rates than Ireland.

*Figure 7.6*   Rural DSL Coverage in the EU15, 2003–08

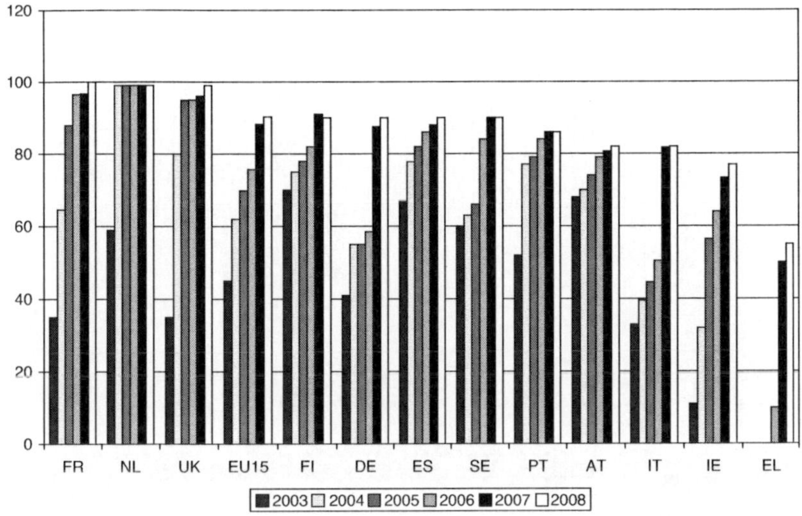

Source: IDATE (2006–2009) and DG AGRI (2006–2009).
Notes: (1) Figures reported are as of December in each year; (2) Belgium, Denmark and Luxembourg are excluded since these countries recorded 100 per cent rural DSL coverage from 2003 onwards.

Another reason for the poor level of broadband availability was the lack of competition, both between and within different broadband platforms (such as cable and DSL). Despite the considerable increase in companies offering broadband services (currently there are almost 200 Internet Service Providers now selling broadband in Ireland),[14] for much of the last decade there was little 'growth in competing platforms, especially cable' and a 'lack of competition and innovation within the DSL market' (Forfás, 2005: 13). As can be seen in Figure 7.7, just over 70 per cent of fixed broadband connections in September 2009 were DSL lines retailed by Eircom or retailed by another operator. Cable broadband connections accounted for less than 15 per cent of fixed connections, a stark contrast to the situation in most other European countries.

The lack of quality broadband services available in Ireland, due to lack of investment by Eircom, low levels of competition in the DSL market and the slow development of cable broadband services, was highlighted by the rapid take-up of broadband services offered by mobile companies such as O2 and Vodafone since the beginning of 2007. Mobile companies can offer broadband access at speeds of 1.4 to 3.6 Mb/s using HSDPA[15]

*Figure 7.7* Competition in Fixed Broadband Access Routes

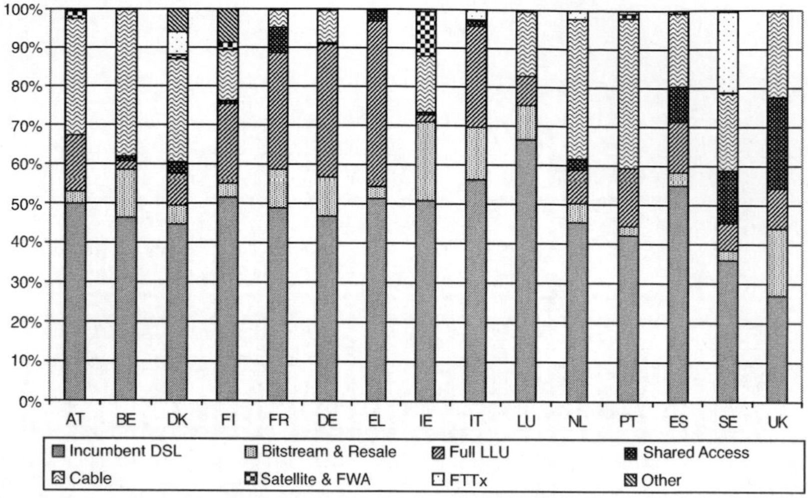
100%
90%
80%
70%
60%
50%
40%
30%
20%
10%
0%
AT
BE
DK
FI
FR
DE
EL
IE
IT
LU
NL
PT
ES
SE
UK
Incumbent DSL
Bitstream & Resale
Full LLU
Shared Access
Cable
Satellite & FWA
FTTx
Other

*Source*: Compiled from ECTA (2009).

technology. In June 2007, ComReg estimated that there were around 45,000 customers of this new service. By December 2009, this figure had increased to 466,969, accounting for almost 30 per cent of total broadband subscriptions in Ireland (ComReg, 2010).

While Ireland's broadband penetration rate has rapidly converged with the EU and OECD averages in the past two years, one of the major issues now facing Ireland is the quality of the broadband services currently on offer rather than availability. Figure 7.8 highlights the fact that Ireland ranked last in the EU15 in terms of average advertised broadband download speed (29th out of 30 OECD countries) as of October 2009. It must be noted, however, that Eircom recently announced a major upgrade to its network which will provide 8Mb/s download speeds to up to one million users in Ireland. The service will be initially available in Dublin only, before being rolled out to other towns and cities across Ireland by December 2010. In addition, Ireland's main cable television provider, UPC, also recently announced major upgrades to its network which will make download speeds of up to 100Mb/s available to approximately half a million homes in Ireland from August 2010.

In general, while faster broadband speeds have been delivered in recent years, these are commonly only available in Dublin and other major cities. In order to avoid an ever widening 'digital divide' between urban and

*Figure 7.8*   EU15 Average Advertised Download Speeds, October 2009

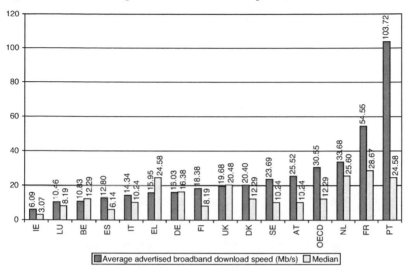

*Source*: OECD Broadband Statistics.
*Note*: Advertised speeds are typically the theoretical maximum for the employed technologies. Users commonly have lower actual speeds. Also, often only parts of the country have been upgraded to the fastest speeds.

rural areas, significant investment in the rollout of high-speed broadband infrastructure in rural and less densely populated suburban areas will be required. The central issue here is whether the private sector will undertake the necessary investment and how quickly such investment will take place. Eircom and other private operators have been reluctant in the past to invest heavily in the current national telecommunications infrastructure in rural areas. Moreover, Eircom's considerable current debt burden of close to €4 billion will severely constrain its capacity to invest significant amounts in its network.

The inadequacy of liberalisation and privatisation policies as a tool of public policy in relation to the provision of rural broadband services is not unique to Ireland and has been recognised in a number of European countries.[16] The inequitable distribution of access to broadband and its consequences in terms of regional development in many countries has invariably meant that governments have had to make funding available for infrastructural investment in such areas. The next section provides an overview of the Irish government's response thus far to the market failure that has emerged in the Irish broadband market.

## 7.5   Irish government response to broadband market failure

The Irish government recognised prior to the decision to privatise Eircom that a competitive market alone would not ensure investment in advanced communications networks to the extent required to contribute to national competitiveness (NDP, 1999: 68). In particular, the government noted that rural areas in Ireland were not attractive for private investment in infrastructure, and would be at a disadvantage to urban areas with obvious implications for regional development. However, the government did not move to correct the market failure that emerged in the provision of broadband infrastructure until 2003, when it began directly investing in rural broadband infrastructure itself through a number of programmes: the Metropolitan Area Networks (MANs) programme, the County and Group Broadband Scheme (CGBS) and the National Broadband Scheme (NBS). A short summary of each programme is provided below.

### 7.5.1   Metropolitan Area Network Programme

MANs are open access fibre-based networks located within cities and towns, designed to foster competition amongst telecommunications operators by reducing the barriers to entry for new operators to provide services either over existing local access networks owned by the private incumbent, Eircom, or via new fibre-connected infrastructure. Essentially, the MANs act as an intermediate loop ('middle mile' connection), providing a link between the national backbone network and the local access network. While alternatives to Eircom's national backbone network existed, there was no competing 'middle mile' network available to provide a link between these networks and local loop infrastructure. The rationale behind the MANs programme was therefore to remove this barrier to entry to Eircom's competitors (DCENR, 2008c).

The first phase of the MANs programme involved 27 different towns in Ireland and commenced construction in 2003, with most of the networks completed in 2005 at a cost of just over €83 million.[17] Due to its success, a second phase, consisting of 94 towns with a population in excess of 1,500 people was announced. Approximately 60 of the second phase MANs in 66 towns across the country were completed by 2009, with the remainder on hold pending the outcome of the government's 2009 policy review of next generation broadband.

The MANs programme has been an important step in terms of regional development and has done much to improve competition, allowing the private sector to offer high-speed broadband services at competitive costs. According to the Industrial Development Agency (Ireland's inward investment promotion agency), the MANs have 'contributed significantly to the competitiveness of regional centres in Ireland and thus their attractiveness to international foreign direct investment, both new and existing' (DCENR, 2008c: 64). This is reflected in the fact that the 27 towns included in the first phase of the MANs project increased their share of IDA inward investment from 24 per cent in 2004 to over 89 per cent in 2007.[18] Some issues emerged in relation to the MANs constructed in a small number of towns where backhaul[19] providers other than Eircom were not available. Eircom consequently faced no competitive challenge and MANs in towns affected by this issue have generally been under-utilised or not utilised at all (DCENR, 2008c).

### 7.5.2 County & Group Broadband Scheme and National Broadband Scheme

The County and Group Broadband Scheme (CGBS) was introduced in 2004 to provide broadband services to rural and low population towns (less than 1,500 people) in Ireland where broadband services were not being provided by the market due to low population density. The scheme involved setting up partnerships between local communities and Internet Service Providers (ISPs), with the state funding up to 55 per cent of the capital expenditure required to provide the service. Although the CGBS proved very effective in communities where projects were rolled out, the uptake of the scheme was far less than anticipated since it required local communities to act on their own initiative. Just over 7,200 subscribers out of a possible 90,000 subscribers availed of the scheme, while the population covered by the scheme exceeded approximately 400,000 people (DCENR, 2008b).

As a consequence of the above, the government announced a National Broadband Scheme (NBS) in May 2007 to replace the CGBS. Rather than depending on local communities to apply for funding, the objective of the NBS is to deliver a service in all areas that are currently without service. Under the planned NBS, the government has recently entered into an agreement with the mobile operator Hutchison 3 Ireland Ltd to provide broadband services to all rural areas that would otherwise not be able to avail of them by 2010. The scheme will provide basic broadband services to roughly 10 per cent of the rural population, spread over approximately 33 per cent of the geographic area of Ireland, and will be delivered primarily using mobile broadband technology over 3G networks. Some €223 million is being provided for the scheme which is being part-financed by the Irish exchequer, the EU and *3* Ireland. The scheme will deliver services with a minimum download speed of 1.2 Mb/s, although a number of upgrades which will enable faster speeds are planned after 2010.[20]

## 7.6   Next generation broadband in Ireland

While the above programmes have done much to improve access to broadband service in rural areas, the fact remains that 'Ireland is lagging at least three to five years behind competitor countries in terms of rolling out infrastructure capable of high speed next generation broadband' (Forfás, 2010: 4). Ireland's dispersed population profile is one of the key obstacles to the development of broadband and next generation network (NGN) infrastructure, and the main reason why private sector investment outside of densely populated urban areas is unlikely to occur at the pace required. The key population differences between Ireland and its European counterparts are:

- Ireland's population is highly dispersed. Approximately 40 per cent of the population live in rural areas, compared to a typical figure of 5–10 per cent for other Western European countries.
- Just under 1.5 million people of a total population of over 4.3 million live in the major urban centres of Dublin, Cork, Galway, Limerick and Waterford.
- Less than 10 per cent of the Irish population live in apartments. In most other developed countries this percentage is generally far higher (for example, almost 40 per cent of Korea's population live in apartments).[21]

The above factors have a significant impact on the financial feasibility of private enterprises investing in the construction of next generation broadband (NGB) infrastructure. The cost of constructing fibre optic networks in rural areas is more expensive than in areas with higher population density due to a far reduced potential for revenue generating connected customers per metre of infrastructure deployed. So far, the government has generally advocated the use of wireless connectivity for the delivery of broadband services in rural areas, (for example, the NBS). While these wireless services will go some way towards bridging the 'digital divide' by providing valuable connectivity, rural areas, will continue to be at a disadvantage to urban areas, which will enjoy far higher bandwidth over fixed-line and cable networks. Even within urban areas, only high-density areas are likely to benefit from the most advanced services available through fibre-to-the-home (FTTH) technologies.

The government's 2008 consultation paper on NGB outlined a number of possible approaches to facilitate the roll-out of NGB infrastructure:

1. Direct government support to build a nationwide NGN or partner with a telecoms operator to provide the same;
2. Government funding to address 'digital divide' issues, regional competitiveness and the use of existing state telecoms assets;
3. Provide indirect support through telecoms related instruments to the private sector (for example, regulatory policy and access to public infrastructure);
4. Support private sector investments through other public policy instruments (for example, use planning regulations to lower barriers to entry for significant infrastructure investments);
5. Stimulate demand for high-speed broadband services (DCENR, 2008a).

Thus far, the government has only committed itself to addressing 'digital divide' issues through the NBS and facilitating access by private operators to publicly-owned telecommunications assets. While the NBS has recently been given the green light and has commenced rollout, there have been no concrete plans set out in relation to bundling existing state-owned telecoms assets and no legislation introduced to ensure that future infrastructure projects (rail, water etc.) will install ducting at the construction phase to facilitate the rollout of a NGN. Furthermore, no legislation is being put forward to facilitate the rollout of new infrastructure in the 'last mile' to enable future expansion of a NGN over private property to the consumer.

Given the importance of NGB infrastructure to the modern 'smart' economy, which Ireland aspires to be, there is now a strong case for the Irish government to take radical action and provide this infrastructure either directly itself, or in partnership with the private sector. If the government continues to wait for the private sector to deliver such services and only engages in limited intervention in rural areas, Ireland will fall even further behind its European comparators. As of September 2009, only 0.6 per cent of fixed broadband connections in Ireland were fibre connections, in stark contrast with the situation in other European countries such as Sweden (20.8 per cent), Denmark (5.9 per cent) and even in newer member states such as Slovenia (18 per cent) and Estonia (10.5 per cent).[22]

### 7.6.1 Development of next generation broadband in other countries

Serious questions have arisen as to the effectiveness of policies based on liberalisation and privatisation measures in relation to network investment. The EU has recognised this by changing its state aid rules to facilitate joint public-private investment in broadband infrastructure in both rural and urban areas. Governments in other European countries and internationally have recognised the importance of investment in fibre-based NGNs by intervening in their broadband markets. Examples of the different strategies being utilised in other countries are:

1. Finland (a country with a similar urbanisation rate as Ireland): The Finnish government has made universal minimum internet access speeds a legal right, committing to a minimum download speed of 1Mb/s per second from July 2010 and to getting 99 per cent of homes within two kilometres of a fibre connection (100Mb/s download speed) by 2015. In areas of the country where the private sector will not deliver, the government has agreed to fund part of the investment.[23]

2. United Kingdom: The former Labour government had planned to set up a Next Generation Access fund (to come from a GBP£6 annual levy on all telephone landlines). The funds generated by the levy would have been used to facilitate the installation of fibre-optic cable in rural and suburban areas where it might otherwise have been unprofitable for the private sector to invest. The new Conservative-Liberal Democrat coalition government elected in May 2010 have since scrapped the plan for a telephone levy and instead plan to fund rural broadband investment using a portion of the annual BBC licence fee.[24]

3. Australia: The government announced a multi-billion fibre-to-the-home project which will provide 100Mb/s connections to 90 percent of homes by 2017. The project is to be run as a joint venture with the private sector where the state will own a minimum of 51 per cent of the project.[25]

4. Singapore: The government is providing almost USD$500 million for a joint venture project with a private sector company to construct the passive infrastructure for a national NGN. A further USD$166 million in funding is being provided for a separate joint venture with Starhub (a subsidiary of Eircom's new owner STT), to build and operate the active infrastructure for the national network and will be completed by 2015.[26]

It is clear that other countries have recognised the strategic importance of high-speed broadband and are taking steps to ensure their countries do not fall behind through various public funding initiatives. While the Irish government has provided some funding for next generation infrastructure through the MANs programme, the MANs essentially only tackle the 'middle mile' of the national network. For Ireland to develop ubiquitous high-speed broadband, further public investment will be necessary since the private sector is unlikely to invest in next generation infrastructure in all but the most lucrative densely populated urban areas.

### 7.6.2   Further government intervention required

The Irish government needs to follow the lead of other European countries and either directly invest in a national NGN itself, facilitate its rollout through cooperative initiatives with the private sector, or use the regulatory instruments available to more effectively drive development of the infrastructure required in all geographical areas of the country. However, given the fiscal constraints that the Irish government currently faces, it is highly unlikely that the government will be willing to provide any funding to subsidise private sector investment.[27] Given Ireland's unique characteristics and current difficult fiscal circumstances, one possible solution, which is worth considering and would require further detailed analysis, is the establishment of a new state-owned NGN company. A new public NGN company could finance any investment through its own borrowings and thus remain 'off balance sheet'.

The case for a state-owned national NGN is further strengthened when one considers that the Irish government is uniquely placed to optimally provide and support the development of a NGN. Most of the cost of constructing fibre optic networks or upgrading existing networks is related to civil engineering works. Any public sector organisation or local authority carrying out major construction projects can potentially be utilised to provide telecommunications infrastructure. Moreover, a number of large-scale transport projects are planned over the next few years. Installing ducting at the construction phase would be a cost-effective way to provide the infrastructure necessary to support the development of a national NGN.

In addition, a number of commercial SOEs already own substantial fibre networks or other ducting infrastructure that can be used for fibre rollout.[28] These existing assets could be used in a more integrated way to provide 'backhaul' connections between local networks and the national backbone network. Bundling these assets together and allowing other operators access to these networks in a less fragmented manner would significantly reduce the cost of deploying next generation services (Forfás, 2010). The transfer of these assets, plus any new infrastructure installed as part of other public sector projects, to a new state-owned national NGN company would allow for the optimal management of all public telecommunication assets. The new NGN company could then be mandated to roll out high-speed broadband infrastructure in all areas of the country where the private sector is unlikely to invest. Fully open access to the new network would then facilitate increased service-based competition in the private sector and ensure Ireland does not continue to fall further behind her European counterparts. The costs of network rollout could be further reduced if a national coordination agency was established to oversee and coordinate investment in all of the state's network companies (electricity, gas, water, rail etc.).

While these suggestions would allow for the better coordination of public investment in the national backbone and middle mile infrastructure, the key obstacle to developing NGB in Ireland remains the critical last mile (local loop) infrastructure, in terms of providing for future ultra high-speed communications capacity beyond the capability of wireless communications. The last mile is a key area of concern given the historical lack of investment by Eircom in this area. Eircom's current local loop infrastructure, which is largely twisted pair copper, is fast becoming incapable of delivering currently available bandwidth-intensive services. The services of the future will require even higher levels of bandwidth. While Eircom has recently invested in upgrading parts of its network, the higher speeds available are generally only available to those living in more urban areas. In order to develop a true national NGN, the deeper rollout of fibre (i.e. to the home or to the kerb), either across Eircom's network, or in a complete green field approach, is necessary for consideration. Eircom's stranglehold on local loop infrastructure continues to be a significant bottleneck in the future development of NGB outside of urban areas.

Eircom recently announced a €20 million pilot project for rolling out fibre-to-the-home in two towns in Ireland on an open-access basis, which would allow other private companies access to the trials. The estimated cost for rolling out fibre-to-the-kerb nationally is €500 million, while the rollout of fibre-to-the-home is estimated at €2.5 billion.[29] Given its substantial debt burden and its current financial difficulties, it is highly unlikely that Eircom will be able to afford such investment alone. The company has indicated that it is interested in collaborating with other operators in building a national fibre-based network. It is currently formulating a business plan, which may include a proposal for establishing a separate network company, thus opening the possibility for other private operators or the government to co-invest in its network.[30] It is difficult to envisage how the required investment can take place without some degree of decisive action by government, which would most likely involve collaboration between the public and private sectors.

## 7.7 Conclusion

The telecommunications liberalisation process initiated and coordinated by the EC since the late 1980s, along with changes initiated primarily by EU member states such as the partial or full privatisation of national telecommunications operators, resulted in the creation of partially or fully market-driven telecommunications industries where firms pursued their own private interests. The liberalisation agenda of the EC was originally concerned with the introduction of competition in order to improve the efficiency – both allocative and productive – of former monopoly incumbents. However, Larouche (2008) highlights how, in terms of improving dynamic efficiency, the dynamic horizon was relatively short-term, with increased efficiency driven by more innovation using the same capital asset base. Now, a decade or more later, most of the former monopoly incumbents have become more efficient. However, their asset base has aged and significant investment in infrastructure is now required. Larouche (2008) argues that EC liberalisation policy is at a crossroads, with public policymakers in EU member states shifting their policy focus from increasing efficiency towards stimulating infrastructure investment in a liberalised environment.

The difficulty in stimulating investment in infrastructure in a liberalised environment is most evident from the considerable divergence in the speed at which high-speed broadband infrastructure has been rolled out across EU member states. Different policy and regulatory approaches across countries have led to vastly different experiences in terms of the development of competition in national telecoms markets and the level of investment in next generation broadband infrastructure. It is clear that a 'one size fits all' policy and regulatory approach at a European level is unlikely to be optimal for every member state, with the best approach to facilitating investment likely to vary, not just from member state to member state, but from one region to another within member states.

Overall, there is little evidence to suggest that privatisation was associated with greater competition in the Irish telecommunications industry, with most developments largely due to the impact of liberalisation
and regulation. Indeed, it would appear that the privatisation of Eircom did in fact have a negative impact on competition, particularly
in the fixed-line and broadband markets due to the lack of LLU, to such
an extent that the government was forced to re-enter the telecommunications market by investing in broadband infrastructure through various
programmes. Given that the government was aware, as far back as 1999,
that the private market would not provide sufficient investment to ensure
the availability of broadband outside urban areas, it is surprising that they
delayed so long in implementing effective public policies, such as the
MANs programme, to complement its liberalisation policy and the
privatisation of Eircom. The delay in the rollout of broadband services
since 2001, coupled with the fact that the quality of services available has
been inferior to the rest of Europe, has arguably hindered the potential
development of SMEs in Ireland, as well as the development of e-business
services.[31]

The government's decision to privatise Eircom as a vertically integrated operation without separating the natural monopoly element
(the network) from the potentially competitive activities is at odds
with its stated goal of enhancing competition in the market, since
any new owner would have an incentive to restrict competition in
potentially competitive activities by limiting the access of rival firms
to its network. Moreover, there was substantial evidence from the
UK in relation to British Telecom which suggested that privatising the
firm as a vertically integrated entity would have serious implications
for future competition even with tight and effective regulation.[32]
While this decision can be attributed to the government's goal of
maximising revenue from the sale, it has arguably come at a high cost
in terms of the subsequent problems in enabling competition in the
industry.

Privatisation and liberalisation policies have become important tools of
economic policy. For 'regional economies' like Ireland, an adequate stock
of infrastructure (including telecommunications infrastructure) is a critical requirement if long run output growth is to be sustained (Krugman,
1997). The privatisation of public enterprises, particularly those operating
in key strategic sectors, leads to a substitution of private markets for the
social welfare and industrial policy objectives that existed previously in
Ireland and the rest of Europe. Where divestiture leads to an influx of
international investors into former state-owned industries, economic

power is transferred out of the country, leading to a decline in government control over the economy (Parker, 1999).

Ireland's experience with the privatisation of the telecommunications industry is a salient example of this loss of control. The decision to relinquish complete control of Ireland's telecommunications network eliminated the scope for the government to prevent any undesirable changes in ownership. The subsequent takeovers by private equity groups in two separate LBOs resulted in a deterioration of the financial structure of the company, with debts soaring to unsustainable levels. This has severely reduced the resources available for capital investment and contributed to the slow rollout of broadband infrastructure described in this chapter. The case of Eircom illustrates how the ownership of strategically important infrastructure by private equity groups is inimical to the development goals of the wider economy and society. This provides a salutary lesson for policymakers charged with decisions in relation to the privatisation of utility network companies.

The government's decision to sell its entire shareholding in 'one go' is in stark contrast to the experience in other European countries. Every other member state opted to float or place partial shareholdings in their national operators, followed by the sales of subsequent partial stakes. Many countries such as France, Germany, Austria, and Belgium still retain sizeable shareholdings in their national telecommunications companies. Of the countries where the state has sold a majority stake, or indeed its entire shareholding in the national operator, many retained a 'golden share' granting them certain veto rights over decisions in relation to changes in company ownership.

# 8
# Nationalisation of the Irish Banking Sector

## 8.0 Introduction

The global financial crisis that came to a head in the autumn of 2008 has had a dramatic impact on the extent of direct state involvement in economies around the world. It remains too early to determine whether the massive state interventions undertaken to rescue banking systems and other major companies will have a lasting effect in terms of extending and deepening the reach of government in the production of goods and services in the global economy. The fact remains, however, that the current crisis has precipitated the re-entry of the state into sectors that it had largely exited, namely the banking and financial sectors of most industrialised countries. This is particularly true in the Irish case. Whereas the state had withdrawn from the Irish banking sector as a result of privatising its three remaining state-owned banks between 2001 and 2002, the current crisis has resulted in a reversal of this position to an extent that was unimaginable up to a few years ago.

Since January 2009, the Irish government has fully or partially nationalised a number of credit institutions. It has also established a new state agency, the National Asset Management Agency (NAMA), to purchase impaired loans from these institutions in order to clean up their balance sheets. These developments have had far-reaching consequences for the composition and size of the SOE sector as well as the assets under its control. The establishment of NAMA has resulted in the Irish government potentially becoming the owner of the largest property portfolio in the country, and constitutes the creation of the largest state-owned entity (in terms of assets) in the history of the state.

This chapter describes the developments that have led to the government's re-entry into the banking market, and outlines how the Irish economy went from boom to bust in less than two decades. It focuses on the banking crisis that emerged as a result of the property market collapse and maps in detail the government's response to date. The catastrophic impact of these events is demonstrated by placing the Irish situation in a comparative historical perspective. We show that the extent and speed of the Irish downturn has been particularly severe, even by current and historical international standards, and the potential costs arising from the government response to date places the Irish exchequer at considerable risk going forward.

## 8.1    Before the crisis: The Celtic Tiger

The term 'Celtic Tiger' has been a widely used metaphor, both nationally and internationally, to describe the period of economic success that began in Ireland during the 1990s. The factors underpinning the emergence of the Celtic Tiger have been the subject of much analysis by a host of different authors (see, for example, Barry (1999), Gray (1997), Honohan and Walsh (2002), Mac Sharry and White (2000), and Sweeney (1999), to name but a few). The reason why Ireland's economic success during the 1990s has been so well-documented is largely due to the fact that its economic growth during this period was so unprecedented. Ireland had experienced a painful recession during the 1980s, reaching its nadir in 1986, when unemployment averaged 17 per cent,[1] the general government deficit as a percentage of GDP stood at 10.6 per cent,[2] and the ratio of general government debt to GDP was 117 per cent.[3]

From the late 1980s onwards, Ireland's economic fortunes began to turn. Over the period 1988–2007, Ireland enjoyed an average annual real growth rate in GDP of 6 per cent, reaching double digits on average during the years 1995–2000 (Honohan and Walsh, 2002). While there has been much debate on the exact causes of Ireland's remarkable economic growth during the 1990s, they are generally ascribed to a number of factors including, *inter alia*: macroeconomic stability, the receipt of EU structural funds, the attraction of increased foreign direct investment (which was helped by a boom in the US economy, the fact that Ireland had a well-educated, English-speaking labour force and a low corporation tax environment), rolling social partnership agreements which restrained wage growth, and increased competition and deregulation.

These factors contributed to a remarkable period of growth. By 2001, unemployment had fallen to less than 4 per cent, while the ratio of general government debt to GDP had decreased to 35 per cent. Ireland's GDP per capita, having been far below that of its European counterparts for decades, converged with the EU15 average during 1997–98 and reached approximately 132 per cent of the EU15 average in 2007, just prior to the onset of the financial crisis.[4]

In examining the nature of Ireland's economic growth from the 1990s onwards, it is necessary to distinguish between two distinct periods before and after the turn of the century. The first period, during the mid- to late-1990s, consisted of largely export-driven growth. In 2000, the ratio of trade (exports plus imports) to GDP was 173 per cent, a figure approached only by Singapore (Honohan and Walsh, 2002). After 2000 however, an unsustainable property and construction bubble took over from exports as the main driver of Irish growth. The domestically driven growth after 2000 masked a number of developments which resulted in Ireland being ill-prepared to cope with the effects of the global financial crisis that brought pressure to bear on the Irish economy in early 2008. These developments included a loss of international competitiveness due to factors such as a 23.4 per cent increase in the trade-weighted exchange rate between 2000 and 2008, as well as increases in the growth rate of labour costs that exceeded the EU average over the period 2004–07 (NCC, 2009). In addition, reckless banking practices in a light-touch regulatory environment, as well as the exchequer's over-reliance on tax revenues from property related sources, stored up a domestic economic crisis that would have resulted in a recession regardless of the global financial crisis (Honohan, 2009a).

## 8.2   The roots of Ireland's economic crisis

In hindsight, it is clear that from the start of the new millennium Ireland was facing a looming economic crisis (Whelan, 2009). The catalyst for the recession was the overheated construction and housing sectors. One of the key features of the post-2000 Celtic Tiger economy was the remarkable housing boom that accounted for increasing levels of economic activity, employment and tax revenues as the country moved into the new millennium. The total stock of dwellings in Ireland had increased gradually from 1.19 million homes in 1991 to 1.41 million homes in 2000. By 2008, this figure had reached 1.93 million homes. Annual house completions increased from 19,539 in 1990 to 49,812 in 2000, peaking at 93,419 in 2006.[5]

Figure 8.1 shows that the increase in the supply of houses did not dampen house prices. Instead, house prices continued to rise as a result of seemingly insatiable demand. Whelan (2009) describes how between 1996 and 2007, house prices in Ireland quadrupled, easily surpassing

*Figure 8.1* New House Completions and New House Prices in Ireland, 1970–2009

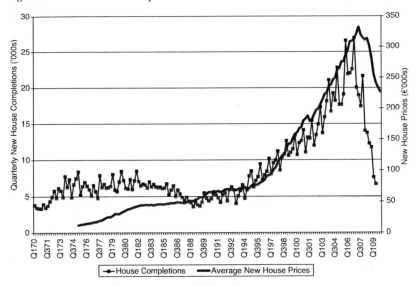

Source: Quarterly data on house completions from Q1 1970 to Q2 2009 sourced from Department of the Environment, Heritage and Local Government housing statistics. Quarterly data on average new house prices (national) from Q1 1975 to Q4 2009 sourced from the CSO.

Note: Data on house completions for the first six months of 2005 was not available in quarterly format. Total house completions for the six-month period were thus divided by two to provide proxy figures for Q1 2005 and Q2 2005.

the doubling of house prices in the USA over the period 1996–2006. The demand for housing in Ireland was driven by a combination of factors such as increased incomes, a growth in population (fuelled by significant inward migration from new EU member states in Eastern Europe), as well as a demographic structure that fed into demand for housing. Two other key features included an environment of low real and nominal interest rates from 1998, aided by Ireland's entry into the EMU, and reckless lending practices by the banks. These factors contributed to increases in prices that significantly overshot fundamental values by 2003–04 (Rae and van den Noord, 2006).

As is evident from Figure 8.1, house completions and prices peaked towards the end of 2006 and have fallen dramatically since then. By March 2010, nominal house prices had fallen by 34 per cent[6] from their peak, and the expectation is that the 'peak-to-trough' fall will reach approximately 50 per cent by 2011 (ESRI, 2010). Such a fall would be comparable to the most severe peak-to-trough declines experienced historically in other countries. For example, following financial crises in their respective countries during the 1990s, Finland, Hong Kong, the Philippines and Colombia, all experienced a decline in real house prices of 50 to 60 per cent, as measured from peak-to-trough (Reinhart and Rogoff, 2008, 2009a).[7]

The slowdown in the housing market has led to a collapse in tax revenues and contributed to a severe fiscal crisis. Prior to the crisis, the exchequer had become heavily reliant on tax revenues from the property market during the years of the construction and housing boom. Indeed, tax revenues from stamp duty, capital gains and VAT as a percentage of total tax revenue rose from 2 per cent in 1988 to 12 per cent in 2006 (Whelan, 2009), while the share of the construction sector in overall employment, having averaged less than 7 per cent from 1990–97,[8] increased rapidly from 1998 onwards. The share of the construction sector in total employment increased from 8.6 per cent in 1998 (the corresponding EU15 average was 7.1 per cent) to 13.3 per cent by 2007 (compared to an EU15 average of 7.6 per cent).[9]

The collapse in the property market and construction sector led to a drastic fall in total tax revenue from 2007 onwards. Total tax revenues fell by 14 per cent in 2008, which was largely explained by a fall in cyclical tax revenues of 36 per cent (Honohan, 2009a).[10] The decline in tax revenues accelerated in 2009 with a 19 per cent decline recorded over the year 2008–09. The general government deficit was 7.3 per cent of GDP in 2008, and increased to 14.6 per cent in 2009. This is particularly disappointing in the context of severe austerity measures taken in three budgets since October 2008. Of particular concern in this regard is the continuing fall in income tax revenue. Despite the imposition of additional income levies, income tax revenues declined by 7 per cent over the 12-month period to March 2009 and a further 10 per cent up to March 2010 (ESRI, 2010).

## 8.3   The role of the banking sector

The Irish banking sector was the critical player in the creation of the property market bubble. Its subsequent collapse has required levels of state support that were unthinkable before the beginning of the current crisis. In this section we detail the credit boom fuelled by the Irish banking sector in the context of a 'light-touch' regulatory framework. Unlike the banking crises that have gripped countries like the USA and the UK, the Irish banking crisis cannot reasonably be attributed to subprime lending in the housing market or trade in complex financial instruments. The cause of Ireland's banking crisis is due to the exposure of Irish banks (and one bank in particular, Anglo Irish Bank) to lending to property developers (Whelan, 2009).

Figure 8.2 shows the rapid increase in private sector credit (PSC) that occurred between 2003 and 2008, with PSC as a percentage of GDP increasing from 115 per cent to 217 per cent over the same period. The increase in PSC during this period was largely driven by property related lending. Between 2002 and 2007, property related lending as a proportion of the total stock of PSC increased from just under 40 per cent to over 60 per cent, reaching a high of 64.1 per cent in June 2007 (CBFSAI, 2007b).[11]

The increase in private sector credit described above occurred in a period where the bubble in property prices was becoming increasingly evident. This did not, however, lead to a tightening of bank regulation. Honohan (2009a) describes how Irish banking regulation appeared compliant with international standards but in fact was 'complacent and permissive'. In addition, it failed to tighten lending standards. By 2006, fully two-thirds of loans to first time buyers had loan-to-value ratios in excess

*Figure 8.2*   Private Sector Credit in Ireland, 1990–2009

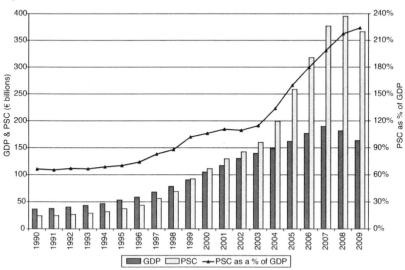

*Source*: Authors' elaboration of data on GDP in current prices (sourced from the CSO national accounts), and data on the stock of private sector credit sourced from CBFSAI monthly statistics (figures used were as of December in each year).

of 90 per cent, while one-third were getting 100 per cent loans (Honohan, 2009a). Whelan (2009) attributes the failure in Irish banking regulation to an over-emphasis on regulating capital requirements. The author argues that while the Irish regulatory system was consistent with the Basel II framework for banking supervision, it over-emphasised capital adequacy rules (which seek to ensure that banks have sufficient capital to absorb losses) at the expense of paying sufficient attention to the issue of 'credit concentration risk' (Whelan, 2009: 13). As a consequence, the exposure of banks to property developers increased disproportionately, especially during the final years of the boom. Moreover, these loans were funded by huge foreign borrowings rather than deposits. By early 2008, net foreign borrowing by Irish banks had jumped to over 60 per cent of GDP from 10 per cent at the end of 2003 (Honohan, 2010).

A government-commissioned report into the causes of the Irish banking crisis by two independent experts published in 2010 (Regling and Watson, 2010) argued that the concentration of risks in bank lending to the property sector, particularly in lending for commercial property (and within this, development loans to a select number of key developers of commercial property), made the Irish banking system particularly vulnerable. The authors stated that:

> Cycles in credit to commercial real estate are prone to particularly wide swings; and in the upswing of the cycle in Ireland, there is wide agreement that property development was well ahead of trends that fundamentals could justify. This put bank capital heavily at risk in some cases. Since this boom was bank-financed, its reversal was bound to be subject to the usual acceleration and deceleration effects that occur when collateral values rise and fall.
>
> (Regling and Watson, 2010: 32)

The banking system was therefore extremely vulnerable to any slowdown in the economy and a downturn in the property sector, particularly given its increasing reliance on wholesale borrowing from the international financial markets. While the global liquidity crisis sparked by the collapse of the US investment bank, Lehman Brothers, in September 2008 brought things in Ireland to a head, both the Honohan (2010) report and Regling and Watson (2010) report conclude that serious stress in the Irish financial system was almost unavoidable, even if the failure of Lehman Brothers had not occurred. Residential property prices had been falling for over 18 months before the collapse of Lehman Brothers, while commercial property prices had been falling for approximately nine months

(Honohan, 2010). Significant losses on development property loans issued at the peak of the market were thus becoming increasingly inevitable.

A deterioration in liquidity conditions in the international financial markets from August 2007 onwards, which progressively deepened throughout 2008 as markets became increasingly wary of any financial risk, led to severe pressure on Irish banks which were overly reliant on wholesale funding. The contagion in the international financial markets after the collapse of Lehman Brothers in September 2008 led to extreme liquidity conditions. After a silent wholesale run, mainly on Anglo Irish Bank (Anglo) but also on a number of other Irish banks, by the end of the month it was feared that Anglo was facing imminent collapse and was in danger of being unable to meet its immediate payment obligations (Honohan, 2010). Had Anglo collapsed, the impact on the rest of Irish banking system, which would likely have experienced an accelerated outflow of funds, would have pushed a number of other banks, including the two largest banks in the state (Allied Irish Banks (AIB) and Bank of Ireland (BoI)), to the brink of collapse (Honohan, 2010). The government's steps to avoid this scenario and the measures it has adopted to resolve the crisis in the Irish banking system are outlined in the next section.

## 8.4 Mapping the Irish government response to the banking crisis

Virtually no country has been left unscathed by the current global financial crisis. While the degree to which governments in Europe and across the world have had to intervene in order to stabilise their financial systems has varied widely, most countries have had to adopt national rescue measures of some sort in order to avoid potential spillover to the wider economy. In the EU15, the emergency measures adopted have ranged from 1) state guarantee schemes, which were introduced in most member states; 2) recapitalisation measures to strengthen the capital base of banks; 3) state loans to support the liquidity positions of banks; 4) the acquisition of impaired assets or the protection of losses from such assets; and 5) the nationalisation of distressed banks with a view to restructuring and eventual reprivatisation (see Petrovic and Tutsch (2009) and Laeven and Valencia (2010) for a detailed overview of the rescue measures introduced in each country).

Following the events of late 2008, the Irish government has utilised almost the full range of measures outlined above. The range of responses adopted sum to a complex web of arrangements that can be difficult to penetrate. The decisions made by the Irish government in response to

Table 8.1   Summary of Major Rescue Measures for Irish Banking System

| Date | Measure | Comment |
|---|---|---|
| 20 Sept. 2008 | Deposit Guarantee | Due to increased liquidity pressures in the Irish banking system and speculation of a possible run on the banks, the government raised the limit under the existing statutory deposit guarantee scheme from €20,000 to €100,000, and increased the coverage of the scheme from 90 to 100 per cent of deposits. |
| 30 Sept. 2008 | Blanket Guarantee | At an emergency meeting on the night of 29/30 September, the government decided to introduce a blanket guarantee on the deposits and most of the liabilities of six domestic banks. The subsidiaries of foreign banks with a significant presence in Ireland were subsequently offered inclusion on the 9 October, with only one bank opting to join. |
| 14 Dec. 2008 | Recapitalisation | The government announced a recapitalisation programme for AIB, BoI and Anglo worth up to €10 billion. |
| 15 Jan. 2009 | Nationalisation | The government announced that Anglo is to be nationalised since recapitalisation alone will not guarantee the bank's viability. |
| 11 Feb. 2009 | Recapitalisation | The government announced the recapitalisation terms to be offered to AIB and BoI. Both banks are offered state investment of €3.5 billion in return for preference shares. |
| 29 May 2009 | Recapitalisation | The government announced it will inject €4 billion into Anglo after the bank reports losses of over €4.1 billion. |
| 31 Jul. 2009 | Asset purchase scheme | Draft legislation for the National Asset Management Agency (NAMA), the state backed asset relief scheme, is published. |

Table 8.1   Summary of Major Rescue Measures for Irish Banking System
– *continued*

| Date | Measure | Comment |
| --- | --- | --- |
| 22 Nov. 2009 | Asset purchase scheme | The National Asset Management Agency Act 2009 is approved by parliament and NAMA is officially established on 21 December 2009. |
| 22 Feb. 2010 | Partial Nationalisation | The state obtains a 15.7 per cent stake in BoI after the bank is forced to pay the annual dividend due on the state's preference share investment in ordinary shares. |
| 31 Mar. 2010 | Nationalisation | The Irish Nationwide Building Society is effectively nationalised after the government has to inject capital into the institution so it can meet the minimum required capital adequacy ratio. |
| 31 Mar. 2010 | Recapitalisation | The government injects €8.3 billion into Anglo to bring its capital levels up to regulatory requirements after the bank incurred record losses. A further €2 billion is injected on 28 May 2010. |
| 13 May 2010 | Partial Nationalisation | The state acquires an 18.3 per cent shareholding in AIB after the bank has to issue ordinary shares in lieu of a cash dividend due to the state on its €3.5 billion preference share investment. |
| 20 May 2010 | Partial Nationalisation | The state increases its shareholding in BoI to approximately 36 per cent after subscribing to a placement of shares. The state's shareholding remained unchanged after a rights issue of new shares in June, where the state subscribed to its full entitlement. |
| 28 May 2010 | Nationalisation | The Educational Building Society is effectively nationalised when the government is forced to recapitalise the building society after it fails to attract private investment to make up its deficiency in required capital. |

the unprecedented banking crisis have proven to be very costly and set Ireland apart from its peers. Early in the crisis, a state guarantee scheme was put in place in order to safeguard the banking system from a possible collapse. The primary measures to support the banking system adopted since the guarantee was introduced include: bank recapitalisations, the nationalisation or partial nationalisation of banks, and the establishment of an asset relief scheme to remove impaired assets from distressed banks. Table 8.1 provides a timeline of the major rescue measures adopted, along with a brief summary of each measure. These measures, and their impacts, are examined in more detail in the following sections, and demonstrate the extraordinary degree to which the Irish state is now the main player in the Irish banking sector.

### 8.4.1   The first response – The bank guarantee

As described earlier, the situation in the Irish banking sector at the end of September 2008 was such that, given the frozen liquidity conditions in the market, one bank (Anglo) was deemed highly unlikely to survive the week, and that if it were to collapse, a number of other banks would have been pushed to the brink. To obviate the risk of such a scenario, the government introduced an extensive guarantee of the deposits and liabilities of six domestic credit institutions, after an emergency meeting on the night of 29/30 September. While almost every EU country introduced deposit guarantees (or increased the level of deposit insurance), and many governments guaranteed the issuing of new debt by banks, the guarantee introduced by the Irish government in September 2008 was unique in that it introduced a blanket guarantee which covered the full stock of existing bank debt, including long-term bonds and some subordinated debt, for a two-year period up until September 2010. The gross amount of liabilities guaranteed by the state totalled approximately €365 billion, almost 2.5 times the level of GNP (Honohan, 2010).

By including banks' existing debt, the Irish government took on significantly more contingent liabilities than any other Eurozone government[12] and exposed the government to substantial financial risk. The decision had enormous ramifications for the state, with the interest cost on sovereign debt increasing significantly as a result.[13] A report by the Governor of the Irish Central Bank on the banking crisis published in June 2010 was critical of the decision to introduce a blanket guarantee since '[t]he inclusion of existing long-term bonds and some subordinated debt [...] was not necessary in order to protect the immediate liquidity position' of Irish banks (Honohan, 2010: 128). The report also noted that:

> In contrast to most of the interventions by other countries, in which more or less complicated risk-sharing mechanisms of one sort or another were introduced, the blanket cover offered by the Irish guarantee pre-judged that all losses in any bank becoming insolvent during the guarantee period – beyond those absorbed by some of the providers of capital – would fall on the State.
>
> (Honohan, 2010: 135)

While the report accepted that an extensive guarantee was required in order to avoid the potential collapse of the Irish banking system at a time when global financial markets were in a severe state of panic, Honohan (2010: 14) nevertheless states that:

> ...the extent of the cover provided (including to outstanding long-term bonds) can – even without the benefit of hindsight – be criticised inasmuch as it complicated and narrowed the eventual resolution options for the failing institutions and increased the State's potential share of the losses.

### 8.4.2   Recapitalisation and nationalisation

With the immediate liquidity pressures faced by the Irish banking system relatively contained after the introduction of the blanket guarantee, the government's focus subsequently shifted to resolving the increasingly evident solvency crisis faced by a number of banks. The primary measures adopted by the government included the nationalisation of Anglo, and capital injections into a number of other banks after a regulatory assessment of each bank's recapitalisation needs was undertaken. As a result of this programme of recapitalisation, the state now owns two building societies, has acquired partial ownership stakes in the two largest banks in the country and is likely to end up with a majority stake in one of these. The measures adopted have resulted in the costliest intervention in the history of the Irish state and have dramatically increased the pervasiveness of state ownership in the Irish economy. The following sections provide details on each of the five credit institutions that have been recapitalised, the level of state investment in each institution, and the government's ownership stake in each institution.

*Anglo Irish Bank*

The rise and fall of Anglo Irish Bank (Anglo) over the last decade in many ways mirrors the economic boom and bust in Ireland during the same period. For years, Anglo was one of the smallest banks operating in Ireland. In terms of its business model, it was essentially a 'monoline' bank that specialised in commercial real estate lending and was not active in retail mortgage lending. Starting in the late 1990s, the bank began lending ever increasing amounts to the commercial property development sector. Anglo's total stock of loans and advances to customers at the end of September 1998 stood at just over €3.5 billion. Between 1998 and 2007, the bank recorded an astounding average annual growth rate in its loan book of almost 40 per cent. By 2008, Anglo's total loans amounted to €72.1 billion, with the bank having made loans of over €10 billion in 2005, and over €15 billion in both 2006 and 2007.[14] Anglo's unparalleled lending growth from 1998 to 2007 led to an increase in its market share from 3 to 18 per cent (of the total assets of the six domestic institutions that were subsequently covered by the blanket guarantee) over the period in question (Honohan, 2009b), making it the third largest bank in Ireland in terms of total assets.

The extent to which Anglo was exposed to a downturn in the Irish and UK property markets is evident from the assets securing its loan book in September 2007. Of its total loan book of €65.9 billion, 93 per cent of loans were secured on real estate, with 39 per cent of loans secured on assets in the UK, and 36 per cent backed by real estate in Ireland (Anglo, 2007). The downturn in both the Irish and UK property markets in 2007 and 2008 had a devastating impact on the quality of Anglo's loan book. The bank was forced to make impairment provisions of €879 million in 2008, and a staggering €15.1 billion in 2009 (€10.1 billion of which related to loans to be transferred to NAMA). Even after the transfer of almost half of its €72 billion loan book to NAMA, almost 40 per cent of the bank's remaining loans were either impaired, or past due but not impaired (Anglo, 2010).

Anglo's share price, having traded at over €10 per share at the beginning of January 2008 (with a market capitalisation of over €8.1 billion), decreased gradually throughout the year and fell below €1 in late November 2008. The share price collapsed during December[15] after details emerged about secret personal loans made to directors which prompted the resignations of the bank's chairman on 18 December, and the bank's chief executive the following day. This prompted the government to announce a €1.5 billion capital injection on 21 December 2008. The capital was to be provided using money from the National Pension Reserve

Fund (NPRF) and would be granted in return for preference shares and a 75 per cent ownership stake. The announcement did little to improve market confidence in the bank, and, on 15 January 2009, the government announced that it was abandoning its plan to inject €1.5 billion into Anglo and had instead decided to fully nationalise it. The decision to nationalise was underpinned by the sustained funding difficulties experienced by the bank and the reputational damage it had suffered following the disclosure of secret loans to directors (Honohan, 2009b). The blanket guarantee introduced by the government in September 2008 effectively meant that it had no option other than to nationalise Anglo, since allowing it to fail would have left the government liable for the bank's deposits and existing liabilities.

In May 2009, Anglo declared a pre-tax loss of €4.1 billion for the six months to the end of March 2009 after incurring an impairment charge of €3.7 billion on its loan book. The state was subsequently forced to inject €4 billion into the bank between June and September 2009 to cover its losses up until that point (Anglo, 2009). In March 2010, Anglo declared a pre-tax loss of €12.7 billion, the largest in Irish corporate history, for the 15-month period to the end of December 2009 following an impairment charge of €15.1 billion on its assets. In order to meet the bank's capital requirements, the government was forced to inject a further €8.3 billion in the form of a promissory note (Anglo, 2010).[16] At the same time, the government also revealed that it may have to inject an additional €10 billion into the bank as a result of further expected losses on loans transferred to NAMA, bringing the total potential cost of bailing out Anglo to €22.3 billion thus far.

Whether or not Anglo will require the additional €10 billion capital will depend on the discounts applied to loans transferred from Anglo to NAMA. However, based on the higher than expected losses incurred by the bank on the first tranche of loans transferred to NAMA in May 2010, there is a strong prospect that Anglo will incur further losses on the remaining loans to be transferred. Indeed, after the losses incurred on the first tranche of loans transferred, the government had to inject a further €2 billion into Anglo in order to bring its capital levels to the minimum demanded by the Financial Regulator.[17] A restructuring plan submitted by the government and Anglo at the end of November 2009, which proposed splitting the bank into a 'good bank' with loans of €13 billion to €15 billion, and a 'bad bank' with loans of €20 billion to be run down over time, was rejected by the EC in March 2010.[18] A revised restructuring plan was submitted at the end of May 2010. While the revised plan still includes a proposed good bank/bad bank split, the EC also requested an assessment of the cost of winding down the bank over a ten-year period, as well as over a period in excess of 20 years.[19] Any decision on the future of Anglo hinges on whether the EC decides the bank has a viable future as a standalone entity.

*Irish Nationwide Building Society*

The Irish Nationwide Building Society (INBS) has been in existence since 1975, the year it replaced the Irish Industrial Benefit Building Society, which had been established in 1873. The society expanded rapidly during the 1980s and 1990s, acquiring the Garda Building Society in 1983, Irish Mutual in 1989, and the Metropolitan Building Society in 1991. In 1998, just prior to the beginning of the property boom in Ireland, the INBS held a loan book of just over €1.66 billion. By 2007 this figure had exploded to over €12.3 billion, with the society recording an average growth of almost 25 per cent in its loan book between 2000 and 2007.[20] Much of the growth was accounted for by commercial loans in the UK and Ireland, which became the primary focus of the society during the boom as it moved away from its traditional residential business. By 2008, approximately 80 per cent of its loan book comprised commercial lending. A substantial amount of the society's lending during the latter years of the boom involved speculative lending for land and development as well as commercial investment loans, which were high-risk and involved inadequate credit checks on borrowers.[21]

The downturn in the property markets and economies of both Ireland and the UK in 2008 thus left the INBS in a very vulnerable position and it incurred heavy losses. The society recorded an after tax loss of €2.5 billion for the year ended 31 December 2009 (INBS, 2010). The majority of the losses incurred were due to substantial impairment charges on the society's UK and Irish commercial loan portfolios. With the society close to insolvent as a result of its losses, the government was forced to effectively nationalise the society after the Financial Regulator determined that the INBS would need €2.7 billion in order to meet its required capital ratio. The state took control of the society on 31 March 2010 after injecting €100 million into the troubled building society in return for a special investment share.[22] On the same date, the government issued a €2.6 billion promissory note to the society in order to meet the remainder of its regulatory capital requirements. The INBS will transfer approximately €9 billion in commercial property loans (almost 80 per cent of its loan book) to NAMA, leaving the society with around €2.4 billion in mainly residential loans (INBS, 2010). In order to receive final EC approval for the €2.7 billion state capital injection, the INBS had to submit a restructuring plan in June 2010 demonstrating that the society had a viable future as a standalone entity. The government has indicated that it is seeking a swift sale of the society or its integration with another entity.[23]

*EBS Building Society*

The EBS was established in 1935 as the Educational (Permanent) Building Society, altering its name to the Educational Building Society in 1949, and subsequently to the EBS Building Society in 1991. The EBS is a mutual building society whose main focus is on residential mortgage lending, as well as the provision of commercial mortgage lending and savings products. The EBS expanded its loan book considerably between 2000 and 2008, with an average annual growth rate in lending of close to 20 per cent recorded over the period. Between 2000 and 2008, total loans and advances to customers increased from €4.4 billion to €16.9 billion.[24] By 2008, approximately 80 per cent (€13.1 billion) of the society's loan book consisted of home loans, while commercial lending and development finance accounted for 14 per cent (€2.4 billion) (EBS, 2009). Despite not engaging as aggressively as other banks in commercial and development finance lending, the EBS nonetheless incurred significant losses on this portion of its loan portfolio.

As a result of the losses incurred and the new capital requirement targets set by the Financial Regulator, the EBS was effectively taken under public ownership in May 2010. EBS received a €100 million capital injection on 28 May 2010 in return for a special investment share after the society failed to attract private investors. As with the INBS, the special investment share gave the Minister for Finance effective economic ownership of the society, with full control over all resolutions. Since the EBS required €875 million to bring its capital reserves up to the required core equity ratio set by the Financial Regulator, the government also undertook to invest further funds of up to €775 million in the form of a promissory note in the event that private capital could not be obtained.[25] In June 2010, the government injected €250 million of the additional €775 million pledged.[26] As with the INBS, the government is looking for a quick sale of the EBS or a possible amalgamation of the society with another financial institution in order to reduce the need for further state investment.

*Allied Irish Banks and Bank of Ireland*

Historically, both Allied Irish Banks (AIB) and Bank of Ireland (BoI) have been the two dominant banks in the Irish banking sector. Despite increased competition from new banks established in the Irish market from the late 1990s onwards, both banks still retained sizeable market shares in their core retail, business and investment activities. In 2008, the combined assets of both banks accounted for over 50 per cent of the total assets in the sector (EC, 2010a). Both banks, in particular AIB, got caught up in the wave of excessive lending to the property sector that occurred towards the peak of the boom.

AIB's total loans and advances to customers increased from just under €40 billion in 1999 to €129.5 billion in 2008. Correspondingly, Bank of Ireland's loan book stood at approximately €36 billion in 1999, before increasing by almost €100 billion in less than a decade to €135.7 billion in 2008.[27] In 2008, approximately 26 per cent of BoI's loan book related to non-residential property lending (the majority of which was investment property lending), while 44 per cent related to mortgage lending (BoI, 2009). In the same year, lending by AIB to the property and construction sector accounted for over 36 per cent of its loan book, with over half of these loans related to commercial investment and development (AIB, 2009).

Rising impairment charges as a result of the downturn in the Irish property market, and problems in securing funding from the international markets as a result of the global financial crisis, led to considerable difficulties for both AIB and BoI. In December 2008, the government announced a recapitalisation programme for both banks, in recognition of their systemic importance to the Irish banking system. In February 2009, the government agreed to inject €3.5 billion through the purchase of preference shares in BoI by the NPRF. The same amount was invested in AIB by the NPRF in May 2009. As part of both investments, the government also obtained warrants giving them the option of subscribing for 25 per cent of the ordinary stock of each bank.

In February 2010, the government took a 15.7 per cent ownership stake in BoI through the NPRF. The NPRF had been due to receive a €250 million dividend on its €3.5 billion preference share investment in BoI. However, BoI was prevented from paying the dividend in cash by the EC, which imposed a dividend and coupon 'stopper' on both BoI and AIB while it considered their restructuring plans and whether or not the banks could pay cash dividends given the circumstances of the state aid they had received. BoI was thus forced to transfer ordinary shares equivalent to the value of the dividend due to the NPRF. The transfer of shares involved the issuing of new shares by BoI, thereby diluting the value of other shareholders' stakes in the bank.[28]

In April 2010, BoI announced a €3.4 billion capital raising programme, involving share placements, a debt for equity offer to existing bondholders, and a rights issue of new ordinary shares. As part of the capital raising exercise, the government (through the NPRF) entered into an agreement with BoI that led to the state increasing its shareholding in BoI to approximately 36 per cent. This increase in state ownership resulted from the NPRF agreeing to subscribe to a substantial placement of ordinary shares in May, followed by a subscription for its full entitlement of new shares during a rights issue of new ordinary stock in June.[29] The NPRF paid for the ordinary shares subscribed to as part of the placement and rights issue through the conversion of approximately €1.66 billion of its original €3.5 billion preference share stock.

The success of the share placements and rights issue, when existing BoI shareholders took up approximately 95 per cent of the new shares on offer,[30] brought BoI's capital requirements above the Financial Regulator's target ratio and it is unlikely that the state will need to increase its stake in BoI beyond its current level. However, this is dependent on whether BoI is able to pay the annual dividends due on the NPRF's remaining preference shares in the next few years in cash. If the bank is unable to do so, it may have to issue more ordinary shares to the NPRF in lieu of a cash dividend. To avoid such a scenario and prevent majority state ownership, BoI have indicated that they hope to redeem some or all of the NPRF's preference stock in the medium-term using some of the net cash proceeds from its capital raising exercise, provided that the bank can maintain its required capital ratios.[31] Whether the bank can afford to do so, particularly given the fact that it is projected to make further losses in the next two years, remains to be seen.

On 13 May 2010, the state obtained an 18.33 per cent stake in AIB after the bank was forced to issue €280 million in ordinary shares to the government in lieu of a cash dividend payment.[32] As with the BoI dividend paid with ordinary shares a few months earlier, AIB was prevented by the EC from issuing a cash payment for the annual dividend due to the government on its €3.5 billion preference share investment.[33] After the Financial Regulator determined that AIB required €7.4 billion in capital to meet its capital ratio targets by the end of 2010, the bank announced plans to raise as much of this capital as it can itself in order to limit the state's future shareholding. AIB will sell its 70 per cent ownership stake in Polish bank, Bank Zachodni WBK, its 22 per cent stake in US bank, M&T, as well as its UK business. Analysts expect the bank to raise approximately €4.5 billion from this asset disposal,[34] indicating that the bank is likely to end up with a majority government shareholding if it cannot make up the remaining shortfall in required capital. The final extent of state ownership will be highly dependent on the size of the proceeds generated from asset sales, the success of any other potential capital raising activities (such as a rights issue or debt for equity swap), and the discount on the remaining loans to be transferred to NAMA.

Overall, the government's intervention in the domestic banking sector has been remarkable in terms of the speed of the events and the size of the intervention. By acquiring full control of three credit institutions, as well as major stakes in the two largest Irish banks, the state has assumed an unprecedented role in the sector. While this is likely to be a temporary state of affairs, these interventions have imposed a considerable burden on the Irish exchequer. We examine the magnitude of the costs associated with this intervention in section 8.5.

### 8.4.3   National Asset Management Agency

While the nationalisation and recapitalisation of banks constitute an extraordinary extension of direct state activity and control in the Irish economy, these measures were accompanied by a further significant government intervention in response to the banking crisis. In April 2009, the government announced its attention to establish the National Asset Management Agency (NAMA) to purchase impaired property related loans from eligible financial institutions at a discount. The decision constitutes one of the most important economic decisions taken in the history of the Irish state. The loans being acquired represent the riskiest element of each participating bank's portfolio, consisting of loans secured on development land and property under development, as well as the largest property backed loans in each bank (NAMA, 2010a). It is envisaged that the removal of these riskier assets from bank balance sheets will free up lending in the banking market and restore confidence in the Irish banking sector.

Any credit institution operating in Ireland, including the Irish subsidiaries of foreign credit institutions, were deemed eligible to apply to join the asset relief scheme. The *National Asset Management Agency Act 2009* was passed into law on 22 November 2009 and came into operation on 21 December 2009. Credit institutions were then given a 60-day window within which they could apply to join the scheme. By the close of the application deadline on 19 February 2010, five credit institutions had applied to join, namely: AIB, Anglo, BoI, the EBS, and INBS.[35]

As of March 2010, loans with an aggregate nominal value of approximately €81 billion from the participating banks were identified as eligible assets for transfer to NAMA. It is estimated that the current market value of these loans is less than €40 billion; however, the approximate purchase price to be paid by NAMA for these loans will total just over

€40 billion (NAMA, 2010c).[36] These loans will be purchased by issuing government guaranteed NAMA bonds that can be exchanged for cash in international markets or at the ECB. The NAMA bonds will be used to pay 95 per cent of the purchase price of all loans, with the remaining 5 per cent paid for through the issue of non-state-guaranteed subordinated debt securities. The subordinated debt securities will be held by the participating credit institutions, thereby exposing them to losses should NAMA lose money.[37]

Approximately 36.4 per cent of the loans to be transferred are backed by land, 27.3 per cent of the loans are backed by development property, and the remainder is made up of associated commercial loans. The majority of the loans to be transferred to NAMA are related to property in Ireland (66.8 per cent), with 20.7 per cent of the loans associated with property in the UK, 6.2 per cent in Northern Ireland, and the remainder in the USA and other countries (EC, 2010b).

Table 8.2 details the breakdown of loans to be transferred by each credit institution. It shows that Anglo and AIB together account for almost 73 per cent of the total value of loans to be acquired by NAMA. Table 8.2 also provides details on the first tranche of shares transferred to NAMA between March and May 2010. The first transfer involved NAMA purchasing loans with an aggregate nominal value of €15.28 billion for a consideration of €7.69 billion, with the average discount applied amounting to almost 50 per cent. It is expected that the transfer of the remaining loans from each bank will be completed by the end of 2010, with a final transfer deadline of February 2011 set by the EC.

The establishment of NAMA will have a significant fiscal impact. The purchase of loans for approximately €40 billion will add roughly 25 percentage points to Ireland's national debt. While this debt will essentially

Table 8.2   Loans to be Transferred to NAMA

|  | AIB | Anglo | BoI | EBS | INBS | Total |
|---|---|---|---|---|---|---|
| Total expected loan transfer (€bn) | 23.0 | 36.0 | 12.0 | 1.0 | 9.0 | 81.0 |
| – as a % of total loans | *28.4* | *44.4* | *14.8* | *1.2* | *11.1* | *100* |
| *First tranche: Mar.–May 2010* | | | | | | |
| Nominal value of loans (€bn) | 3.29 | 9.25 | 1.93 | 0.14 | 0.67 | 15.28 |
| Total consideration (€bn) | 1.90 | 4.16 | 1.26 | 0.09 | 0.28 | 7.69 |
| Discount (%) | *42.1* | *55.1* | *34.6* | *36.8* | *58.1* | *49.7* |

*Source*: NAMA (2010b).

be 'off-balance sheet' due to a decision by Eurostat in October 2009,[38] it nevertheless exposes the state to significant costs should the agency fail to break even. The next sections turn to the issue of fiscal costs and examine the fiscal outlays associated with the measures undertaken to date. This is then set in context by comparing the costs incurred thus far in Ireland to those of other countries, both during the current crisis and historically.

## 8.5    Fiscal costs of banking crises

Estimating the net fiscal costs related to banking crises can be problematic. Even when assessing the fiscal costs of historical crises, where one would imagine that the passage of time would allow for a complete analysis, it is often difficult to source reliable data on the amounts paid out by the exchequer and the rate of recovery. It is even more difficult to examine the fiscal costs associated with ongoing crises, where the costs related to guarantees, recapitalisations, nationalisations and liquidity schemes will not become apparent for a number of years. Notwithstanding these difficulties, this section examines the fiscal costs of the Irish banking crisis and compares it to current estimates of the costs incurred in other European countries. Some historical perspective is then provided by comparing current cost projections with those experienced by other countries during previous banking crises.

Table 8.3 summarises the total amounts provided by the government for bank recapitalisation to date, as well as an estimate of the amount to be paid by NAMA for loans to be acquired. The total investment provided by the state for the recapitalisation of the banks (existing and estimated) to date amounts to almost €33 billion, or just over 20 per cent of GDP. The approximate €40 billion to be paid by NAMA for the impaired loans of the five participating banks equates to roughly 25 per cent of GDP. In terms of estimating the final fiscal cost of these measures, it is useful to separate the potential costs into three components: (1) the recapitalisation of AIB, BoI and the EBS; (2) the recapitalisation of Anglo and the INBS; and (3) NAMA (ESRI, 2010).

With regard to the recapitalisations of AIB, BoI, and the EBS, there is a possibility that the state may recoup its investment in these institutions in the medium- to long-term, by selling the stakes that it has acquired (which may increase in the future) once the banks return to profitability. However, as pointed out by the ESRI (2010: 56) 'the gross assets (shares in the banks) and the related liabilities of the State are likely to be large and minor difference[s] in rates of return on these assets could see the State

Table 8.3   Summary of Government Support to Banking Sector

|  | Total state investment (€ billions) | Total investment (% of 2009 GDP) | Source of funding |
|---|---|---|---|
| AIB | 3.5 | 2.15 | NPRF |
| Anglo | 22.3 | 13.70 | *Exchequer:* €4bn already provided in 2009 €10.3bn promissory note in 2010 Further €8bn likely to be required |
| BoI | 3.5 | 2.15 | NPRF |
| EBS | 0.88 | 0.54 | *Exchequer:* €0.1bn special investment share €0.78 promissory note |
| INBS | 2.7 | 1.66 | Exchequer: €0.1bn special investment share €2.6bn promissory note |
| *Total Recap.* | *32.88* | *20.18* |  |
| NAMA | 40 | 25 | Issue of government guaranteed NAMA bonds |

*Notes*: (1) the amount to be paid by NAMA for the assets acquired is an estimate. The final amount to be paid will depend on the size of the discounts applied to the remaining loans to be transferred to the agency; (2) the €8 billion in additional capital likely to be required by Anglo could increase or decrease depending on the discounts applied by NAMA to the remaining loans to be transferred by the bank.

realising either a significant gain or a significant loss in the long term.' The one component of the response to the banking crisis where there is agreement that the state will definitely incur a considerable fiscal cost is the recapitalisation of Anglo and the INBS. The approximate €25 billion to be invested by the state in these institutions (the equivalent of over 15 per cent of GDP) holds little prospect of ever being recovered, and as such it is this component of the government's response to the banking crisis that is likely to account for the majority of the eventual fiscal cost for the state (ESRI, 2010).

In relation to NAMA, it is possible that, over the next decade, the eventual returns generated by the agency on the assets acquired may equal the price paid for them. However, the sheer magnitude of the sums being acquired mean that even a small unexpected loss could lead to a substantial cost to the exchequer. Whether or not the agency can generate the required break-even return on its portfolio of assets is heavily reliant on future developments in the property market, the timing of asset sales and a range of other factors. Should NAMA end up being unable to recover the amount of money paid for the loans acquired, the government has indicated that a tax surcharge will be applied to the five participating institutions to make up the shortfall.

Of the members of the EU15, both Ireland and the UK have experienced the worst banking crises and have had to adopt the costliest range of rescue measures to stabilise their banking systems. Outside of the EU15, the closest comparator is the USA, which has also had to adopt wide ranging rescue measures to counter the crisis. Table 8.4 provides an indication of the relative size of the financial support extended to the banking systems in Europe and the USA between 2007 and 2009. The table provides details on direct fiscal outlays (net of any repayments made by the end of 2009), which mainly relate to government funds used

Table 8.4   Financial Sector Support in EU15 and USA 2007–09 (as % of GDP)

| Country | Direct fiscal outlays (Net) (1) | Asset guarantees (2) | Deposit & liability guarantees (3) |
|---|---|---|---|
| Austria | 4.1 | 0.6 | 30.1 |
| Belgium | 5.0 | 7.7 | 26.4 |
| Denmark | 3.1 | ... | ... |
| France | 1.0 | 0.3 | 16.4 |
| Germany | 1.4 | 6.1 | 18.0 |
| Greece | 3.6 | ... | 6.2 |
| Ireland | 7.6 | ... | 198.1 |
| Italy | 2.7 | ... | ... |
| Luxembourg | 7.7 | ... | ... |
| Netherlands | 6.8 | 10.8 | 33.6 |
| Portugal | ... | ... | 12.0 |
| Spain | 1.8 | ... | 15.8 |
| Sweden | 0.7 | ... | 47.5 |
| UK | 8.7 | 14.5 | 53.2 |
| USA | 4.9 | ... | 10.6 |

*Source*: Laeven & Valencia (2010) and IMF (2010) for columns (1) and (2) and IMF (2009) for column (3).

*Notes*: (i) The amounts in column (1) mainly relate to funds used for the recapitalisation of banks in each country and exclude asset purchases and direct liquidity support from the treasury. These funds can be significant in some countries, for example, the Special Liquidity Scheme in the UK swapped GBP£185 billion in treasury bills with banks in return for securities; (ii) Column (3) excludes deposit insurance provided by deposit insurance agencies; (iii) Figures in columns (1) and (2) are as a percentage of 2009 GDP. Figures in column (3) are as a percentage of 2008 GDP.

to recapitalise banks and purchases assets. The table also provides information on the financial risk that governments have exposed themselves to through asset guarantees, as well as deposit and liability guarantees. While such guarantees do not involve any direct fiscal outlays, they nevertheless subject governments to potential losses arising from the contingent liabilities assumed.

The estimated direct fiscal outlays for Ireland in Table 8.4 differ from our estimates provided in Table 8.3 since the analysis of Laeven and Valencia (2010) only covers the period up until the end of 2009. The direct fiscal cost of 7.6 per cent of GDP for Ireland in Table 8.4 therefore only includes the amounts injected into AIB, BoI and Anglo in 2009, and does not include the funds provided for the recapitalisation of the EBS, INBS and the additional capital injections into Anglo. The cost of asset purchases by NAMA is also excluded. Were these amounts to be included in Table 8.4 it is clear that the direct fiscal outlay associated with the Irish banking crisis (approximately 20 per cent of GDP for recapitalisations and 25 per cent of GDP for NAMA) would be far in excess of those incurred elsewhere during the current crisis. Even when compared to a country such as the UK, which has experienced a severe banking crisis, with the government forced to nationalise a number of banks, inject significant amounts of capital into some of the country's largest banks, and introduce an asset guarantee scheme, the direct fiscal costs in Ireland are shown to be markedly higher.

A number of studies have attempted to estimate the direct fiscal outlays associated with systemic banking crises over the past number of decades. Caprio *et al.* (2005) provide estimates of the direct fiscal costs associated with 56 crises over a 50-year period. For systemic crises, the authors find that the median fiscal cost was 13.1 per cent of GDP (mean 16.8). Laeven and Valencia (2008) find that the mean fiscal cost of 42 systemic crises in their database is 13.3 per cent. Honohan (2008) extended the sample of Caprio *et al.* (2005) and found that the median fiscal cost for the 78 systemic crises in his sample was 15.5 per cent (mean 19.1). The direct costs incurred by the Irish government to date would therefore appear to be in line with those experienced historically, albeit far higher than those incurred by other governments during the current financial crisis.

Interestingly, Honohan and Klingebiel (2003) found that fiscal costs were systematically higher the more accommodating the response to the crisis was. For example, countries that introduced blanket guarantees for depositors and other creditors were found to incur higher fiscal costs than countries that avoided such responses. The current experience in Ireland would thus tend to support the findings of Honohan and Klingebiel

(2003). Ireland was the only EU15 country to introduce a blanket guarantee that included existing bank liabilities, and the details provided earlier show that the direct fiscal costs incurred by the government to date greatly surpass those experienced in other countries. It is therefore not surprising that the same author, Patrick Honohan, who was appointed as Governor of the Irish Central Bank in September 2009, in his recent report into the Irish banking crisis, was critical of the decision to introduce a blanket guarantee in September 2008 (discussed in section 8.4.1).

## 8.6   Indirect costs of banking crises

While estimating the net fiscal cost of current or historical banking crises is problematic, it is even more difficult to identify the indirect economic costs related to such crises. Many studies have attempted to measure indirect costs by examining the impact of banking crises on key variables such as output, unemployment, fiscal balances and government debt. However, when examining the impact of a crisis on such variables it is difficult to disentangle the impact of other underlying factors. For example, a downturn in economic activity in a country that experiences a banking crisis can often be due to an endogenous or exogenous economic shock that also contributes directly to the recession. It is therefore difficult to determine the precise contribution of a banking crisis to a recession. Nevertheless, this section briefly examines the empirical evidence in relation to the indirect costs related to systemic banking crises and places the Irish experience to date within the context provided.

Connolly (2009) examined 12 banking crises that occurred in developed countries between the 1970s and 1990s. The author found that the banking crises were generally preceded by financial deregulation which sparked credit growth and asset price inflation. During the boom period, the author found that the lending standards of banks generally deteriorated and prudential regulation was inadequate. The aftermath of the most serious crises involved deep and protracted downturns in economic activity, followed by muted recovery. Connolly (2009) found that the peak-to-trough decline in real GDP in their sample of both systemic and non-systemic banking crises in advanced economies ranged from a low of 5 per cent to a high of 14 per cent. Reinhart and Rogoff (2009a, 2009b) document average peak-to-trough declines in real GDP per capita of approximately 9.3 per cent over an average period of two years for their sample of countries that experienced severe systemic crises.

When the ongoing crisis in Ireland is placed in the context of the historical perspective provided above, it already ranks amongst the worst on record. Real GDP fell by 3 per cent in 2008, by 7.1 per cent in 2009, and is projected to fall by approximately 0.5 per cent in 2010 (ESRI, 2010).[39] The peak-to-trough fall in real GDP currently stands at a staggering 14.5 per cent.[40] The severity of this downturn ranks Ireland as one of the worst in the OECD, along with Turkey and Iceland, in terms of the percentage decline in real GDP from peak-to-trough during the current global recession (OECD, 2010: 264). When measured in terms of real GNP, arguably a more relevant indicator for Ireland, the peak-to-trough decline thus far is 19 per cent.[41] It must be noted that this cumulative decline in output cannot be entirely attributed to the banking crisis in Ireland. A major recession in Ireland would undoubtedly have occurred without the banking crisis as a result of the property market bubble and the global economic downturn. Nevertheless, the banking crisis has significantly exacerbated the downturn in Ireland, imposing considerable fiscal costs on the government at a time when it can least afford them, and constraining a swifter economic recovery, thus ensuring that the pain of the crisis is prolonged.

In relation to the impact of banking crises on other key macro-economic variables, Reinhart and Rogoff (2009a, 2009b) find that, on average, unemployment rises for almost five years following a systemic crisis, with an average increase in the unemployment rate of approximately 7 percentage points. In Ireland, the unemployment rate was 4.6 per cent in 2007, the year prior to the crisis. By 2009, the unemployment rate had increased to 11.8 per cent and it is projected to reach 13.75 per cent in 2010, before declining slightly in 2011 (ESRI, 2010). The unemployment rate is therefore set to increase by over 9 percentage points in the three years following the crisis. An OECD analysis of the increase in unemployment rates recorded between 2008 and 2009 ranks Ireland and Spain as the two worst performers in the OECD, with the percentage point increases in the unemployment rate in both countries double that of the next highest ranked country (OECD, 2010: 271).

Declining tax revenues and higher expenditures associated with a combination of bank bailout costs, increased social welfare transfers, and debt servicing costs lead to a rapid deterioration in fiscal balances. Reinhart and Rogoff (2009a, 2009b) find that fiscal deficits increase significantly in the aftermath of systemic financial crises. Two countries in their sample experienced double-digit percentage point increases in their fiscal deficits, as measured by the difference between the general government balance as a percentage of GDP in the year before the crisis and the peak annual deficit-to-GDP ratio recorded in the years following the crisis.[42] In the case of Ireland, the government recorded a minor surplus of 0.1 per cent of GDP in 2007. The peak deficit recorded in the aftermath of the crisis (thus far) occurred in 2009, with the general government deficit as a percentage of GDP reaching 14.3 per cent.[43] The rapid fiscal deterioration in Ireland would thus appear to rank amongst the worst recorded by any advanced economy in history.

The generation of large fiscal deficits in the years following a banking crisis naturally leads to a substantial increase in a country's national debt. Reinhart and Rogoff (2009a, 2009b) document an average increase in real public debt levels of 86 per cent in the three years following a banking crisis in their sample of historical systemic crises. The authors examine the percentage increase in debt levels, rather than debt-to-GDP ratios, since the decline in GDP following crises complicates the interpretation of such ratios. The increases in debt observed are generally shown to be the result of considerable decline in tax revenues and, in many cases, significant increases in government expenditures where fiscal stimulus packages are used to combat the recession. In a number of cases, the costs associated with bank bailouts were shown to be only a relatively minor contributor to the overall increase in post-crisis debt.

In Ireland, national debt levels almost doubled between 2007 and 2009, increasing from €37.6 billion to €75.2 billion over the two-year period.[44] National debt is set to increase further in 2010, with the general government deficit expected to amount to approximately €19 billion (ESRI, 2010),[45] as well as in subsequent years where the government is projected to run continued, albeit declining, deficits up until 2014. As a percentage of GDP, Ireland's general government debt increased from just over 25 per cent in 2007 to 65 per cent in 2009, and the debt-to-GDP ratio is expected to reach almost 80 per cent in 2010 (ESRI, 2010). It must be noted that the figures for the level of national debt and the ratio of debt to GDP quoted in this section exclude the increase in debt due to NAMA. The approximate €40 billion to be paid out by NAMA over the next year is equivalent to 25 per cent of forecasted GDP in 2010.[46]

## 8.7   Conclusion

The global financial crisis has provoked a catalogue of responses from governments around that world that would have been unimaginable prior to the events of late 2008. The impact of the crisis on the performance of individual economies and their banking and financial sectors can justifiably be described as seismic. In relative terms, the downturn in economic fortunes experienced in Ireland ranks as one of the most dramatic. Poor economic management and the failure to control the unsustainable growth in the property market meant that the Irish economy was likely to have faced considerable problems regardless of international events. However, these domestic factors combined with the openness of the Irish economy meant that the economy was per-ilously exposed to the downside risks of any crisis in the international economy. Since late 2007, the Irish economy has contracted by over 14 per cent (in real GDP terms from peak-to-trough), and experienced such a rapid deterioration in its public finances that the possibility of a sovereign debt crisis remains a real risk.

The roots of the Irish economic crisis can largely be traced back to the reckless behaviour of the domestic banking sector, which was facil-itated by an ineffective system of financial regulation. The potential collapse of the Irish banking system in September 2008 resulted in a number of state interventions on a scale that is scarcely credible. The fiscal costs of these interventions to date are of a magnitude that ranks Ireland amongst the countries worst affected by the crisis. Both the direct and indirect costs incurred are likely to hinder the prospects for economic recovery for some time to come.

The principal government responses to the banking crisis have had a considerable impact on the size and scope of the Irish SOE sector. Three credit institutions have been effectively nationalised and the state has taken significant ownership stakes in the country's two largest banks. In addition, the state has established a new SOE, NAMA, for the purpose of purchasing impaired loans from the same almost-failed credit institutions. In terms of the value of assets managed, NAMA is now the largest SOE in Ireland. Taken together these measures consti-tute the biggest government intervention in the Irish economy since independence in 1922.

These actions raise a question that has relevance throughout the global economy: do the spate of nationalisations witnessed over the last two years signal a new era of state capitalism? The answer to this question is unlikely to be straightforward. In the Irish context, however, the tentative conclusion that we draw is that the unprecedented increase in the extent of direct state ownership in the Irish economy is unlikely to be per-manent. The actions taken by the Irish government have been significantly shaped by largely failed attempts at keeping the banking sector in private ownership. This overarching aim has been explicitly articulated by the

Minister for Finance, Brian Lenihan, who stated that the government 'believes that it is important, where possible, that the banking sector has a market presence and that it operates within market disciplines and constraints'.[47]

The massive state interventions discussed in this chapter have been far-reaching. Although unintended, the re-entry of the state in the Irish financial sector is consistent with a historical pattern of state rescues in the case of market failure, and is likely to have effects that will be manifest for decades.

## *Postscript* – revised estimates of the cost of government support to the banking sector

Since this manuscript was submitted in July 2010 further information in relation to government support to the banking sector has entered the public domain. Following a statement from the government and Central Bank on 30 September 2010, the full *potential* cost of support to the banking sector is estimated at €90.8 billion (57 per cent of GDP in 2009). The potential cost of recapitalising individual institutions is as follows:

Anglo Irish Bank:    €34.3 billion (total cost to date €29.3 billion).
Allied Irish Bank:    €7.2 billion (total cost to date €3.5 billion).
Bank of Ireland:    €3.5 billion (total cost to date €3.5 billion).
INBS:    €5.4 billion (total cost to date €5.4 billion).
EBS:    €0.4 billion (total cost to date €0.4 billion).

In addition, the payment planned for loans transferred to NAMA is estimated at €40 billion. This brings the total potential cost of government support to the banking sector to €90.8 billion.[48]

The enormous cost of support to the banking sector and attendant crisis in the public finances has had calamitous effects. Sustained increases in the yield on Irish government debt were recorded during October and November 2010. The spread of Irish 10 year bonds over the benchmark German bonds widened and hit a record high of 652 basis points on 11 November.[49] Ten days later the Irish government requested financial support from the EU and the IMF. At the time of writing it appears that this support will be provided under a €85 billion programme and a central element of the plan will be to address the future capital needs of the banking sector as well as facilitate its restructuring.

# 9
# Lessons from Privatisation and the Future of SOEs

## 9.0 Introduction

There is no doubt that the privatisation policies implemented over the last 30 years have had an enormous impact on reducing the extent of direct state intervention in economies around the world. These policies were part of a set of wider public sector reforms that were designed and implemented by several governments in Europe and beyond, in response to a powerful consensus that was critical of the state's role as the main provider of public services. These included services of general interest, such as health, education and housing, as well as infrastructure-based services such as rail and the distribution of water, electricity and gas, which were commonly provided by SOEs.

As described in Chapter 2, criticisms of SOEs, and the public sector in general, had their intellectual origins in theories of property rights and public choice. These had been hugely influential in underpinning the critical review of the state that started in the UK in the 1970s, and led to two distinct lines of public sector reform. The first was the privatisation of SOEs, with vast swathes of such enterprises transferred to private ownership by means such as high-profile flotations, trade sales and, in some cases, management buyouts. The second came under the general heading of new public management (NPM) (Hood 1991, 1995), which covers a range of reforms aimed at improving the efficiency of public services that could not be directly privatised. Services such as health, education and those traditionally provided by local government were subjected to the transplanting of private sector management techniques and quasi-market reforms based on competition, purchaser-provider splits, contracts, incentives and prices.

Although there were earlier examples (for example, Italy in the 1920s), privatisation policies were pioneered by the Thatcher governments in the UK before being adopted with similar zeal in countries such as New Zealand and Chile. It was then spurred by the collapse of centrally planned economies and imposed on developing countries through conditions attached to IMF, World Bank and USAID[1] loans (Martin, 1993). In Chapter 1 we saw that, in regional terms, Western Europe ranks highest from the point of view of the revenues raised from sales. A marked slowdown in privatisation activity in Europe in the early part of the new century suggested that the process of privatisation had come to a halt. Chapter 1 shows that this was not the case, however. Since 2004 there has been a resurgence of privatisation activity, with Germany, Italy and, in particular, France, disposing of shares in SOEs through sales to the public and the direct placement of shares with private equity funds. A likely impact of the global financial crisis is that further momentum will be given to privatisation policies, as governments will look to privatisation as a means of raising much needed exchequer revenues in order to tackle burgeoning levels of sovereign debt. There is already evidence that further privatisation is under consideration in countries such as Portugal, Ireland, Greece and the UK, which all face acute fiscal crises.

Whether privatisation has succeeded in achieving its goals remains a topic of intense debate. In Chapter 2 we saw that the results from economic analyses of the impact of privatisation on economic efficiency have not been equivocal. There is certainly evidence which shows that privatisation is associated with improved company performance but this does not apply in all cases. When the wider social welfare impacts of privatisation are considered, there is evidence to suggest that privatisation can lead to unintended consequences, especially in terms of distributional effects. In some cases, the supply of specific services by private companies in competitive markets has been incompatible with the nature of the sectors involved due to problems related to equity and universality of provision. In such cases, market-based solutions may involve prices and methods of provision that have a negative impact on citizens and customers. Possible problems in this regard include fuel, water and energy poverty, which pose difficulties for the achievement of social cohesion (Poggi and Florio, 2010).

While one might argue that the problems above can be addressed by effective regulation, this poses challenges in itself. The realisation of these problems and challenges has meant that there are now examples of services that have been the subject of reverse privatisation, with the public sector once again taking direct or indirect responsibility for their provision.[2] Such events remind us that the state continues to play a sizeable and important direct role in public service delivery, a fact that can get lost when one considers the phenomenal history of privatisation over the last three decades. The following sections demonstrate how the state remains very much 'in business', and discusses some of the key issues of relevance to SOEs in the early part of the twenty-first century.

## 9.1   The continuing presence of SOEs

Notwithstanding the rollback of direct government involvement in economic activity, the state remains a significant player, often retaining full or dominant control of enterprises in key sectors such as energy and transport. This holds true for developed and developing countries alike. According to the OECD (2005: 23), the SOE sector in industrialised countries is 'remarkable for its size, economic impact and the "strategic sectors" in which it operates'. Although countries differ in terms of the size and scope of their SOE sectors, the OECD estimates that in some countries the sector contributes 20 per cent to GDP and around 10 per cent of employment.

Shapiro and Globerman (2009) point out that, prior to the global financial crisis, the total number of commercial SOEs in the OECD area was in the region of 1,000 firms. While significant, it is still less than the number of SOEs listed on China's stock markets. The central government in China is responsible for 17,000 SOEs, and local governments for 150,000. There are 240 SOEs in India (outside of the financial sector). The SOE sector also continues to play an important part in emerging and transition markets. According to the World Bank (2006, cited in Shapiro and Globerman, 2009), the state sector accounts for between 20–40 per cent of total output in Central and Eastern European countries.

This data was collected prior to the onset of global financial crisis in September 2008, which has resulted in widespread state intervention in economies around the world. The extent of nationalisation and private company rescues has been extraordinary in the context of trends towards privatisation observed over the last 30 years. It is difficult to argue, however, that this heralds the beginning of an era of renewed state intervention in modern capitalist economies. The fact remains that public enterprise has continued to play a substantial role in developed and developing countries, the high level of privatisation witnessed since the early 1980s notwithstanding. The ubiquity of SOEs since the late nineteenth century is described by Wettenhall and Thynne (2002: 6), who observe that 'new public enterprises continue to appear, just as old ones continue in existence.' In speculating as to the future of public enterprise in the twenty-first century, the same writers make the following prescient observation:

> It is, moreover, by no means clear that governments, when put to the test by the failure of economically significant private enterprises, will be able to resist demands for the state to enter into rescue missions. For one of the long understood rationales for public enterprise has been as 'ambulance for sick industry', and history shows that such state interventions have sometimes succeeded in producing good 'turnrounds'. The rejuvenated entities have often remained in government hands, while others have subsequently become the targets of privatization initiatives.
>
> (Wettenhall and Thynne, 2002: 6)

The current spate of nationalisations and government bailouts can realistically be interpreted as the continuation of a well-established pattern of such interventions that often occur as pragmatic responses to market failures. They represent the latest stage in the ebb and flow of SOE creation, privatisation and reconfiguration witnessed for more than a century. Privatisation and new public management reforms have, of course, significantly altered the objectives, governance and structure of SOEs. The nature and performance of SOEs in the early years of the twenty-first century are markedly different to those observed 40 years ago. Yet, a number of challenges lie ahead for governments and SOEs. Principal among these are ongoing efforts to improve corporate governance and the challenges arising from the increasing internationalisation of SOE activities. The latter presents challenges for the owners of SOEs extending their activities abroad, as well as governments playing host to foreign SOEs in their jurisdictions.

## 9.2   SOE corporate governance: An ongoing challenge

The question of governance has been at the heart of much of the economic analysis of the SOE sector in recent decades. A number of relevant contributions to the literature were reviewed in Chapter 2. These focused on principal-agent relations in SOEs and problems arising from the misalignment of objectives, information asymmetries, and the roles of incentives and contracts. Among the governance problems commonly identified with SOEs are multiple and sometimes conflicting objectives (for example, social and economic), too many layers of principal-agent relations (for example, citizen, government, minister, board, enterprise managers), political interference, corruption, and the absence of mechanisms that serve to monitor and incentivise managers (for example, the threats of bankruptcy and takeover). Shapiro and Globerman (2009) point out that there is general agreement on the requirements for good governance. These include:

1) Strong internal controls that ensure effective monitoring by principals;
2) Independent boards free from political interference;
3) High levels of transparency and disclosure;
4) Strong external constraints on managerial discretion including the monitoring of capital markets;
5) Threats of bankruptcy and takeover.

There is a widely held view that SOEs commonly fail to satisfy these requirements and are therefore susceptible to governance failures. Concerns in this regard are held by multilateral agencies such as the OECD and the World Bank, both of which have issued guidelines on corporate governance in recent years.

Although such concerns appear valid, the current global financial crisis poses difficult questions for those who might argue that governance concerns apply exclusively to the public sector. It is also worth noting some more positive views on the state of corporate governance in SOEs. Musacchio and Flores-Macias (2009), for example, assert that a host of changes over the last decade and a half have contributed to improved corporate governance. Measures including the appointment of outside directors to state boards, the use of performance-related incentives, and the professionalisation of management have helped improve internal governance. In addition, the part-privatisation of companies that are listing shares on the stock exchange, as well as issuing bonds, has strengthened external governance mechanisms and forced SOEs to meet higher standards of accounting and disclosure. As a consequence, it has become harder for managers or politicians to divert enterprise resources for personal or political purposes.

Looking forward, Wettenhall and Thynne (2002) provide some pointers in relation to potentially key issues of governance of SOEs. They envisage the development of an 'enlightened' form of governance in response to community interests and needs. New forms of governance will recognise market virtues such as flexibility and diversity, but will appreciate that responsiveness to market forces must be complemented by a commitment to enhancing the role of civil society (Thynne, 2001, as cited by

Wettenhall and Thynne, 2002). This enlightened form of governance will give rise to an increase in 'organisational pluralism' that will involve 'various types and bases of organisation criss-crossing state, market and civil society boundaries' (Wettenhall and Thynne, 2002: 12). These will include contracts, partnerships and other forms of collaborative action, while organisations will adopt a combination of public, private and not-for-profit sector approaches to management and employment. The authors also highlight the growing tendency of public companies, both before and after privatisation, to operate in the international arena, a development that makes governance issues such as accountability and public control difficult to address in a way that ensures the legitimacy of state action. In fact, the growing internationalisation of public enterprises has become a hot topic for discussion in recent years and constitutes another key issue for public enterprise in the twenty-first century.

## 9.3   Internationalisation of SOEs

The increased tendency for SOEs to extend their activities across borders can be attributed to a number of factors including, for example, the increased integration in the international economy of countries with large SOE sectors (for example, China and India). The OECD (2009b) notes that in China, the internationalisation of the SOE sector was codified in the Central Committee's *'Go Global Strategy'* in 2000. In addition, the increasing international profile of sovereign wealth funds (SWFs) and recent government rescues of financial and some manufacturing enterprises with international reach have also contributed to the global dimension of some SOEs. These developments can cause concern for host countries due to issues such as foreign ownership of key industries and the impact of foreign SOEs on the competitiveness of domestic markets. They also pose new challenges in terms of accountability and control of domestic SOEs whose activities flow over national boundaries.

Wettenhall (1993) noted that the globalisation of activities is not a new feature of SOE activity. He provided examples such as British Petroleum and the Finnish state mining company, Outokumpu, to illustrate that some SOEs have had a high degree of global reach for decades. As he predicted, however, the tendency towards internationalisation was set to increase and attract more attention among academics and policymakers alike. A recent development in this regard is the growth of SWFs. These have existed for some time, and some of the largest funds – such as the Abu Dhabi Investment Authority (ADIA), and Singapore's Government Investment Corporation (GIC) and Temasek – have been active for decades (Fotak *et al.*, 2008). In recent years, however, SWFs have attracted enormous attention due to the rapid increase in their number, with 60 per cent of funds currently active having been established in the last decade (Monk, 2010).

Although there is a lack of agreement on the precise definition of SWFs, Fotak *et al.* (2008: 1) assert that most definitions suggest these are 'state-owned investment funds (not operating companies) that make long-term domestic and international investments in search of commercial returns'. Their high profile can be traced back to early 2007, when a Chinese state-owned fund purchased a USD$3 billion non-voting equity stake in Blackstone Group, the global investment and advisory firm. In late 2007, and again in early 2008, SWFs became the focus for even more attention as funds, mostly based in the Persian Gulf, purchased some USD$60 billion worth of newly issued stock in top American and European banks at the height of the sub-prime mortgage crisis. It is estimated that SWFs now control USD$3 trillion in assets worldwide (Fotak *et al.*, 2008).

Although funds commonly described as SWFs have different characteristics, they do have common origins insofar as they were initially set up as 'stabilisation funds' in countries where government revenues were dependent on one underlying commodity. Such funds were established to facilitate a diversification of investments in an effort to stabilise government revenues. Fotak *et al.* (2008) explain that SWFs have, therefore, been commonly established in countries that are rich in natural resources. Oil rich countries such as the Arab Gulf states, ex-Soviet republics and Norway, have established SWFs, as have some commodity rich countries in Africa and South America.

The evidence suggests that most of these funds are invested in their home countries, and that most of their capital is not directed towards controlling investments (Shapiro and Globerman, 2009). Nonetheless, investments by SWFs have provoked defensive reactions in a number of countries including Thailand, Germany and the USA, where there has been particular concern expressed about investments by funds from China and Russia. Although academic research into the role and impact of SWFs is very much in its infancy, there is little doubt that they will be the subject of increased analysis as their growth contributes more and more to the internationalisation of the public sector.

Shapiro and Globerman (2009) note that, despite examples of increased internationalisation, SOEs have played a relatively minor economic role across international borders (at least up until the outbreak of the global financial crisis). In 2008, SOEs accounted for just 13 of the top

100 multinational enterprises (MNEs) and most of these SOEs have minority state ownership. Moreover, just two of these SOEs originate from emerging and transition economies. Nevertheless, the importance of this increasing trend of internationalisation is becoming more and more evident, not least because it is occurring in sectors of great significance to competitiveness and societal welfare (for example, natural resource industries and public utilities).

Clifton *et al.* (2007) have undertaken a comprehensive analysis of what they refer to as an important transformation of network services in transport, communications, energy and water sectors. They highlight the rise of 'network giants' which have become some of the world's leading MNEs:

> By the beginning of the twenty-first century, some of the same network services – France Telecom, E. On, RWE, Suez-Gaz de France, Telefónica, Deutsche Post, Endesa, Deutsche Telekom, Enel, Telecom Italia, Nacional Grid Tasco and so on – emerged as the world's leading TNCs. Some of these were privatised, whilst others remained in state hands, at least partially.
>
> (Clifton *et al.*, 2007: 6)

There are a number of commonly voiced concerns about the development of the cross-border operations of SOEs. These include political unease about foreign ownership and management of foreign direct investment (FDI) in socially important public network services. Such concerns have already manifested themselves in terms of governments taking action to prevent FDI by SOEs. For example, the proposed takeover of US oil company Unocal by CNOOC (Chinese National Offshore Oil Co.) was rejected on the grounds that the presence of a foreign SOE was a threat to US national security (Clifton *et al.*, 2007). Other concerns include the possibility that privately-owned business might face unfair competition from foreign SOEs that may have access to government support in the form of subsidies or preferential access to finance. In addition, there are issues in relation to FDI resulting in effective renationalisation of formerly privatised SOEs by foreign governments (OECD, 2009b).

The trend towards increased internationalisation by SOEs looks set to increase and may well have accelerated as a result of the global financial crisis. This will pose challenges for home and host countries, as well as for the enterprises themselves. It remains unclear how individual states and regulatory bodies are likely to react to having foreign

SOEs enter their jurisdictions in pursuit of their commercial goals. Fears are more likely to be allayed if the corporate governance practices of SOEs in the home jurisdiction are in keeping with accepted 'good practice'. In this regard, it is important that there is sufficient transparency and disclosure to allow relevant stakeholders to monitor performance in relation to these good practices, thereby improving accountability and providing legitimacy for the actions of increasingly global SOEs.

To sum up, policies of privatisation and liberalisation have changed the environment in which SOEs operate, as well as the activities, objectives and governance of these enterprises. It remains the case that SOEs will continue to play a major part in modern economies and the lives of ordinary citizens. This applies in the context of developed, emerging and transition economies. Ireland is no different. The following section summarises the key lessons from Ireland's privatisation programme and, looking forward, it highlights some of the important issues for the Irish SOE sector in the context of the international developments reviewed above.

## 9.4 Lessons from Ireland's privatisation experience

The Irish privatisation experience has, to a large degree, been dominated by the transfer of the national telecommunications operator, Eircom, to private ownership. The flotation of shares in Eircom was characterised by a number of mistakes that serve important lessons for all policymakers faced with decisions in relation to the sale of public utility companies. Principal among these mistakes was the decision to divest the government's entire shareholding when the IPO was conducted in July 1999.

This decision had important consequences in a number of respects. First, the failure to stagger the sale of government-held shares resulted in the exchequer foregoing substantial levels of revenues. The big advantages associated with selling shares in different tranches were noted in Chapter 5. These include the establishment of a market price following the issue of the first tranche, which allows later prices to be set with some accuracy. This approach was taken in the cases of the first two Irish divestures (Irish Sugar and Irish Life), with discounts of 11.3 per cent (Irish Sugar) and 4.8 per cent (Irish Life) recorded for the first sales. The discounts in the second tranches were 4.4 per cent and 5.4 per cent respectively. However, the discount recorded in the case of Eircom amounted to 18.5 per cent of gross proceeds (€778 million). In this regard, the decision not to stagger the sale of shares is difficult to fathom. International and domestic experience provided clear demonstration of the advantages of selling in stages and, in the weeks prior to the Eircom flotation, the expectation was that the government would retain a percentage of its shareholding. The last-minute decision to sell its shares in 'one go' was unexpected and has proven to be immensely costly in terms of revenues foregone and the relinquishment of control over the future of the telecommunications sector in Ireland.

A second consequence of the government's decision not to retain a significant shareholding was its subsequent inability to prevent a number of undesirable changes in ownership following privatisation. These changes resulted in a massive deterioration of the financial structure of the company which was almost debt-free at the time of flotation, but now holds over €3.5 billion of debt. As Chapter 7 describes, the legacy of these changes has been considerable underinvestment in Ireland's telecommunications infrastructure. Government plans to create a so-called 'smart economy', as well as the desire to achieve goals such as regional development, have been severely undermined by the slow rollout of high-speed broadband services. As a result, Ireland is perennially ranked among the worst performers in the EU across most broadband development indicators. The negative consequences of the Eircom flotation are widely recognised. Almost, ten years after full privatisation, the current Minister for Communications, Mr. Eamonn Ryan, asserted that '[w]e privatised a highly profitable, debt-free, heavily investing Eircom and the result on prices, services, and broadband has been disastrous'.[3]

This outcome may have been prevented if the Irish government had decided to retain an ownership stake in the company at the time of the initial offering of shares. Such a decision would have been consistent with the pattern of privatisation of utility companies observed among industrialised countries. In a recent report on privatisation in the twenty-first century it is noted that, in recent years, many of the sales of equity in public utilities by OECD governments have been characterised as 'partial privatisation' because governments have sought to maintain control of these companies. It is also noted that 'in some countries the state is even required by law to retain holdings above certain thresholds in certain utilities companies' (OECD, 2009a: 9).[4]

The decision not to retain a minority share large enough to block undesirable bids is all the more remarkable in light of the findings by Bortolotti and Faccio (2008), who reported that governments maintain control of two-thirds of privatised firms in the EU by a variety of means including partial sell-offs, golden shares and certain regulatory and contractual requirements. The case of Eircom is clearly an outlier given the pervasiveness of retained control by EU governments, and provides useful lessons for policymakers facing similar decisions. In fact, there is evidence that the Irish government has learned some lessons from the Eircom flotation. When shares in Aer Lingus were floated in 2006, the government retained a minimum shareholding of 25.1 per cent. This was explained on the basis of the need to protect the airline's ownership of valuable landing slots at Heathrow Airport. Within days of the flotation the value of this minority shareholding was demonstrated when it was used by the government to thwart an unwelcome takeover from rival airline, Ryanair.

Another key lesson from the Eircom case centres on the question of ownership of former public utilities by private equity groups. Since full privatisation was completed, Eircom has been owned by two separate private equity funds, Valentia (2001–04) and Babcock and Brown (2006–10). This places Eircom among a group of former public telecommunications utilities (including TDC in Denmark and BTC in Bulgaria) that were taken over by such funds in highly leveraged buyouts (LBOs). Chapter 6 details how the principal objective of private equity funds conducting LBOs is to maximise short-term profits rather than invest in the long-term growth of the target firms. LBOs are typically followed by enterprise restructuring, financial engineering which leads to substantial increases in debt, the extraction of cash from the business, and a resale of the firm, typically within 3–5 years.

Melody (2008) analysed the cases of Eircom, TDC, and BTC and concluded that fund ownership led to the companies being forced to take on high levels of debt, which imposed strict constraints in terms of making long-term investments in network development. This problem was amplified by strategies focused on making short-term cash gains arising from cost-cutting measures, underinvestment and the resale of the operators. Moreover, managers of the utilities were given incentives that were inimical to taking long-term perspectives, since personal rewards were high if management facilitated the takeovers.

In recent years, private equity funds have become increasingly attracted to former public utilities, especially airports and telecommunications companies. However, transferring ownership to these funds is incompatible with the public interest role served by public utilities, which generally involves the provision of essential public services and, in some cases, carrying out important public service responsibilities (for example, universal service obligations). The case of Eircom exemplifies the dangers inherent in allowing private equity funds attain ownership of such operations.

A key lesson from the Eircom experience is that governments must consider these risks and adopt suitable measures to protect strategic interests (for example, telecommunications network development) as well as wider social welfare. Possible measures include the retention of control by maintaining a significant shareholding, or designing appropriate regulatory instruments. Melody (2008) suggests the strengthening of regulatory powers in EU states to enable effective governance over utilities. In particular, he advocates extending regulatory powers and bringing matters relating to financing, ownership and management under the remit of regulators:

> ...regulators will need to be empowered to prevent financial practices and transactions that are contrary to the public interest in long term infrastructure and services development [...] Most utility regulatory agencies in the US and Canada have strong regulatory powers over the financial practices of public utilities precisely because they are 'businesses affected with a public interest'.
>
> (Melody, 2008: 282)

The case of Eircom provides a salient example of where such powers might have served to avoid the disastrous consequences of full privatisation.

Overall, the impact of privatisation on enterprise performance in Ireland has been less than impressive. In the run up to divestiture most companies demonstrated improved performance by accruing static efficiency gains that are commonly observed in privatisation programmes. Sustaining improved performance has, however, proved to be problematic in most cases. Following privatisation, companies such as Eircom, Irish Sugar/Greencore and Aer Lingus have operated in increasingly competitive markets and have not succeeded in maintaining the rates of improved performance witnessed before divestiture. It is important to note, however, that sustained improvements might equally not have materialised if these firms remained under public ownership. The multidimensional character of performance should be recognised. Ownership is just one of an amalgam of relevant factors including market competition and internal organisational aspects such as structure and leadership.

Our findings in relation to Ireland's former state-owned banks merit special attention, especially in light of the recent global financial crisis and the problems faced by banking sectors worldwide. The time-frame of our analysis of the performance of privatised banks in Ireland precedes the current crisis and a cautionary note must be sounded in relation to our findings. Two of the three former state banks included in our analysis demonstrated some improvements in financial performance in the post-privatisation period. However, these improvements were recorded on the basis of enormous growth in the size of these institutions, which were absorbed into bigger institutions under private ownership. Our analysis of the Irish banking crisis in Chapter 8 highlights clearly how much of this growth was unsustainable. The interpretation of performance indicators in this context should therefore be conducted with care.

Our analysis of performance has been confined to the level of the enterprise. From a policymaking perspective it is, however, important to understand that privatisation can have important distributional effects that have an important bearing on wider social welfare. A full analysis of such effects is beyond the scope of this book, but it is instructive to consider how privatisation has impacted on key groups of stakeholders such as consumers, shareholders and employees.

Irish consumers have certainly benefited from lower prices for telecommunications and airline services both before and after privatisation, but this can be explained by increased competition in these markets as a result of liberalisation policies. Other divestitures, including those in the financial sector, had little impact in terms of consumer prices. In relation to shareholders, it is clear that they stand to make appreciable gains or losses as a result of privatisation policies. From a policymaking perspective, this is especially relevant in relation to ordinary citizens, who have often been targeted by governments seeking to increase the proportion of the share-owning population. This has been an important issue in Ireland's privatisation programme, but mainly in the case of Eircom where over 570,000 small shareholders purchased shares in the company, receiving some 55 per cent of the total offering. Significantly, when Eircom was broken up in 2001 and separate sales were completed for its mobile telephone (Eircell) and fixed-line businesses, the number of small shareholders was 450,000. These structural changes and the collapse of the Eircom share price resulted in these small shareholders losing approximately a third of their original investment. This was a significant negative distributional effect of privatisation that dampened subsequent enthusiasm for such sales among shareholders and politicians.

Employees are also key stakeholders in the privatisation process. A commonly held view is that privatisation policies are normally associated with reductions in employment levels and deteriorations in conditions of work (Martin, 1993). In the Irish case there is no clear pattern of increases or decreases in employment as a result of privatisation. The employment effects vary from company to company (Palcic and Reeves, 2005). An important distributional impact in relation to employees has, however, arisen as a result of the ESOPs established in privatised firms since 1998. Chapter 6 demonstrated that some employees in some companies have accrued significant gains with the value of shares transferred to date ranging from approximately €31,000 to €145,000 per employee.

A full discussion of ESOPs is provided in Chapter 6 where we show how the transfer of large shareholdings to employees has been a distinctive feature of the Irish privatisation programme. Although the allocation of shares to employees is common in the context of privatisation, the size of the ESOPs created in the Ireland, and the degree of power conferred on trade unions and employees in terms of the strategic direction of some companies, make the Irish case an interesting one.

The experience with ESOPs has provided a number of lessons for employees, trade unions and policymakers alike. For trade unions and employees, the cases of Eircom and Aer Lingus have shown that sizeable ESOPs significantly increase their importance and power as stakeholders in the newly privatised companies. This poses the challenge of articulating a coherent agenda for the ESOP and striking a balance between acting in the wider public interest and maximising the returns to ESOP members.

The question of the public interest is of particular importance in the context of privatised utility companies. The efficiency, quality and availability of services provided by such enterprises have important societal impacts. They typically hold monopoly power over the provision of essential public services and require large-scale investment in physical infrastructure that must be maintained and developed over time. Moreover, they frequently contribute to social cohesion by fulfilling universal service obligations. Whether trade unions and employees should adopt a 'stewardship role' that attaches a high level of importance to the public interest poses an important question of governance for these stakeholders in the context of sizeable ESOPs. In the case of Eircom, however, the evidence suggests that the balance was tipped in favour of protecting the interests of members. Issues such as the ESOP's support for the breakup of the company, two separate takeovers by private equity groups, and the payment of large dividends, as well as the huge personal rewards accrued by ESOP representatives on the Eircom board of directors, are difficult to justify in terms of serving the public interest. The latter has also been at odds with trade union objectives of equity and fairness (Sweeney, 2004).

Internal governance issues have also arisen in relation to the appointment of ESOP representatives on the Eircom board of directors. Since its establishment, the ESOP has nominated either two or three directors to the Eircom board. Over time, these nominations have included a senior manager at Eircom, a private stockbroker and a private business consultant. Although these individuals might well have brought valuable expertise to the table, they were not representative of employees (Sweeney, 2004).

Questions can also be asked in relation to the voting rights of ESOP members. Whereas members were allowed to cast their votes on the takeovers and the sale of the mobile phone division, Eircell, in 2001, this was not the case when the Valentia consortium restructured the debt of the company and paid a dividend of €446 million in 2003. This decision was justified by the ESOP on the grounds that a ballot would delay the issuance of bonds and that favourable market conditions would not be exploited in the event of delay. Whereas this may have been the case, the argument put forward by the ESOP reveals the high priority it attached to the financial advantages of refinancing. The absence of a ballot, however, prevented a detailed debate of the wider issues, such as the potential extraction of cash from the company and the implications of the increase in indebtedness that would accompany the refinancing. Issues in relation to internal governance, as well as the wider objectives of ESOPs, are likely to arise in the case of future sales and these present important challenges for employees and trade unions.

Privatisation has proved to be an important instrument of economic policy in Ireland over the last 20 years. Although comparatively slow *vis-à-vis* pioneers of privatisation such as the UK and New Zealand, a number of Irish governments made the decision to sell SOEs, with the effect that the Irish state has fully withdrawn from direct production in sectors such as telecommunications, shipping, steel and sugar production, while it retains a minority stake in the former state-owned airline, Aer Lingus.

The likelihood is that there will be further divestitures in the coming years. In May 2010, the Irish government announced its intention to sell the state-owned health insurance company, Voluntary Health Insurance. In addition, the fiscal crisis faced by the country as a consequence of chronic mismanagement of public expenditure and the collapse in tax revenues due to reliance on an overheated property market, has increased the probability of further sales.[5] This prospect underscores the importance of learning lessons from the privatisation programme to date, and focusing attention on the best way forward for the remaining SOEs that continue to hold strategic importance for the wider economy. In light of the principal findings from our analysis we now turn our attention to those enterprises that remain under public ownership in Ireland.

## 9.5   Looking forward: Key issues for the Irish SOE sector

Chapter 8 detailed the re-emergence of the state in the banking sector since January 2009. This development highlights the need to avoid simplistic assertions that the adoption of privatisation policies signals the end of state involvement in the direct provision of goods and services. Table 9.1 lists the enterprises that remain under state ownership in Ireland. Despite privatisation, the state remains active, and in many cases dominant, in sectors of huge importance to society such as electricity, gas, rail and postal services. In addition, the state owns ports and bus companies as well as others in the health insurance,

Table 9.1   Commercial SOEs in Ireland in 2010

| Company and sector | Established | Principal activity |
| --- | --- | --- |
| *Communications* | | |
| An Post | 1984 | Postal Services |
| Raidió Teilifís Éireann | 1960 | Broadcasting |
| *Energy* | | |
| Bord Gáis Éireann | 1976 | Gas Distribution |
| Bord na Móna | 1946 | Energy-Renewables |
| Electricity Supply Board | 1927 | Electricity |
| *Natural Resources* | | |
| Arramara Teo | 1949 | Seaweed Processing |
| Coillte Teo | 1989 | Forestry |
| *Transport* | | |
| Aer Lingus (25 per cent) | 1936 | Air Transport |
| Dublin Airport Authority | 1937 | Airports |
| Córas Iompair Éireann | 1944 | Rail and Bus Transport |
| 10 Port and Harbour Companies | 1996 | Ports |
| *Banking* | | |
| Anglo Irish Bank | 2009 | Banking |
| Educational Building Society | 2010 | Banking |
| Irish Nationwide Building Society | 2010 | Banking |
| *Other* | | |
| Voluntary Health Insurance | 1957 | Health Insurance |
| Irish National Stud | 1946 | Horse Breeding |
| National Asset Management Agency | 2009 | Asset Management |

*Note*: The state took ownership of the three credit institutions over the period 2009–10.

broadcasting and forestry sectors. The effective nationalisation of three financial institutions (one bank and two building societies) over the period 2009–10 has added considerably to the state's portfolio of enterprise. Moreover, when measured in terms of the value of its asset base, the newly established National Asset Management Agency constitutes the largest SOE in the state portfolio.

Compared to other industrialised countries, the extent of SOE activity in the Irish economy is low. The OECD (2008) provides an indication of the extent of SOE activity in comparative terms. It finds that Ireland ranks towards the bottom for two measures adopted: (i) the scope of public enterprise in their economies[6] (fourth from bottom), and (ii) public ownership (seventh from bottom). However, Ireland ranks highly (sixth from top) for 'government involvement in the infrastructure sector' (energy, transport and telecommunications). This reflects the nature of the Irish privatisation programme which, to date, has not extended to these sectors (with the exception of telecommunications).

Ireland's status as a 'regional economy', with heavy reliance on its export base and attracting FDI, means that the goal of improving competitiveness is very much at the centre of Irish economic policy. A major challenge over the last 20 years has been addressing deficits in the size and quality of Ireland's stock of infrastructure in areas such as roads, public transport, telecommunications (including broadband), water and waste management. Despite recording one of the highest rates of investment (as a percentage of GDP) in physical infrastructure among EU countries over the last decade, Ireland still ranks poorly in terms of the stock of physical infrastructure per capita and perceptions of quality of infrastructure (NCC, 2009).

The continued strategic importance of the SOE sector for a small regional economy, particularly in infrastructure industries, means that the performance of SOEs will continue to have an enormous bearing on the prospects for the wider economy. A number of issues in relation to the operation, structures and ownership of the SOE sector will require close consideration in the short to medium term. These include the governance of the SOE sector and government policy with respect to ownership and regulation.

### 9.5.1   Governance of SOEs

Wettenhall and Thynne (2002) remark that in the era of NPM there was a suggestion that concerns about corporate governance originated in the private sector. They dispute such a suggestion and draw attention to long-standing interest in the roles and responsibilities of the boards of public enterprises. Their observation has resonance in the Irish context. Bristow (1982) highlighted the governance concerns of Sean Lemass who, as Minister for Industry and Commerce and later as Taoiseach, oversaw the establishment of a number of SOEs in the 1950s and 1960s. In an article written for the Irish journal *Administration*, Lemass (1959) devoted a full section to the 'problems and dangers' with public enterprises. These included the 'the relationship between Ministers and boards; the composition of boards, the distinction between state-sponsored bodies and civil service departments, the limits of parliamentary power in regard to these bodies etc.' (Bristow, 1982: 167). It is now over 50 years since Lemass identified these governance issues as matters for consideration in the Irish context but questions of governance continue to be important for SOEs in Ireland and abroad. This is evidenced by the ongoing attention paid to the governance of SOEs by multilateral agencies such as the OECD and World Bank.

In their survey of the corporate governance of SOEs in member countries, the OECD (2005) identified three prevailing models of ownership of SOEs:

1)  In the *decentralised model*, SOEs are the responsibility of different ministries. This model exists in a small number of OECD countries such as Finland and, to a lesser extent, Germany. The greater availability of sectoral expertise is one of the main advantages of this model. One of its main drawbacks is the problem of separating the ownership function from the regulatory one. In addition, there is a danger that government might interfere with day-to-day operations.

2)  The *dual model* has been adopted in many OECD countries including New Zealand, South Korea, Greece and Italy. In this model, 'sector ministries' and a 'common ministry', such as the Department of Finance, share responsibility for exercising ownership rights. Both ministries can nominate representatives to the company board of directors. They also share responsibility for strategic plans and decisions on major transactions (Vagliasindi, 2008). An advantage of the dual model is that it can curb undesirable increases in the power of the Department of Finance. Also, there is a greater likelihood of better monitoring if both ministries compete. An important disadvantage is that there is a danger that the responsibilities of the two ministries can be blurred (too many principals) leading to a lack of clear direction.

3)  In the *centralised model*, responsibility for the government's stake in all SOEs is vested in one ministry or agency. In most cases, this

is the Ministry of Finance (Denmark, the Netherlands, Spain) or the Ministry of Industry (Norway and Sweden). This model offers the advantage of establishing a clear line of accountability between the SOE and government. However, there is a risk that the single ministry may not have a sufficient depth of sectoral expertise.

In recent years, the question of governance has been addressed in a number of contributions to the debate on SOEs in Ireland (Sweeney, 2004; ICTU, 2005; MacCarthaigh, 2009; Fine Gael, 2010). In broad terms, these contributions point to the merits of a move from the dual model, which currently characterises Irish SOE governance, to the centralised model recommended by the OECD.

Sweeney (2004) and ICTU (2005) propose the most concrete proposal put forward in the Irish context to date. They advocate a special organisational model based on a 'holding company', which is a variant of the centralised model. Under this model the shareholding of each commercial SOE would be transferred from the Department of Finance to the new holding company. The new state holding company would be legally owned by a new board with statutory responsibility. The new shareholders would be a new State Holding Company Investment Board (SHCIB), the National Treasury Management Agency (NTMA),[7] private pension funds and ESOPs. Skilled representatives would be appointed to a small board (eight members) by the SHCIB and NTMA, with other representatives coming from private pension funds and the social partners. The state holding company would be accountable to a joint Oireachtas (parliamentary and senate) committee.

ICTU (2005) asserts that this structure resolves a number of governance problems that have stymied the progressive development of Irish SOEs. These include the problem of political interference, which is possibly the most cited global governance problem in relation to SOEs. In the Irish case, a particularly noteworthy example in this regard arose in connection with the international activities of the electricity utility, the ESB. In 2002, the ESB sought to diversify its operations in response to the development of competition in the domestic electricity generation market. It proposed to extend its activities to Poland through the purchase of eight power distribution companies. Although it was selected as the preferred bidder for the companies, it was instructed by the Irish government to withdraw from its planned investment (Sweeney, 2004).

Other arguments advanced in favour of the holding company model include the advantage of addressing the problem of the Irish government's effective moratorium on investing new equity in SOEs. Under the proposed structure, the board of the holding company would have full discretion on raising finance for SOEs. ICTU (2005) proposes that this could be a mixture of bonds and equity, with private pension funds also providing substantial equity especially at the initial stages. While placing minority stakes on the stock exchange is not ruled out, it is clear that this proposal is designed to ensure that problems with accessing capital cannot be used as a reason for large-scale privatisation. ICTU also asserts that private pension funds will improve the monitoring of SOEs. Moreover, accountability can be safeguarded in legislation, which can specify structures for reporting to the Department of Finance and the Oireachtas. The proposal also adopts the OECD (2005) recommendation that there should be a transparent payment from the exchequer for any social and uneconomic roles allocated to SOEs.

The 'holding company' proposal certainly appears to have the potential to address governance problems commonly identified with SOEs in Ireland and abroad, not least in connection with access to finance. On a cautionary note, the model is relatively untested, with the Austrian Industries Holding Model (ÖIAG) being one of the few examples of holding company models in the OECD. In her review of different models of SOE governance, Vagliasindi (2008) finds that the holding company model has shown its limitations. She concludes that the model has not proved to be efficient in terms of corporate restructuring or financial management. In addition, the Italian holding company, IRI, was not efficient in achieving its principal goal of regional development.

Notwithstanding these conclusions, ICTU's proposal is specifically designed to remedy governance problems in the Irish context. Moreover, it is largely consistent with the recommendations of the OECD. It is unlikely to be adopted in the short term, however. A new version of the *Code of Practice for the Governance of State Bodies* was published by the Irish government in June 2009 and makes no reference to the proposals made by ICTU (2005) or the OECD (2005). Radical departures do not appear to be on the policy agenda.

The theoretical and empirical case for privatisation is weak where an enterprise holds market power. This is particularly relevant in Ireland where most of the enterprises that remain under public ownership are dominant in their relevant markets. Economic policy faces challenges in regulating these industries if privatisation occurs. The effectiveness of the regulatory framework in Ireland has been questioned by a number of commentators and interest groups, not least in the context of the massive regulatory failure that contributed to the country's current banking crisis. A number of important issues that ought to be addressed in terms of regulating SOEs and utilities in particular include:[8]

1) The proliferation, cost and lifespan of regulators and the consequent case for rationalisation – Sweeney (2004) suggests a single regulatory commission with three divisions (energy, transport and communications (including broadcasting)) that would be separate from the Competition Authority;
2) The increased prices of regulated services – In recent years, the prices of gas and electricity paid by consumers and business in Ireland have been amongst the highest in Europe;
3) Over-emphasis on price regulation – Regulators need to take a broader view and pay closer attention to the cost of capital and long-term investment needs;
4) The need to regulate the financial practices of public utilities to prevent and to place limits on the ownership stakes of private equity funds focused on short-term profits;
5) The need to take Ireland's small size, geographical location and lack of interconnection into account when designing regulatory structures.

Ultimately, the regulatory challenge centres on separating the government's dual role as owner and regulator. The ongoing process of European integration and liberalisation of markets means that the challenge of limiting managerial discretion becomes more complex. It was noted earlier that SOEs, and utility companies in particular, are operating with a more commercial ethos that encourages internationalisation, mergers, acquisitions and other forms of collaboration. The complex regulatory challenge in this context is to ensure that the maximisation of company interests is not at odds with the interests of the public at large (Lane, 2002).

Finally, the future of ESOPs represents an important issue in terms of the future governance of SOEs. The origins, rationale and impact of ESOPs were discussed in detail in Chapter 6. Although the case for employee share ownership in SOEs appears to have merit, the experience to date raises a number of issues. First, the precise objectives of ESOPs remain unclear. If the purpose of ESOPs is to increase employee commitment or allegiance to their companies, it must be recognised that there is no available evidence which shows that this outcome has occurred in the Irish case. If the objective of ESOPs is, however, to transfer financial gains to employees, the evidence shows that ESOPs have been successful in this regard. However, the gains made by employees have been sizeable and have been increased by the fact that allocations of shares are not liable for tax. Whether these gains are justifiable or not cannot be objectively assessed and some value judgements are required.

Assuming that ESOPs are created principally to secure financial benefits for employees, one option that could be considered is allocating shares to individuals rather than structured ESOPs. This may not gain acceptance by trade unions, however. It is evident that trade unions have embraced the ESOP approach instead of allocating shares to individuals because this approach confers power on the ESOP and allows it to use the entire share-holding in order to influence key decisions. The evidence presented in Chapter 6 demonstrates that this has posed challenges for trade unions in terms of striking the balance between the financial interests of members and the wider public interest. The issues are complex, but it is worth noting that ESOPs will play a key part in the future of Irish SOEs, and the issues we highlight require careful consideration by policymakers and trade unions.

## 9.6   Future policy on privatisation

The principal focus of this book has been on the Irish experience with privatising SOEs. Our findings add to the now sizeable literature on privat-isation experiences that demonstrate that privatisation has not always achieved the improvements in quality and efficiency of public services suggested by its proponents. The era of privatisation has not come to an end, however. In the Irish context, the current fiscal crisis has already led to calls for privatisation and one planned divestiture has been officially announced. Moreover, in July 2010 the Irish government established a Review Group on State Assets to advise the government on the possible sale of SOEs.

These developments provide a suitable context for making a number of policy recommendations on the basis of our analysis of Ireland's privatisation experience and similar international developments. These recommendations, which we discuss below, are as follows:

1) SOEs should not be privatised for the principal purpose of raising exchequer revenues;
2) Decisions in relation to privatisation should be made in the context of a comprehensive strategy for the overall SOE sector;
3) A 'holding company' model of governance should be adopted for the SOE sector;

4) Selling partial stakes in SOEs should be considered in some cases;
5) The network elements of all SOEs should remain under public ownership;
6) The sale of stakes in SOEs to private equity groups should be avoided;
7) A new network coordination agency should be established.

Our analysis shows that raising revenue for the exchequer is not a sufficient reason to sell SOEs, particularly if the company is of strategic importance or serves an important role in the economy or society. Moreover, such revenues are rarely maximised due to a combination of share discounts and expenses associated with executing sales. A fire-sale of SOEs as a response to Ireland's fiscal crisis is ill-advised. Instead, we recommend that future decisions in relation to privatisation are taken in the context of a coherent and clearly articulated strategy for Ireland's SOE sector. This strategy should consider all aspects in relation to the SOE sector and deliver a clear statement of the objectives of each enterprise that highlights both their economic and social functions. Any assessment of the performance of SOEs must be clearly based on consideration of these objectives.

Questions that should be considered in the formulation of a comprehensive strategy include those concerning the governance of the sector as well as issues in relation to the internationalisation of SOE activities, and the regulation of individual SOEs and their relevant sectors. Serious consideration should be given to the holding company model recommended by the OECD (2005) and ICTU (2005). A key advantage of this model derives from its potential to provide SOEs with finance for commercially viable investments. Adopting the holding company model does not rule out privatisation. The sale of partial stakes in SOEs offers advantages, including the governance-enhancing feature of subjecting SOE management to monitoring by equity markets. In addition, partial privatisation creates a basis for establishing a market price for shares in SOEs and limiting the potential for underpricing if additional shares are sold in the future.

Our findings demonstrate clearly that many of the problems encountered in the Eircom case stemmed not from privatisation *per se*, but from the decision to sell the company in one fell swoop. In light of the Eircom experience, we recommend that a strategy for Ireland's SOE sector gives careful consideration to industries that are of strategic importance to Ireland's economy. Network utilities (for example, electricity, gas, rail and water) are of particular importance in this regard. Among the lessons to arise following the privatisation of Eircom are: (i) the network elements of SOEs should be retained under public ownership, (ii) parts of strategically important SOEs should not be sold in one go:

the retention of government shareholdings in such enterprises is consistent with the approach taken in most other European countries, and (iii) the sale of significant stakes to private equity groups should be avoided. The Eircom experience as well as similar experiences in some other countries demonstrates that strategies adopted by such investors (for example, asset sweating and the extraction of cash) are inconsistent with the long-term perspective required in the management of these assets.

The strategic importance of Ireland's network industries is such that a networks coordination agency should be established. The main function of this agency would be to coordinate elements of the activities of organisations responsible for networks such as electricity, gas, rail, roads and water. The merits of establishing such an agency include increased efficiencies as result of a coordinated approach to network management and investment.

Ultimately, the principal role of modern Irish SOEs is to ensure the efficient and equitable provision of quality infrastructure and public services. The fulfilment of this role is of huge importance to the competitiveness of Ireland's regional economy. In historical terms, there has always been an ebb and flow to the objectives and scope of public enterprise across different countries. Ireland has been no different. The last 30 years or so has witnessed a continuation in this regard, but the principal factors that have shaped the direction of change in Western Europe since the 1970s have undoubtedly been commercialisation, deregulation and privatisation. These measures have brought many benefits. In many cases, 'sleepy' SOEs have been woken from their slumber and have improved their efficiency and effectiveness. Privatisation has, however, resulted in some unintended consequences, including underinvestment in vital infrastructure and some negative distributional impacts. Important aspects such as competition policy and regulation therefore require careful consideration when planning privatisation policies in the future.

These important issues notwithstanding, it remains the case that SOEs continue to play a vital role in economies around the globe. Importantly, they retain the characteristics that have always provided a strong rationale for their existence. It is inevitable that policymakers in Ireland and abroad will adopt further privatisation measures and it is important that they seek to learn lessons from experience. The Irish experience provides one such set of lessons which will prove useful to policymakers dealing with the challenge of managing SOEs in the future.

# Notes

## Chapter 1    Privatisation in Europe

1   Additional details on these sales that do not appear in Megginson *et al.* (1994) were sourced from an article published in 1964 in Ireland's main national newspaper, the *Irish Times* (Mercator (1964) 'Eurocomment', *Irish Times*, 14 November, p. 6). Interestingly, this article marked the first time the word 'privatisation' was used in the national Irish media in any context.

2   Chile also experimented with privatisation briefly in the 1970s. However, the programme was poorly executed and a lot of the companies were rena-tionalised in the early 1980s (Megginson *et al.*, 1994).

3   Interestingly, Bishop and Kay (1989) note that when the Conservatives came to power after the 1979 general election, the first companies to be privatised were in fact companies that operated in competitive markets and played little or no role in broader public policy objectives. The influence of trade unions was not an issue in any of these cases.

4   Ridley was connected with the Centre for Policy Studies, a think tank estab-lished by Keith Joseph and Margaret Thatcher (Parker, 2009).

5   See Parker (1999) for a comprehensive review of the specific rationale behind the privatisation programmes of each EU member state.

6   The author defines Southern Europe as consisting of Italy, Greece, Spain and Portugal.

7   The EU15 consists of Austria, Belgium, Denmark, Finland, France, Germany, Greece, Ireland, Italy, Luxembourg, the Netherlands, Portugal, Spain, Sweden and the UK.

8   Bortolotti and Milella's definition of Western Europe includes the EU15 plus Iceland, Malta, Monaco, Norway, Switzerland and Turkey.

9   Authors' own estimate based on Bortolotti and Milella (2008) and Privatiza-tion Barometer (2008).

10  For the purpose of this review, the data relating to the EU15 excludes Luxembourg given the small size of its economy and limited scope for privat-isation. The data on privatisation revenues used to create each of the figures in this chapter was sourced from the *Privatization Barometer* database (accessed in November 2009). It must be noted that *Privatization Barometer* data includes data on both direct and indirect privatisation revenues. With regard to direct privatisations, where the government sells a partial or full shareholding in an SOE, the sale proceeds accrue directly to the exchequer. Indirect privatisations comprise the sale of subsidiaries by SOEs or privatised SOEs, or the transfer of shares from financial institutions partly owned by the state (Privatization Barometer, 2005a). With indirect privatisations, the proceeds flow to the divesting company and not necessarily to the exchequer. The distinction between these two categories has important revenue implications, particularly in the cases of countries such as Germany (for example, the sale of Postbank by Deutsche Post), Italy (for example, the sale of Terna, the electricity grid, by

Enel) and France (for example, the sale of Pages Jaunes by France Telecom), where considerable revenues have been raised from indirect privatisations. In 2004, some 45 per cent of the privatisation activity in Europe related to indirect privatisations (Privatization Barometer, 2005a). In total, approximately USD$82.8 billion of the USD$308.2 billion raised between 2004 and 2008 in the EU15 is accounted for by indirect privatisation proceeds (authors' own calculation from *Privatization Barometer* database and various *Privatization Barometer* reports).

11  *Source*: Authors' calculation based on data sourced from *Privatization Barometer* database.

12  In current prices, the total revenues raised by France and Italy have now surpassed those of the UK privatisation programme, while total proceeds in Germany are almost on a par with the UK (see Figure 5.1). However, much of the revenues generated by France, Italy and Germany relate to divestitures that took place in recent years whereas the majority of UK privatisations took place in the 1980s and 1990s.

13  Presentation by Dénis Samuel-Lajeunesse, General Director of APE, to the *Privatization Barometer Workshop* 'The Future of Privatization in Europe' (Privatization Barometer, 2005b).

14  Hope, K. (2010) 'Greece pushes ahead with privatisation', *Financial Times*, 2 June, available: www.ft.com/cms/s/0/15fa34e6-6e7b-11df-ad16-00144fea-bdc0. html.

15  Ministério das Finanças e da Administração Pública, *Stability and Growth Programme 2010-2013*, submitted to European Commission 29 March 2010.

## Chapter 2    Privatisation Objectives: Theory and Evidence

1  Performance measurement is discussed in a number of papers, for example, Barrow and Wagstaff (1989), Molyneux and Thompson (1987), Muellbauer (1986), and Pestieau (1989).

2  Dewenter and Malatesta (2001) updated the work of Boardman and Vining (1989) with a larger sample and their results strongly supported the hypothesis that public enterprises display inferior profitability compared to firms in the private sector.

3  Krugman, P. (2009) 'How Did Economists Get It So Wrong?', *The New York Times*, 6 September, available: http://www.nytimes.com/2009/09/06/magazine/06Economic-t.html [accessed 15 September 2009].

## Chapter 3    Public Enterprise and Privatisation in Ireland

1  While Ireland did not follow the trend towards privatisation that was set in the UK in the early 1980s, Sweeney (1990) identifies one earlier case of privatisation, that of Bord Bainne (The Irish Dairy Board), which was privatised in 1972.

2  Irish Sugar, 'Minutes of Meeting of Directors', May 1989.

3  Irish Sugar, 'Minutes of Meeting of Directors', February 1990.

4  Irish Sugar, 'Minutes of Meeting of Directors', March 1990.

5 The privatisation of both Irish Sugar and Irish Life involved an initial public offering (IPO) of a majority stake in each firm, followed by two separate seasoned public offerings of the government's remaining shares.

6 Dáil Éireann Debates (1991) Vol. 414, 10 December: *B&I Line Bill: Second Stage*, cols. 824–5 (Brennan, S., Minister for Tourism Transport and Communications).

7 Dáil Éireann Debates (1996) Vol. 463, 3 April: *Irish Steel Limited Bill, 1996 [Seanad]: Second Stage*, col. 1969.

8 *Ibid.*, col. 1962.

9 The fixed Euro conversion rate for the Irish Punt is IRP£1 = €1.2697381.

10 PTT Telecom and Telia were the national telecommunications operators of the Netherlands and Sweden respectively.

11 Dáil Éireann Debates (1999) Vol. 500, 18 February: *Postal and Telecommunications Services (Amendment) Bill, 1998: Second Stage*, col. 1275.

12 Deposit Interest Retention Tax (DIRT) is a tax deducted at source by deposit takers from interest paid or credited on deposits of Irish residents.

13 The mandatory off-take regime was introduced by the government in 1982 to ensure the survival of the Whitegate oil refinery, which the INPC had just acquired. It obliged all oil companies operating in Ireland to purchase a proportion of their oil from the INPC at a premium price.

14 Chief Executive Officer, Chief Financial Officer and Chief Operations Officer.

# Chapter 4 Privatisation and Performance in Ireland

1 Joint Parliamentary and Senate Committee.

2 Shanahan, E. (1981) 'Plan to axe Tuam plant meets wave of protests', *Irish Times*, 12 September, p. 1.

3 The government's decision, in the face of intense pressure from workers, civic and religious leaders in the Tuam region and opposition parties, was a defining point, not just for Irish Sugar, but for Irish state-sponsored bodies in general. The controversy over the closure of the Tuam plant sparked a national debate as to the role of SOEs in Ireland and whether they should be run on more commercial lines or to facilitate wider social objectives.

4 Employment levels were more than halved between 1980 and the end of the decade, falling from 3,558 to 1,757 workers. This significant reduction in the workforce ranked Irish Sugar as the second largest shedder of labour in the commercial SOE sector during the 1980s (Sweeney, 1991).

5 Ireland's entry into the EEC in 1973 meant that Irish Sugar became part of the European sugar Common Market Organisation (CMO). The CMO was set up in 1968 in order to protect EEC sugar companies and ensure self-sufficiency in the Community. Import levies were used to protect firms from cheaper international imports and production quotas were created to keep production in line with internal demand. The EEC (and the EC post-Maastricht) operated a system of support prices within sugar quotas, setting an intervention price for quota sugar each year, which along with a storage levy, provided sugar manufacturers with a guaranteed minimum price for sugar, known as the effective support price. The EC also set minimum prices that sugar manufacturers had to pay to beet farmers for sugar beet (EC, 2004).

6  Dáil Éireann Debates (1991) Vol. 414, 10 December: *B&I Line Bill, 1991: Second Stage*, col. 825 (Brennan, S., Minister for Tourism, Transport and Communications).

7  Prior to the sale, ICG and its main subsidiary, Irish Ferries, had operated an Ireland-France ferry and freight service. The company had performed reasonably well in its niche market in the years prior to the acquisition of B&I Line. However, its operations were relatively smaller than B&I Line, with turnover of €39.26 million in 1991 compared to €92.09 million in the same year for B&I Line (B&I Line, 1991; ICG, 1991). The purchase of B&I Line and its substantial Ireland-UK operations provided ICG with the scale necessary to compete in the mainstream ferry and shipping business.

8  For the years where accounts can be directly compared, there is strong evidence of the significance of B&I Line's contribution to ICG's overall operations. Between 1992 and 1994, B&I Line accounted for 69.96, 71.05 and 65.44 per cent respectively of ICG's turnover. Moreover, in 1993 and 1994, B&I Line accounted for 79.41 and 80.75 per cent respectively of the 1.35 million passengers carried by ICG in each of those years (B&I Line and ICG annual reports, 1992–94).

9  The details in this section on the losses made by Irish Steel and the terms of the sale of the company to ISPAT rely heavily on information provided by Bruton, R. (Minister for Enterprise and Employment) in Dáil Éireann Debates (1996) Vol. 463, 3 April: *Irish Steel Limited Bill, 1996 [Seanad]: Second Stage*, cols. 1851–7.

10  Dáil Éireann Debates (1982) Vol. 334, 13 May: *Supplementary Estimates, 1982: Vote 50: Industry and Energy*, cols. 1098–9 (Barrett, S., Minister of State at the Department of Finance).

11  The fixed Euro conversion rate for the Irish Punt is IRP£1 = €1.2697381.

12  Since the deal with ISPAT involved a state aid package, the sale could only go ahead with the approval of the EC and EU Industry Council. The EC approved the package, however, although 14 of the 15 members of the Council accepted the deal, the UK refused to accept the package on the grounds that it would impact negatively on the operations of British Steel. After lengthy negotiations, the UK government eventually backed down on the condition that Irish Steel/ISPAT be subjected to limits on its production and sales in the EU market.

13  After five years in operation, ISPAT Ireland's accumulated losses stood at approximately €12.7 million (McManus, J. and P. Yeates (2001) 'ISPAT plans to close Cork plant with 400 job losses', *Irish Times*, 16 June, p. 1).

14  Hogan, D. (2001) 'Concern over health and safety record', *Irish Times*, 16 June, p. 17.

15  It also emerged that a union proposal to set up a safety committee was vetoed by ISPAT and the former plant safety manager was refused a budget of €15,000 to introduce an improved fire-safety training regime (Roche, B. (2005) 'Plant's 62 years spanned boom and bust as economy evolved', *Irish Times*, 22 August, p. 2).

16  EU directives on the liberalisation of telecommunications markets gradually introduced competition into the market from 1990 onwards. The most important development in the liberalisation of the European telecommunications market occurred in March 1996, when the EC issued a final directive forcing member states to remove the remaining barriers to competition in voice

telephony services by 1 January 1998. The Irish government received a temporary two-year derogation from the directive; however this was waived by the government within a year and the Irish market was fully liberalised in December 1998.

17 The Telecommunications (Miscellaneous Provisions) Act of 1996 established an independent regulatory body, the Office of the Director of Telecommunications Regulation (ODTR), which took over responsibility for the regulation of the Irish telecommunications market. As part of its remit, the ODTR also became responsible for implementing a price cap on Telecom Éireann's tariffs established by the 1996 Telecommunications Tariff Regulation Order. The Order introduced a price cap formula, CPI-X, similar to the one used for British Telecom in the UK.

18 Tosco was purchased by Phillips Petroleum in 2001, who themselves were in the process of merging with Conoco Petroleum. The merger was completed in 2002 with the establishment of ConocoPhillips, one of the largest oil companies in the world.

19 Authors' calculation from company annual reports (INPC, 1995–2000).

20 Although the pre- and post-privatisation entities are technically different given that the accounts for the INPC prior to 2001 also include the operations of NORA, which was not included in the sale; the results pre- and post-divestiture are nevertheless comparable since the terminal and refinery operations accounted for the vast majority of the INPC's assets and operations prior to divestiture.

21 As a result of the banking crisis that emerged in 2008, the state has had to nationalise three credit institutions, and partially nationalise two other banks. These developments are discussed in detail in Chapter 8. For the purpose of this chapter, the use of the term 'state banks' refers to the ACC, ICC and TSB banks only.

22 Dáil Éireann Debates (2000) Vol. 528, 14 December: *Sale of ICC Bank: Motion*, col. 694 (McCreevy, C., Minister for Finance).

23 *Source*: ICC (2001) and BoSI (2001).

24 IL&P was established in 1999 after the merger of the former state-owned insurance company, Irish Life, with Irish Permanent building society.

25 Deposit Interest Retention Tax (DIRT) is a tax charged on the payment of interest on savings in deposit taking financial institutions that was introduced in Ireland in 1986. Many of the largest banks in Ireland facilitated DIRT tax evasion during the 1980s and 1990s by setting up bogus non-resident accounts for customers.

26 The *surplus arising* method was used by Irish Life up until 1991. The surplus arising in a year is the amount by which the change in the life fund exceeds the change in actuarial reserves prior to any distribution of surplus. One of the major flaws of this method is that it gives no indication of how profitable new business is. After 1991, Irish Life switched to the *embedded value* method which attempts to calculate the profits that will arise on new business written during the period by projecting the profits that will be earned over the life of the policy and discounting it back to give a present value for these profits (Irish Life, 1991).

27 Authors' calculation from data on Irish Life's share price and the ISEQ index sourced from the Irish Stock Exchange. The ISEQ (Irish Stock Exchange Quotient) is the published index of shares for the Irish Stock Exchange.

## Chapter 5   The Financial Costs of Privatisation

1   As an indicator of the annual fiscal deficit, the PSBR was a key fiscal target during the early years of the Conservative Party governments that first came to power in the UK in 1979.

2   Their analysis, however, excludes the costs borne by the companies themselves, which were substantial in some cases. For example, BT is estimated to have spent over GBP£8 million in advisory fees and approximately GBP£25 million on its flotation advertising campaign (Vickers and Yarrow, 1988: 182).

3   Furthermore, the analysis of Harris and Lye (2001) does not include costs borne by the companies themselves during the process of sale and thus may be further understated.

4   Harris and Lye (2001) illustrate this point with reference to the example of Commonwealth Serum Laboratories (CSL), where total costs amounted to 2.2 per cent of proceeds. This amount was markedly lower than other Australian privatisations and this can be attributed to the fact that the sale was not underwritten.

5   Indeed, Buckland (1987) estimates that the cost of underpricing associated with the sale of 50 per cent of BT alone amounted to some GBP£1.2 billion. The author claims that 'had 10 per cent of BT been sold at the quotation stage, at a (pessimistic) discount of 10 per cent, followed by further sales totalling 40 per cent at a (pessimistic) discount of 5 per cent on the same market price, discounting costs would have been GBP£924 millions lower' (Buckland, 1987: 247).

6   Aer Lingus Prospectus, 2006.

7   This figure is based on the €4.2 billion raised by the government as part of the IPO. The total proceeds for the sale of Eircom, which are detailed in Table 5.3, also include payments received from the Comsource consortium and the ESOP for their respective stakes.

8   For example, when Irish Sugar was floated, both employees and beet growers were given the opportunity to subscribe for a portion of shares at a 20 per cent discount (Hogan, D. (1991) 'Irish Sugar employees to receive £250 in free shares', *Irish Times*, 21 March, p. 12).

9   McGrath, B. (1991) 'B&I Line is going for a poor song', *Irish Times*, 16 December, p. 4.

10   Dáil Éireann Debates (1991) Vol. 414, 10 December: *B & I Line Bill, 1991: Second Stage*, col. 841.

11   Gallagher, J. (1991) 'ICG may take over B&I before end of year', *Irish Times*, 23 August, p. 14.

12   Dunne, J. (1990) 'Secret shipping merger plan shelved', *Irish Times*, 14 March, p. 1.

13   It is noteworthy that Irish Sugar had been a loss maker up until 1986 but after returning to profitability in the four years prior to flotation and eliminating its accumulated losses, its sale generated significant revenues for the exchequer.

14   Murdoch, B. (1990) 'State pulls the plug on B&I loss making', *Irish Times*, 24 September, p. 12.

15   McGrath, B. (1991) 'B&I Line is going for a poor song', *Irish Times*, 16 December, p. 4.

16 Over €9 million was paid to ISPAT by way of compensation for the future restrictions on production and sales imposed by the EC in return for state aid to be granted (Dáil Éireann Debates (1996) Vol. 463, 3 April: *Irish Steel Limited Bill, 1996 [Seanad]: Second Stage*, col. 1856).

17 The fixed Euro conversion rate for the Irish Punt is IRP£1 = €1.2697381.

18 Dáil Éireann Debates (1996) Vol. 463, 3 April: *Irish Steel Limited Bill, 1996 [Seanad]: Second Stage*, col. 1857.

19 The privatisation of the INPC had unique characteristics. Only the Whitegate refinery and Bantry terminal subsidiaries were divested in 2001, with the INPC continuing as a going concern after the sale. The costs and write-offs associated with the sale of the refinery and terminal operations and the creation of an ESOP were charged to the profit and loss account of the company and as such were not directly incurred by the exchequer.

20 €98 million was also received in repayment of the intercompany balances of the two subsidiaries sold (INPC, 2002).

21 *Source*: INPC annual reports, 2002–05.

22 Hancock, C. (2001) 'Whitegate oil refinery needs $400m investment', *Irish Times*, 23 June, p. 19.

23 The €116 million sale price accepted in 2001 also included the oil storage terminal operation at Whiddy Island in Bantry (Cork), as well as an office block in Dublin.

24 The legal case against the ACC arose out of its involvement as the lead bank of a consortium of lenders in a Dublin city hotel development. The development ran over budget causing the banks to lose money and the ACC was subsequently sued by a number of banks involved in the consortium.

25 McGrath, B. (2001) 'Dutch Rabobank pays €165m for ACCBank', *Irish Times*, 6 December, p. 14.

26 The plan consisted of 2,500 redundancies as well as other cost-cutting measures over a period of 5 years.

27 Eircom agreed to contribute €127 million in return for employees agreeing to contribute 5.3 per cent of their salaries towards their pension schemes which prior to then had been funded entirely by Eircom.

28 In every other EU15 country a partial stake was either floated on the stock market or placed with institutional investors, followed by subsequent sales of partial stakes. Moreover, many European governments still retain sizeable shareholdings in their national telecommunications operators (*Source*: *Privatization Barometer*).

29 With the exception of Sweden, Belgium and Austria, the flotation of every other national telecommunications operator in the EU15 preceded the Eircom IPO (*Source*: *Privatization Barometer*).

# Chapter 6   Employee Share Ownership Plans

1 Keeling, M. (2008) 'Employee Ownership in the United States: Focus on the Employee Stock Ownership Plan, or ESOP, Model', Excerpt from remarks given by J. Michael Keeling, President of the ESOP Association and the Employee Ownership Foundation (Washington D.C.), to attendees at a conference on employee ownership in Granada, Spain on 5 June 2008, available: http://

www.esopassociation.org/about/about_esop_overview.asp [accessed: 27 January 2010].

2  See Kruse (2002) and NCEO (2007) for a review of the empirical evidence on the impact of employee ownership on company performance in the USA.

3  Irish Sugar employees each received some €317 worth of free shares and the option of subscribing for additional shares on the basis of one share per €11.40 of pensionable income or 500 shares (whichever was the greater) at a 20 per cent discount (Hogan, D. (1991) 'Irish Sugar employees to receive £250 in free shares', *Irish Times*, 21 March, p. 12). Irish Life employees each received approximately €650 in free shares along with priority access to the purchase of a further €950 worth of shares where tax relief was granted if they held on to the shares for five years (Gallagher, J. (1991) 'Small investors take bulk of Irish Life public offering', *Irish Times*, 19 July, p. 14).

4  This was replaced by the National Centre for Partnership and Performance (NCPP) in 2000.

5  Employees in Eircom's subsidiary Cablelink (a cable television company) were unable to participate in the ESOP. As part of the privatisation of Eircom, it was agreed that Cablelink would have to be sold separately in order to promote sectoral competition. As compensation, Cablelink employees received an ex-gratia payment worth approximately €51,000 each. Such deals are less attractive to employees and their unions since employees must pay tax on the lump sum payment, whereas ESOP participants receive gradual payments over time which avoids such tax liabilities.

6  Participants assume full ownership over shares once they have reached a 'retention date'. This is reached once the shares have been held in the ESOT for two years and the participant has been a member of the ESOP for the same period of time. Shares are distributed on a tax-free basis if the ESOT has held the shares for a period of three years (the 'release date') and the participant has been a member of the ESOP for the same period of time.

7  Much of the information in this section is taken from information provided by Martin Cullen, the then Minister of State at the Department of Finance (Dáil Éireann Debates (2001) Vol. 546, 13 December: *Disposal of ACC Shares: Motion*, cols. 1069–71).

8  This section relies heavily on details provided by Charlie McCreevy, the then Minister for Finance (Dáil Éireann Debates (2000) Vol. 528, 14 December: *Sale of ICC Bank: Motion*, cols. 695–7).

9  The purchase price paid by the ESOP for its 9.9 per cent stake was based on a valuation of the firm carried out at the end of 1999, which valued the bank at €254 million (Dáil Éireann Debates (2000) Vol. 528, 14 December: *Written Answers – ICC Bank*, col. 903).

10  This figure is calculated based on the fact that there was an average of 358 employees employed at the ICC in February 2001 (ICC, 2001). It must be noted that in order to qualify for the full allocation of shares, employees had to have joined the bank by January 1st 1998. Those with a shorter service received reduced allocations. Given that the average number of ICC employees was 340 in 1998, it is likely that the majority of employees qualified for a full allocation of shares.

11  This section relies heavily on detail provided by Charlie McCreevy, the then Minister for Finance (Dáil Éireann Debates (2001) Vol. 529, 31 January: *Trustee Savings Banks (Amendment) Bill, 2000*, cols. 799–801).

12  The purchase price paid by the ESOP was based on a valuation of the bank carried out in early 2000 by financial advisers PriceWaterhouseCoopers, which valued the TSB at €254 million (Dáil Éireann Debates (2001) Vol. 529, 31 January: *Trustee Savings Banks (Amendment) Bill, 2000: Second Stage*, col. 828).

13  This calculation is based on approximate average employee numbers of 1,200 (Dáil Éireann Debates (2001) Vol. 529, 31 January: *Trustee Savings Banks (Amendment) Bill, 2000: Second Stage*, col. 799).

14  The INPC remained as a going concern after the sale of its refinery and terminal operations; however, its activities were reduced to managing Ireland's strategic stock of petroleum products.

15  This calculation is based on an average number of 229 employees as of December 2000 (INPC, 2001).

16  The details provided in this section rely heavily on Aer Lingus (2002, 2006) and Aer Lingus ESOP (2003).

17  This calculation is based on a figure of 4,665 employees provided as the approximate number of staff participating in the ESOP in a number of Aer Lingus ESOP documents from 2006. The value of the ESOP excludes the cost of borrowing approximately €35 million, which was used to purchase shares during the IPO. The amount borrowed was to be repaid through a profit sharing agreement ratified before the IPO.

18  It should be noted that by law ESOPs are only allowed to invest in their host firms.

19  Most of the information on ICC ESOP share distributions was sourced from an interview with the ICC ESOP Manager in May 2010.

20  *Source*: IPSA (2007) 'Irish ProShare Association Technical and Legislation Tracker', Issue 1 December 2007, Dublin: Irish ProShare Association (IBEC).

21  It must be noted that the USD$12.77 million in shares that had yet to be distributed could rise or fall in value depending on movements in ConocoPhillips' share price after December 2007.

22  The process involved splitting Eircell from Eircom into a new company called Eircell 2000. Eircom shareholders then got one share in Eircell 2000 for every share they held in Eircom while continuing to hold their existing Eircom shares. Vodafone then acquired Eircell 2000 by giving each shareholder 0.9478 Vodafone shares for every two Eircell 2000 shares that they held.

23  McManus, J. (2000) 'Eircom defends €4.5bn price tag Vodafone pins on Eircell', *Irish Times*, 22 December, p. 16.

24  McManus, J. (2001) 'Basic questions unanswered by MacSharry and his board', *Irish Times*, 12 May, p. 19.

25  Valentia was offering warrants covering more than 5 per cent of the company with a guarantee that it would buy back its warrants for 4 cents in 12 months, and for 7 cents in 36 months. The present value of those future warrants was deemed to be a generous 5.8 cents, and, when added to the cash offer, this put Valentia marginally above the eIsland bid. Although eIsland was also offering warrants, these were not guaranteed and a similar exercise could not be conducted on their offer. Estimates put a value of 6 to 12 cents on the warrants however, and it is surprising that the board opted to go with the Valentia bid over the eIsland offer on the basis of their debatable calculations (McManus, J. (2001) 'Fuzzy maths relies heavily on cash and warrant considerations', *Irish Times*, 12 June, p. 16).

26  EBITDA – Earnings (turnover minus operating expenses) before interest, taxes, depreciation and amortisation measures the cash flow generated from operating activities that is used to pay interest and taxes.

27  This approximate value is based on an initial equity investment of €676 million and proceeds to equity investors of approximately €872 million (McManus, J. (2004) 'Eircom comes to market… again', *Irish Times*, 5 March, p. A3). The estimated proceeds in this article were based on an expected flotation share price of €1.62. Since Eircom was eventually floated at a share price of €1.55, the estimated proceeds were adjusted downwards and totalled approximately €834 million.

28  *Source*: BCM Ireland Finance Ltd (Eircom), Quarterly and pro forma 12-months results announcement, June 2007.

29  Quoted in CWU General Secretary Circular GSE 19-09 'ESOP Ballot Update', 19 November 2009. available: http://www.cwuconnect.org/index.php?option=com_content&task=view&id=563&Itemid=36 [accessed 7 March 2010].

30  Oliver, E. (2006) 'Aer Lingus Esot accuses Ryanair of faulty claims', *Irish Times*, 27 October, p. A2.

# Chapter 7   Telecommunications: A Tale of Privatisation Failure

1  Authors' own calculation from *Privatization Barometer* data.

2  The remaining 49.9 per cent stake was made up of the 14.9 per cent ESOP and the shares held by the *Comsource* consortium (*Comsource* acquired a further 15 per cent of the company prior to the flotation, increasing their stake from 20 to 35 per cent).

3  For example, when the Spanish government sold its remaining shareholding in Telefónica in 1997, it retained a ten-year golden share in the company which it used to exert considerable influence over the direction of the company, even preventing a potential merger with KPN in 2000 by threatening to use its golden share to veto the deal (Bel and Trillas, 2005).

4  O'Rourke, M. (Minister for Public Enterprise) in Dáil Éireann Debates (1999) Vol. 504, 13 May: *Telecom Éireann ESOP IPO: Motion*, col. 1129.

5  It is worth noting that Eircom's dominance of the fixed-line market has not resulted in comparatively higher prices. The company still faces price cap regulation on certain services and has faced increasing competitive pressure from mobile voice telephony and to a lesser extent from voice over internet (VoIP) services. In September 2007, 49 per cent of all voice calls in Ireland originated from mobile phones, by December 2009 this figure exceeded 57 per cent (ComReg, 2010). As a result of the above, prices for both residential and business fixed-line calls remain less expensive than the average across all EU member states.

6  The 'local loop' consists of the copper wires that connect buildings to the nearest telephone exchange.

7  Information and communication technologies (ICT) such as broadband are of vital importance to economic growth and enabling higher productivity. This was illustrated by van Ark *et al.* (2003) who found that labour productivity growth in various ICT-using service industries was far higher in the

USA than in Europe between 1995 and 2000, and the authors argue that this is mainly due to the lower levels of ICT investment in European countries.

8  AT = Austria, BE = Belgium, DK = Denmark, FI = Finland, FR = France, DE = Germany, EL = Greece, IE = Ireland, IT = Italy, LU = Luxembourg, NL = Netherlands, PT = Portugal, ES = Spain, SE = Sweden.

9  *Source*: ECTA (2009).

10  In October 2008 the monthly rental price was €16.43 for fully unbundled lines (EU average was €9.28) and €8.41 for shared access lines (EU average was €2.62) (EC, 2009). In January 2010, Eircom agreed to a ComReg ruling to reduce the monthly price for shared access lines from €8.41 to €0.77. In February 2010, ComReg set the maximum monthly rental price for fully unbundled lines that Eircom could charge at €12.41.

11  For fully unbundled loops the alternative operator is the only one connected to the loop. For shared access lines, the alternative operator only has access to the high frequency part of the line while Eircom continues to use the low frequency part of the line.

12  Authors' elaboration of data from ECTA (2009).

13  *Source*: Authors' calculation from Eircom financial reports.

14  Authors' calculation from ComReg's Electronic Register of Authorised Undertakings.

15  High Speed DownLink Packet Access (HSDPA) is a 3G mobile telephony communications protocol which allows higher data transfer speeds and capacity.

16  For example, Nunes (2006), in an analysis of the Portuguese broadband market found that private telecommunications companies had only invested in more lucrative urban markets with dense populations and had neglected rural areas. The author argued that the Portuguese government needed to rethink the role of public funding for services such as broadband after years of market liberalisation which have led to market failures originating from pro-competitive policies between private operators.

17  This figure includes capital expenditure, administration and consultancy costs (DCENR, 2008c).

18  *Source*: elnet (2008) 'MAN's Work – Fibre Network Helps IDA Secure DTS Investment For Limerick' 3 December, elnet News Archive 2008.

19  Backhaul refers to access from a local network to a communications backbone and onwards to the national network.

20  *Source*: Department of Communications, Energy and Natural Resources and Department of Finance.

21  *Source*: DCENR (2008a).

22  Percentages calculated as number of FTTH/B connections (both incumbent and entrant) divided by total fixed broadband connections as of September 2009. Data was sourced from ECTA (2009).

23  *Source*: BIS (2010).

24  *Source*: BIS (2010); Parker, A. and B. Fenton (2010) 'Telephone tax dropped in proposals to fund rural internet', *Financial Times*, 23 June, available: http://www.ft.com/cms/s/fe850518-7e5e-11df-94a8-00144feabdc0.html [accessed 26 June 2010].

25  *Source*: BIS (2010) and Berkman (2009).

26  *Source*: *Infocomm Development Authority of Singapore* (state body responsible for the development and growth of the communications sector in Singapore).

27   The Irish economy is currently experiencing a severe recession due to a property bubble crash and resulting banking crisis in 2008, as well as the impact of the global downturn (see Chapter 8). Ireland's General Government Deficit in 2009 was 14.3 per cent (highest in EU) and 7.3 per cent in 2008 (second highest in EU).

28   The national electricity (ESB), gas (Bord Gáis) and rail (CIE) operators as well as the National Roads Authority (NRA) and water network (Waterways) all own considerable fibre optic and ducting networks which have been deployed alongside their respective networks over the past number of years.

29   Hancock C. (2010) 'Eircom to invest in trials of "ultra fast" broadband', *Irish Times*, 16 June, p. 21.

30   Hancock, C. (2010) 'Competition and effects of slump spur Eircom to act', *Irish Times*, 10 July, p. 17.

31   For example, a survey commissioned by ComReg in 2006 found that 87 per cent of SMEs surveyed in Ireland at the end of 2005 were connected to the internet. However, just 57 per cent of SMEs were connected via DSL (ComReg, 2006). Eurostat data from January 2006 shows that although broadband take-up in Irish SMEs had improved considerably, Ireland still only ranked 16th out of 20 countries for businesses that employed 10–49 people, and 17th out of 20 for companies that employed 50–249 people.

32   Even though British Telecom was privatised in 1984 and has been subject to tight regulation since divestiture, the company still dominated the fixed-line market up until recently and while developments in technology have eroded its dominance in densely populated areas, this did not happen in less densely populated areas (Saal, 2003).

# Chapter 8   Nationalisation of the Irish Banking Sector

1   *Source*: Central Statistics Office. This figure was estimated as the average of the unemployment rate (ILO standardised definition) based on seasonally adjusted Live Register figures for the 12 months in 1986.

2   *Source*: Eurostat.

3   *Source*: Somers (1992).

4   *Source*: Authors' calculation from Eurostat data on GDP per capita in Purchasing Power Standards.

5   *Source*: Department of the Environment, Heritage and Local Government, Housing Statistics. To put the 2006 figure for house completions in perspective, the 93,419 houses completed during that year surpassed the total amount of houses completed over the period 1994–96, and almost equalled the total amount of houses built between 1986 and 1990.

6   *Source*: Permanent TSB/ESRI House Price Index, Quarter 1 2010 figures. The peak in new house prices occurred in Q4 2007. In real terms, house prices have fallen by approximately the same amount (the CSO consumer price index (base December 2006=100) for March 2010 was 100.5, almost the same price level recorded at the end of 2006 when house prices peaked).

7   Reinhart and Rogoff (2008, 2009a) examine a number of major banking crises which were preceded by housing booms. The duration of the downturn in house prices following the crises generally ranged from 4–6 years, while the peak to trough fall in real house prices averaged 35 per cent.

8 Authors' calculation from data on employment in building and construction sourced from the *ESRI Databank*.

9 *Source*: Authors' calculation from Eurostat ESA95 National Account data (NACE code F – construction).

10 The contribution of cyclical taxes (corporation tax, stamp duties and capital gains tax) to total tax revenues had increased steadily from 8 per cent in 1987 to 30 per cent in 2006. By 2008, the contribution of these cyclical taxes to total tax revenue had fallen to 20 per cent (Honohan, 2010), and in 2010 this figure is expected to fall to approximately 14 per cent (Authors' calculation from Department of Finance *Cumulative Profile of Expected Exchequer Tax Revenue Receipts in 2010*).

11 The CBFSAI define property related lending as the sum of lending to real estate activities, construction and the personal sector for housing. In the years ending June 2006 and June 2007, property related lending accounted for almost 80 per cent and 75 per cent respectively of the annual increase in PSC (CBFSAI, 2006b, 2007a). By the end of 2007, Ireland had the highest level of personal sector credit as a percentage of GDP in the Eurozone (CBFSAI, 2007b).

12 The ECB (2009: 68) shows that the Irish government took on more contingent liabilities than any other Eurozone government (equivalent to 214.8 per cent of GDP, excluding guarantees on retail deposits). Belgium (where the government guaranteed contingent liabilities equal to 21 per cent of GDP) and Luxembourg (where the government took on contingent liabilities equivalent to 12.8 per cent of GDP) were ranked second and third to Ireland in terms of the potential fiscal risk that Eurozone governments exposed themselves to as a result of guarantee schemes.

13 The announcement of the blanket guarantee did not have an immediate impact on Irish sovereign bond yields. The yield on Irish ten-year sovereign bonds averaged 4.62 per cent between 1 October and 31 December 2008, compared to an average of 4.76 per cent between 1 July and 30 September 2008. It was only after the government nationalised Anglo Irish Bank in January 2009, thereby exposing it to increased financial risk, that Irish sovereign bond yields started to increase rapidly. The yield on Irish ten-year sovereign bonds hit a high of 6.18 per cent (288 basis points higher than the yield on German ten-year sovereign bonds) on the 26 January 2009, just days after the Irish government officially nationalised Anglo Irish Bank [Source for sovereign bond yields: *Reuters EcoWin Pro*].

14 Authors' calculations from information on total loans and advances to customers sourced from Anglo Irish Bank annual reports for the years 1999 to 2009.

15 By the end of December 2008, Anglo's shares were trading at less than €0.20 (with a market capitalisation of approximately €130 million), representing a fall in value of over 98 per cent since the beginning of the year (Information on share price and market capitalisation sourced from the Irish Stock Exchange).

16 The promissory note was structured by the government to extend over a period of ten to 15 years in order to reduce the impact on the exchequer by stretching the payments out into the future. The note is structured to allow 10 per cent of the principal to be redeemed each year at the request of the bank. Despite the fact that the capital issued is drawn down gradually over time, the Financial Regulator accepted the full amount of the note when assessing the bank's required core equity target.

17  Carswell, S. (2010) 'State gives further €2 billion in capital', *Irish Times*, 1 June, p. 18. The additional €2 billion was provided by adjusting the previous €8.3 billion promissory note up to €10.3 billion.

18  Carswell, S. (2010) 'Closure of Anglo over year would cost €42bn', *Irish Times*, 17 June, p. 20.

19  Letter from Vice President of the EC, Joaquín Almunia, to Ireland's Minister for Foreign Affairs, Micheál Martin, in relation to 'State aid NN12/2010 and C11/2010 (ex N667/2009) – Ireland: Second recapitalisation of Anglo Irish Bank and restructuring of Anglo Irish Bank', 31 March 2010, available: http://ec.europa.eu/competition/elojade/isef/case_details.cfm?proc_code= 3_C11_2010 [accessed 9 July 2010].

20  Authors' elaboration of figures sourced from various INBS annual reports.

21  An example of the risky lending practices pursued by the INBS was provided by its new chief executive who stated that the building society had, in a substantial number of cases, provided loans worth more than 100 per cent of the value of the land backing them, with the society then taking a share of the profit when it was resold in the rising property market (Carswell, S. (2010) 'Fingleton's successor says events at INBS an outrage', *Irish Times*, 20 April, p. 1.)

22  The special investment share transferred effective ownership of the INBS to the Minister for Finance, granting him full control over all resolutions, and granting the state the right to any surplus proceeds generated as part of a winding-up or sale of the society.

23  Hancock, C. (2010) 'Irish Nationwide submits its plan for restructuring', *Irish Times*, 23 June, p. 17.

24  *Source*: Authors' calculations from various EBS annual reports.

25  Lynch, S. (2010) 'State takes control of EBS after investor talks fail', *Irish Times*, 29 May, p. 1.

26  Lynch, S. (2010) 'State injects further €250m into EBS', *Irish Times*, 17 June, p. 20.

27  *Source*: AIB and BoI annual reports. Between 1999 and 2008, the average annual growth rate in loans and advances to customers was approximately 15 per cent in AIB, and 16 per cent in BoI. During the peak years of the boom (2004–07), AIB made over €20 billion in loans annually, or €62.8 billion in the space of three years, while BoI loaned out €57.5 billion over the same period.

28  Slattery, S. and C. O'Brien (2010) 'Shares in Bank of Ireland drop 6% as State takes 15.7% stake', *Irish Times*, 23 February, available: http://www.irishtimes. com/newspaper/finance/2010/0223/1224265033987.html [accessed 24 February 2010].

29  As part of the share placement in May, Bank of Ireland repurchased all of the warrants that had been issued in conjunction with the 2009 preference share investment, in return for €491 million in cash (representing the profit generated by the difference between the exercise price of the warrants and the closing price of the ordinary stock before the placement, plus a fee of €12 million). Following the placement, the NPRF held an approximate 36 per cent stake in BoI (BoI (2010) 'Rights Issue Prospectus' 26 April). The state's ownership stake in BoI remained unchanged after the bank's rights issue of new ordinary stock in June 2010. The NPRF opted to subscribe for

its full entitlement of rights issue stock, which it paid for through the conversion of part of its preference share stock. Following the rights issue, the NPRF's remaining preference share investment in BoI amounted to approximately €1.84 billion (BoI (2010) 'Announcement of Rights Issue Terms', 17 May).

30 The remaining new shares which were not taken up by existing shareholders were successfully sold off in the market (Carswell, S. (2010) 'BoI shares not taken up in rights issue offloaded in market', *Irish Times*, 10 June, p. 23).

31 BoI (2010) 'Announcement of Capital Raising', 26 April, available: http://www.bankofireland.com/investor/capital_raising/ [accessed 22 May 2010].

32 AIB (2010) 'Allied Irish Banks, plc. – Interim Management Statement', 13 May, available: http://www.ise.ie/app/announcementDetails.asp?ID=10490402 [accessed 22 May 2010].

33 AIB had hoped to agree a restructuring plan with the EC prior to the 13 May due date for the payment of the annual dividend on the state's €3.5 billion preference shares. This would have allowed it to pay the dividend in cash rather than in ordinary shares, thereby preventing the state from taking an ownership stake in the bank.

34 Hancock, C. (2010) 'AIB sells off family silver', *Irish Times*, 14 May, available: http://www.irishtimes.com/newspaper/finance/2010/0514/1224270365025.html [accessed 15 May 2010].

35 AIB and BoI are the two largest banks in the state, holding a combined share of approximately 51 per cent of total Irish banking assets in 2008. In the same year, Anglo Irish was the third largest bank in terms of assets (12.1 per cent of total bank assets), while EBS and INBS were relatively smaller, with assets equalling 2.9 and 2 per cent of total bank assets respectively (EC, 2010b: 3).

36 NAMA estimates that the long-term economic value of the assets to be acquired equals €44.7 billion. Long-term economic value is defined as 'the value, as determined by NAMA, that it can reasonably be expected to attain in a stable financial system when the crisis conditions prevailing are ameliorated and in which a future price or yield of the property is consistent with reasonable expectations having regard to the long-term historical average' (NAMA, 2010c: 21).

37 The government could withhold the full capital amount owed by NAMA to credit institutions on the subordinated debt should NAMA fail to recover the cost of purchasing loans.

38 The creation of a privately controlled Special Purpose Vehicle with responsibility for the purchase, management and disposal of NAMA loans, facilitated debts arising from the creation from NAMA being accounted for 'off-balance sheet' and not counting towards general government debt or the general government balance.

39 Correspondingly, real GNP fell by 2.8 per cent in 2008, 11.3 per cent in 2009, and is projected to remain stable in 2010 (ESRI, 2010).

40 This estimate is based on quarterly GDP figures at constant market prices (chain linked annually and referenced to 2008) sourced from the CSO. The peak quarter was Q4 2007 while the trough quarter is Q4 2009. Initial estimates for real GDP in Q1 2010 show a return to positive growth; however, it remains to be seen whether this continues. The ESRI (2010) predicted a decline in real GDP in the first half of 2010 before recovering in the second half of the

year. The final peak-to-trough fall in GDP may differ from our current estimate.

41  This estimate is based on quarterly GNP figures at constant market prices (chain linked annually and referenced to 2008) sourced from the CSO, where the peak quarter was Q4 2007 and the trough quarter (thus far) was Q1 2010. Thus, the final peak-to-trough fall in real GNP may end up being slightly higher, depending on developments in 2010.

42  Finland's general government balance went from a surplus of 1 per cent of GDP prior to its crisis in 1991 to a deficit of 10.8 per cent of GDP in 1994, an 11.8 percentage point increase in its deficit. Sweden went from a surplus of 3.8 per cent of GDP in the year preceding its crisis in 1991, to an 11.6 per cent deficit-to-GDP ratio, a 15.4 percentage point increase (Reinhart and Rogoff, 2009a: 231).

43  *Source*: EC (2010a). The government had forecast a deficit of 11.8 per cent for 2009. However, they were forced to revise this upwards to 14.3 per cent in April 2010, after Eurostat reclassified the €4 billion (2.5 per cent of GDP) capital injection into Anglo Irish Bank in June 2009 as a capital transfer. This had previously been omitted from the calculation of the general government deficit on the basis that the government argued it was an investment. The projected deficit-to-GDP ratios for 2010 and 2011 are 11.7 and 12.1 respectively (EC, 2010a). However, the 2010 deficit could increase substantially, depending on the EC's ruling in relation to the promissory notes issued to recapitalise Anglo and the INBS (see note 45).

44  *Source*: National Treasury Management Agency.

45  In addition to this, the promissory note of €10.3 billion issued to Anglo (to date, an additional €8 billion may be required), the €2.6 billion note issued to the INBS, and the €775 million promissory note issued to the EBS are all recorded as increasing Ireland's general government debt by the full amount in 2010, despite the fact that the amounts promised will be funded through sovereign bond issuance in subsequent years (Dáil Éireann Debates (2010) Vol. 707, 28 April: *Priority Questions*, cols. 660–1). The EC are currently examining the restructuring plans of all three institutions. Critically, if the EC decide that the state is unlikely to get a return from the €10.3 billion Anglo note and the €2.6 billion INBS note, they cannot be counted as an investment (financial transaction), and must therefore be classified as a capital transfer (non-financial transaction). This would then mean that the amounts issued would count towards the general government deficit in 2010. Given the amounts involved, this could lead to a substantial increase in Ireland's 2010 deficit, although it must be stressed that if the notes issued to Anglo and the INBS have to be accounted for in the 2010 deficit, it would significantly overstate the actual borrowing requirement of the government in that year.

46  This estimate takes no account of the value of the assets acquired by NAMA. A proper estimate would offset these assets against the liabilities assumed by NAMA. Since the true value of the assets transferred to NAMA will not emerge for some time, such an estimate is not possible.

47  Opening Statement to Joint Committee on Finance and the Public Sector by the Minister for Finance, Mr Brian Lenihan, 26 May 2009, available: http:// www.finance.gov.ie/viewdoc.asp?DocID=5793 [accessed 24 September 2009].

48  *Source*: ESRI (2010) *Quarterly Economic Commentary Autumn 2010*, Dublin: Economic and Social Research Institute.
49  *Source*: Bloomberg.

## Chapter 9   Lessons from Privatisation and the Future of SOEs

1  US Agency for International Development.
2  High profile examples of reverse privatisation include Air New Zealand which was privatised in 1989 and renationalised in 2001. British Rail was privatised between 1994 and 1997. Railtrack, the private company that ran the rail network, went into 'railway administration' in 2001 before being bought by Network Rail, a newly created 'not for dividend' company. There are also numerous examples of reverse privatisation in the case of municipal services in the USA (Hefetz and Warner, 2007).
3  Editorial (2009) 'Eircom's Broadband', *Irish Times*, 18 March, p. 15.
4  In Switzerland, federal law stipulates that public ownership in Swiss Telecom may not fall below 50 per cent plus one share (OECD, 2009a: 41).
5  Leahy, P. (2010) 'Government lines up sale of semi-states', *Sunday Business Post*, 13 June, p. 1.
6  The scope of public enterprise is measured as the proportion of sectors in which the state controls at least one firm (OECD, 2008).
7  The NTMA manages assets and liabilities on behalf of the Irish government. It was established at the end of 1990 to borrow for the exchequer and manage the national debt. Its remit now includes the management of the National Pensions Reserve Fund, the National Development Finance Agency, the National Asset Management Agency and the State Claims Agency. Certain banking system functions of the Minister for Finance have also been delegated to the NTMA.
8  A number of these points are made by Sweeney (2004) and MacCarthaigh (2009).

# Bibliography

ACC (1994–2005) *Annual Report & Accounts*, Dublin: ACCBank.

Aer Lingus (1995–2009) *Annual Report & Accounts*, Dublin: Aer Lingus Group, plc.

Aer Lingus (2002) *Aer Lingus Employee Share Ownership Plan: Outline of Summary Terms*, Dublin: Aer Lingus Group plc.

Aer Lingus (2006) *Initial Public Offering Prospectus*, Dublin: Aer Lingus Group plc.

Aer Lingus ESOP (2003) *Aer Lingus ESOP Explanatory Booklet*, Dublin: Aer Lingus ESOP Trustee Limited.

AIB (2000–2008) *Annual Report & Accounts*, Dublin: Allied Irish Banks, plc.

AIB (2009) *Annual Financial Report 2008*, Dublin: Allied Irish Banks, plc.

Alchian, A. A. (1965) 'Some Economics of Property Rights', *Il Politico*, 30(4), 816–29.

Alchian, A. A. and Demsetz, H. (1972) 'Production, Information Costs, and Economic Organization', *American Economic Review*, 62(5), 777–95.

Allen, K. (2000) *The Celtic Tiger: The Myth of Social Partnership*, Manchester: Manchester University Press.

Allen, K. (2007) *The Corporate Takeover of Ireland*, Dublin: Irish Academic Press.

Anglo (1999–2008) *Annual Report & Accounts*, Dublin: Anglo Irish Bank.

Anglo (2009) *Interim Report: Six Months Ended 31 March 2009*, Dublin: Anglo Irish Bank.

Anglo (2010) *Annual Report & Accounts 2009*, Dublin: Anglo Irish Bank.

B&I Line (1985–1994) *Annual Report & Accounts*, Dublin: B&I Line Limited.

Barrow, M. and Wagstaff, A. (1989) 'Efficiency Measures in the Public Sector: An Appraisal', *Fiscal Studies*, 10(1), 72–97.

Barry, F. (ed.) (1999) *Understanding Ireland's Economic Growth*, London: Macmillan.

Bel, G. (1998) 'Los Costes Financieros de la Privatización en España', *Información Commercial Española*, 772, 125–44.

Bel, G. (2006) 'The Coining of "Privatization" and Germany's National Socialist Party', *Journal of Economic Perspectives*, 20(3), 187–94.

Bel, G. (2009a) 'From Public to Private: Privatization in 1920's Fascist Italy', *European University Institute Working Paper*, No. RSCAS 2009/46.

Bel, G. (2009b) 'Against the Mainstream: Nazi Privatization in 1930s Germany', *The Economic History Review*, 63(1), 34–55.

Bel, G. (2009c) 'The First Privatization Policy in a Democracy: Selling State-Owned Enterprises in 1948–50 Puerto Rico', *Universitat de Barcelona Research Institute of Applied Economics Working Paper*, No. 2009/15.

Bel, G. and Trillas, F. (2005) 'Privatization, Corporate Control and Regulatory Reform: The Case of Telefonica', *Telecommunications Policy*, 29(1), 25–51.

Berkman (2009) *Next Generation Connectivity: A Review of Broadband Internet Transitions and Policy from around the World*, Cambridge, MA: The Berkman Center for Internet & Society at Harvard University.

BIS (2010) *Consultation on Proposals for a Next Generation Fund*, London: Department of Business, Innovation and Skills.

Bishop, M. and Kay, J. A. (1989) 'Privatization in the United Kingdom: Lessons from Experience', *World Development*, 17(5), 643–57.

Bishop, M. and Thompson, D. (1992) 'Regulatory Reform and Productivity Growth in the UK's Public Utilities', *Applied Economics*, 24(11), 1181–90.

Boardman, A. E. and Vining, A. R. (1989) 'Ownership and Performance in Competitive Environments: A Comparison of the Performance of Private, Mixed, and State-Owned Enterprises', *Journal of Law & Economics*, 32(1), 1–33.

BoI (2000–2008) *Annual Report & Accounts*, Dublin: Bank of Ireland Group.

BoI (2009) *Report & Accounts for the Year Ended 31 March 2009*, Dublin: Bank of Ireland Group.

Boiteux, M. (1971) 'On the Management of Public Monopolies Subject to Budgetary Constraints', *Journal of Economic Theory*, 3(3), 219–40.

Borcherding, T. E., Pommerehne, W. W. and Schneider, F. (1982) 'Comparing the Efficiency of Private and Public Production: The Evidence from Five Countries', *Zeitschrift für Nationalökonomie*, 42(2), 127–36.

Bortolotti, B., D'Souza, J., Fantini, M. and Megginson, W. L. (2002) 'Privatization and the Sources of Performance Improvement in the Global Telecommunications Industry', *Telecommunications Policy*, 26(5 6), 243–68.

Bortolotti, B. and Faccio, M. (2008) 'Government Control of Privatized Firms', *The Review of Financial Studies*, 22(8), 2907–39.

Bortolotti, B. and Milella, V. (2008) 'Privatization in Western Europe: Stylized Facts, Outcomes, and Open Issues' in G. Roland (ed.) *Privatization: Successes and Failures*, New York: Columbia University Press, 32–75.

Bortolotti, B. and Siniscalco, D. (2004) *The Challenges of Privatization: An International Analysis*, Oxford: Oxford University Press.

Bös, D. (1987) 'Privatization of Public Enterprises', *European Economic Review*, 31(1–2), 352–60.

Bös, D. (1991) *Privatization: A Theoretical Treatment*, Oxford: Clarendon Press.

BoSI (2001–2005) *Directors' Report and Consolidated Financial Statements*, Dublin: Bank of Scotland (Ireland) Limited.

Boubakri, N. and Cosset, J.-C. (1998) 'The Financial and Operating Performance of Newly Privatized Firms: Evidence from Developing Countries', *Journal of Finance*, 53(3), 1081–110.

Boycko, M., Shleifer, A. and Vishny, R. W. (1996) 'A Theory of Privatisation', *The Economic Journal*, 106(435), 309–19.

Breen, R., Hannan, D. F., Rottman, D. B. and Whelan, C. T. (1990) *Understanding Contemporary Ireland: State, Class and Development in the Republic of Ireland*, Dublin: Gill and Macmillan.

Bristow, J. A. (1982) 'State-Sponsored Bodies' in F. Litton (ed.) *Unequal Achievement: The Irish Experience 1957–82*, Dublin: Institute of Public Administration, 165–82.

Buchanan, J. M. (1978) 'From Private Preference to Public Philosophy: The Development of Public Choice' in J. M. Buchanan, C. K. Rowley, A. Breton, J. Wiseman, B. Frey and A. T. Peacock (eds.) *The Economics of Politics*, London: Institute of Economic Affairs, 1–20.

Buckland, R. (1987) 'The Costs and Returns of the Privatization of Nationalized Industries', *Public Administration*, 65(3), 241–57.

*Budget Book* (1990) Dublin: Stationery Office.

*Building on Reality* (1984) Dublin: Stationery Office.

Burk, K. (1988) *The First Privatization: The Politicians, the City and the Denationalization of Steel in 1953*, London: Historian's Press.

Cahill, N. (2000) *Profit Sharing, Employee Share Ownership and Gainsharing: What can they Achieve?*, Dublin: National Economic and Social Council.

Caprio, G., Klingebiel, D., Laeven, L. and Noguera, G. (2005) 'Banking Crisis Database' in P. Honohan and L. Laeven (eds.) *Systemic Financial Crises*, Cambridge: Cambridge University Press.

Caves, R. E. (1990) 'Lessons from Privatization in Britain: State Enterprise Behavior, Public Choice, and Corporate Governance', *Journal of Economic Behavior & Organization*, 13(2), 145–69.

CBFSAI (2005) *Financial Stability Report 2005*, Dublin: Central Bank and Financial Services Authority of Ireland.

CBFSAI (2006a) *Financial Stability Report 2006*, Dublin: Central Bank and Financial Services Authority of Ireland.

CBFSAI (2006b) *Sectoral Developments in Private-Sector Credit – June 2006*, Dublin: Central Bank and Financial Services Authority of Ireland.

CBFSAI (2007a) *Sectoral Developments in Private-Sector Credit – June 2007*, Dublin: Central Bank and Financial Services Authority of Ireland.

CBFSAI (2007b) *Sectoral Developments in Private-Sector Credit – December 2007*, Dublin: Central Bank and Financial Services Authority of Ireland.

CEEP (1994) *Les Entreprises à Participation Publique dans l'Union Européenne, Annales du CEEP*, Brussels: Centre Européen des Enterprises à Participation Publique.

Chubb, B. (1982) *The Government and Politics of Ireland*, London: Longman.

Clifton, J., Comín, F. and Diaz Fuentes, D. (2003) *Privatisation in the European Union: Public Enterprises and Integration*, Dordrecht: Kluwer Academic Publishers.

Clifton, J., Comín, F. and Diaz Fuentes, D. (eds.) (2007) *Transforming Public Enterprise in Europe and North America: Networks, Integration and Transnationalization*, Basingstoke: Palgrave Macmillan.

ComReg (2006) *Business Telecommunications Survey Wave 2, 2005: Report and Analysis*, Dublin: Commission for Communications Regulation.

ComReg (2007) *Irish Communications Market Quarterly Key Data Report: March 2007*, Dublin: Commission for Communications Regulation.

ComReg (2010) *Irish Communications Market Quarterly Key Data Report: Data as of Q4 2009*, Dublin: Commission for Communications Regulation.

Connolly, E. (2009) 'Banking Crises and Economic Activity: Observations from Past Crises in Developed Countries', *Economic Papers*, 28(3), 206–16.

ConocoPhillips (2001–2006) *Directors' Report and Consolidated Financial Accounts*, Cork: ConocoPhillips Ireland Limited.

Daßler, T., Parker, D. and Saal, D. S. (2002) 'Economic Performance in European Telecommunications 1978–1998: A Comparative Study', *European Business Review*, 14(3), 194–209.

DCENR (2008a) *Consultation Paper on Next Generation Broadband*, Dublin: Department of Communications, Energy and Natural Resources.

DCENR (2008b) *Value for Money and Policy Review of the Group Broadband Schemes*, Dublin: Department of Communications, Energy and Natural Resources.

DCENR (2008c) *Value for Money and Policy Review of the Metropolitan Area Networks (Phase I)*, Dublin: Department of Communications, Energy and Natural Resources.

De Alessi, L. (1980) 'The Economics of Property Rights: A Review of the Evidence', *Research in Law and Economics*, 2, 1–47.

Dewenter, K. and Malatesta, P. (1997) 'Public Offerings of State-Owned and Privately-Owned Enterprises: An International Comparison', *Journal of Finance*, 52(4), 1659–79.

Dewenter, K. and Malatesta, P. (2001) 'State-Owned and Privately Owned Firms: An Empirical Analysis of Profitability, Leverage, and Labor Intensity', *American Economic Review*, 91(1), 320–34.

DG AGRI (2006–2009) *Rural Development in the European Union: Statistical and Economic Information Report*, Brussels: European Commission (Directorate General for Agriculture and Rural Development).

D'Souza, J. and Megginson, W. L. (1999) 'The Financial and Operating Performance of Privatized Firms During the 1990s', *Journal of Finance*, 54(4), 1397–438.

Dunsire, A., Hartley, K. and Parker, D. (1991) 'Organizational Status and Performance: Summary of the Findings', *Public Administration*, 69(1), 21–40.

Dunsire, A., Hartley, K., Parker, D. and Dimitriou, B. (1988) 'Organizational Status and Performance: A Conceptual Framework for Testing Public Choice Theories', *Public Administration*, 66(4), 363–88.

EBS (2001–2008) *Annual Report & Accounts*, Dublin: Educational Building Society.

EBS (2009) *Annual Report & Accounts 2008*, Dublin: Educational Building Society.

EC (2004) *The Common Organisation of the Market in Sugar*, Brussels: European Commission (Directorate-General for Agriculture and Rural Development).

EC (2009) *Progress Report on the Single European Electronic Communications Market 2008 (14th Report)*, Brussels: European Commission.

EC (2010a) *European Economic Forecast – Spring 2010*, Brussels: European Commission (Directorate-General for Economic and Financial Affairs).

EC (2010b) *Establishment of a National Asset Management Agency (NAMA): Asset relief scheme for banks in Ireland (State Aid Case No. N725/2009)*, Brussels: European Commission (Directorate-General for Competition).

ECB (2009) 'The Impact of Government Support to the Banking Sector on Euro Area Public Finances' in *ECB Monthy Bulletin July 2009*, Frankfurt: European Central Bank.

ECTA (2004–2009) *ECTA Broadband Scorecards*, Brussels: European Competitive Telecommunications Association.

ECTA (2009) *ECTA Broadband Scorecard Q3 2009*, Brussels: European Competitive Telecommunications Association.

Eircom (2000–2001) *Annual Report & Accounts*, Dublin: Eircom, plc.

Eircom ESOP Trustee (2001a) 'Proposed Demerger and Sale of Eircell', *ESOP Extra*, Issue 1(May).

Eircom ESOP Trustee (2001b) 'The Recommended Revised Offer for Eircom plc from Valentia Telecommunications Limited and the Offer for Eircom plc from eIsland plc', *ESOP Extra*, Issue 4(August).

ESRI (2010) *Quarterly Economic Commentary Spring 2010*, Dublin: Economic and Social Research Institute.

Fine Gael (2010) *NewERA*, available at: http://www.new-era.ie/NewERA2010.pdf.

Florio, M. (2004) *The Great Divestiture: Evaluating the Welfare Impact of the British Privatizations 1979–1997*, Cambridge, MA: The MIT Press.

Forfás (2005) *Benchmarking Ireland's Broadband Performance*, Dublin: Forfás.

Forfás (2006) *Overview of Ireland's Broadband Performance*, Dublin: Forfás.

Forfás (2010) *Ireland's Broadband Performance and Policy Actions*, Dublin: Forfás.

Foster, C. (1994) 'Rival Explanations of Public Ownership: Its Failure and Privatization', *Public Administration*, 72(4), 489–503.

Fotak, V., Bortolotti, B. and Megginson, W. L. (2008) 'The Financial Impact of Sovereign Wealth Fund Investments in Listed Companies', paper presented at *UBC Summer Finance Conference*, Sauder School of Business, University of British Columbia (CA), July 27–29.

Frydman, R., Gray, C., Hessel, M. and Rapaczynski, A. (1999) 'When Does Privatization Work? The Impact of Private Ownership on Corporate Performance in the Transition Economies', *Quarterly Journal of Economics*, 114(4), 1153–91.

Galal, A., Jones, L., Tandon, P. and Vogelsang, I. (1994) *The Welfare Consequences of Selling Public Enterprises*, New York: Oxford University Press for the World Bank.

Gathon, H. J. and Pestieau, P. (1993) 'The Implications of European Union for the Performance of Public Enterprises', *Administration*, 41(2), 149–65.

Gray, A. W. (ed.) (1997) *International Perspectives on the Irish Economy*, Dublin: Indecon.

Greencore (1991–1999) *Annual Report & Accounts*, Dublin: Greencore Group.

Hager, W. (1982) 'Industrial Policy, Trade Policy, and European Social Democracy' in J. Pinder (ed.) *National Industrial Strategies and the World Economy*, London: Croom Helm, 236–64.

Harris, M. D. and Lye, J. N. (2001) 'The Fiscal Consequences of Privatisation: Australian Evidence on Privatisation by Public Share Float', *International Review of Applied Economics*, 15(3), 305–21.

Hart, O., Shleifer, A. and Vishny, R. W. (1997) 'The Proper Scope of Government: Theory and an Application to Prisons', *Quarterly Journal of Economics*, 112(4), 1127–61.

Haskel, J. and Szymanski, S. (1992) 'A Bargaining Theory of Privatisation', *Annals of Public and Cooperative Economics*, 63(2), 207–27.

Haskel, J. and Szymanski, S. (1993) 'Privatisation, Liberalisation, Wages and Employment: Theory and Evidence for the UK', *Economica*, 60(238), 161–82.

Hefetz, A. and Warner, M. (2007) 'Beyond the Market vs. Planning Dichotomy: Understanding Privatisation and its Reverse in US Cities', *Local Government Studies*, 33(4), 555–72.

Honohan, P. (2008) 'Risk Management and the Costs of the Banking Crisis', *National Institute Economic Review*, 206, 15–24.

Honohan, P. (2009a) 'What Went Wrong in Ireland?', paper prepared for the World Bank, May 2009, available: http://www.tcd.ie/Economics/staff/phonohan/What%20went%20wrong.pdf [accessed 23 September 2009].

Honohan, P. (2009b) 'Resolving Ireland's Banking Crisis', *The Economic and Social Review*, 40(2), 207–31.

Honohan, P. (2010) *The Irish Banking Crisis – Regulatory and Financial Stability Policy 2003–2008 (A Report to the Minister for Finance by the Governor of the Central Bank)*, Dublin: Central Bank & Financial Services Authority of Ireland.

Honohan, P. and Klingebiel, D. (2003) 'The Fiscal Cost Implications of an Accommodating Approach to Banking Crises', *Journal of Banking & Finance*, 27(8), 1539–60.

Honohan, P. and Walsh, B. (2002) 'Catching Up with the Leaders: The Irish Hare', *Brookings Papers on Economic Activity*, 2002(1), 1–57.

Hood, C. (1991) 'A Public Management for All Seasons?', *Public Administration*, 69(1), 3–19.

Hood, C. (1995) 'The "New Public Management" in the 1980s: Variations on a Theme', *Accounting Organisations and Society*, 20(2/3), 93–109.

Hotelling, H. (1938) 'The General Welfare in Relation to Problems of Taxation and of Railway and Utility Rates', *Econometrica*, 6(3), 242–69.

Huang, Q. and Levich, R. M. (1999) 'Underpricing of New Equity Offerings by Privatized Firms: An International Test', *NYU Working Paper*, No. FIN-99-075.

Hulsink, W. (1999) *Privatisation and Liberalisation in European Telecommunications*, London: Routledge.

ICC (1993–2001) *Annual Report & Accounts*, Dublin: ICC Bank, plc.

ICG (1990–1994) *Annual Report & Accounts*, Dublin: Irish Continental Group, plc.

ICTU (2005) *A New Governance Structure for State Companies*, Dublin: Irish Congress of Trade Unions.

IDATE (2006–2009) *Broadband Coverage in Europe: Final Report – Study for DG INFSO (European Commission)*, Montpellier (FR): IDATE Consulting & Research.

IL&P (2000–2007) *Annual Report & Financial Statements*, Dublin: Irish Life & Permanent, plc.

IMF (2009) 'The State of Public Finances Cross-Country Fiscal Monitor: November 2009', *IMF Staff Position Note*, No. SPN/09/25.

IMF (2010) *A Fair and Substantial Contribution by the Financial Sector, Interim Report for the Meeting of G-20 Ministers April 2010*, Washington D.C.: International Monetary Fund.

INBS (2001–2009) *Annual Report & Accounts*, Dublin: Irish Nationwide Building Society.

INBS (2010) *Annual Report & Accounts 2009*, Dublin: Irish Nationwide Building Society.

INPC (1992–2006) *Annual Report & Accounts*, Dublin: Irish National Petroleum Corporation.

Irish Ferries (1994–1998) *Annual Report & Accounts*, Dublin: Irish Ferries Limited.

Irish Life (1984–1998) *Annual Report & Accounts*, Dublin: Irish Life.

Irish Sugar (1980–1990) *Annual Report & Accounts*, Dublin: Irish Sugar.

Jenkinson, T. and Mayer, C. (1988) 'The Privatisation Process in France and the UK', *European Economic Review*, 32(2–3), 482–90.

Jenkinson, T. and Mayer, C. (1994) 'The Costs of Privatization in the UK and France' in M. Bishop, J. Kay and C. Mayer (eds.) *Privatization and Economic Performance*, New York: Oxford University Press, 290–8.

Jeronimo, V., Pagan, J. A. and Soydemir, G. (2000) 'Privatization and European Economic and Monetary Union', *Eastern Economic Journal*, 26(3), 321–33.

JOCSSB (1980a) *Joint Committee on State-Sponsored Bodies Thirteenth Report, Comhlucht Siuicre Eireann, Teoranta*, Dublin: Stationery Office.

JOCSSB (1980b) *Joint Committee on State-Sponsored Bodies Eleventh Report, Industrial Credit Company, Limited*, Dublin: Stationery Office.

Jones, S. L., Megginson, W. L., Nash, R. C. and Netter, J. M. (1999) 'Share Issue Privatizations as Financial Means to Political and Economic Ends', *Journal of Financial Economics*, 53(2), 217–53.

Kay, J. (1987) 'Public Ownership, Public Regulation or Public Subsidy?', *European Economic Review*, 31(1–2), 343–5.

Kay, J. (1993) 'Privatisation in Western Economies' in D. E. Fair and R. Raymond (eds.) *The New Europe: Evolving Economic and Financial Systems in East and West*, Dordrecht: Kluwer Academic Publishers, 69–85.

Kay, J. and Thompson, D. (1986) 'Privatisation: A Policy in Search of a Rationale', *The Economic Journal*, 96(381), 18–32.

Kikeri, S. (1998) 'Privatization and Labor: What Happens to Workers When Governments Divest?', *World Bank Technical Paper*, No. 396.

Kim, E. H. and Ouimet, P. (2009) 'Employee Capitalism or Corporate Socialism? Broad-Based Employee Stock Ownership', *U.S. Census Bureau, Center for Economic Studies, Working Paper*, No. 09-44.

Krugman, P. R. (1997) 'Good News from Ireland: A Geographical Perspective' in A. W. Gray (ed.) *International Perspectives on the Irish Economy*, Dublin: Indecon Economic Consultants, 38–53.

Kruse, D. (2002) 'Research Evidence on the Prevalence and Effects of Employee Ownership', *Journal of Employee Ownership Law and Finance*, 14(4), 65–90.

Laeven, L. and Valencia, F. (2008) 'Systemic Banking Crises: A New Database', *IMF Working Paper*, No. WP/08/224.

Laeven, L. and Valencia, F. (2010) 'Resolution of Banking Crises: The Good, the Bad, and the Ugly', *IMF Working Paper*, No. WP/10/146.

Laffont, J.-J. and Tirole, J. (1991) 'Privatization and Incentives', *Journal of Law, Economics, and Organization*, 7, 84–105.

Lane, J.-E. (2002) 'Transformation and Future of Public Enterprises in Continental Western Europe', *Public Finance and Management*, 2(1), 56–80.

Larouche, P. (2008) 'Europe and Investment in Infrastructure with Emphasis on Electronic Communications' in G. Arts, W. Dicke and L. Hancher (eds.) *New Perspectives on Investment in Infrastructures*, Amsterdam: Amsterdam University Press, 241–70.

Lavdas, K. (1996) 'The Political Economy of Privatization in Southern Europe' in D. Braddon and D. Foster (eds.) *Privatization: Social Science Themes and Perspectives*, Dartmouth (UK): Aldershot.

Lee, J. J. (1989) *Ireland 1912–1985: Politics and Society*, Cambridge: Cambridge University Press.

Leibenstein, H. (1966) 'Allocative Efficiency vs. "X-Efficiency"', *American Economic Review*, 56(3), 392–415.

Lemass, S. F. (1959) 'The Role of the State-Sponsored Bodies in the Economy', *Administration*, 6(4), 277–95.

Litton, A. J. (1962) 'The Growth and Development of the Irish Telephone System', *Journal of The Statistical and Social Inquiry Society of Ireland*, XX(V), 79–115.

MacCarthaigh, M. (2009) *The Corporate Governance of Commercial State-owned Enterprises in Ireland, CPMR Research Report No. 9*, Dublin: Institute of Public Administration.

Mac Sharry, R. and White, P. (2000) *The Making of the Celtic Tiger: The Inside Story of Ireland's Boom Economy*, Cork: Mercier Press.

Mahboobi, L. (2001) 'Recent Privatisation Trends' in OECD (ed.) *Financial Market Trends No. 70*, Paris: OECD.

Manning, M. and McDowell, M. (1984) *Electricity Supply in Ireland: The History of the ESB*, Dublin: Gill and Macmillan.

Martin, B. (1993) *In the Public Interest? Privatisation and Public Sector Reform*, London: Zed Books.

Martin, S. and Parker, D. (1995) 'Privatization and Economic Performance Throughout the UK Business Cycle', *Managerial and Decision Economics*, 16(3), 225–37.

Martin, S. and Parker, D. (1997) *The Impact of Privatisation: Ownership and Corporate Performance in the UK*, London: Routledge.

Mayer, C. and Meadowcroft, S. (1985) 'Selling Public Assets: Techniques and Financial Implications', *Fiscal Studies*, 6(4), 42–56.

McCarthy, D. (2007) *The Role of Privatisation and Employee Share-Ownership in Determining Organisational Change: A Case Study of Eircom*, unpublished thesis (Ph.D), University of Limerick.

McCarthy, D., Reeves, E. and Turner, T. (2010a) 'The Impact of Privatisation and Employee Share-Ownership on Employee Commitment and Citizen Behaviour', *Economic and Industrial Democracy, in press* (doi:10.1177/0143831X09351213).

McCarthy, D., Reeves, E. and Turner, T. (2010b) 'Can Employee Share-Ownership Improve Employee Attitudes and Behaviour?', *Employee Relations, in press*.

Megginson, W. L. (2006a) 'Major Deals of 2H2005' in B. Bortolotti (ed.) *The Privatization Barometer Newsletter, Issue N. 4*, Milan: Fondazione Eni Enrico Mattei, 14–19.

Megginson, W. L. (2006b) 'Major Deals of 1H2006' in B. Bortolotti (cd.) *The Privatization Barometer Newsletter, Issue N. 5*, Milan: Fondazione Eni Enrico Mattei, 17–20.

Megginson, W. L., Nash, R. C. and Van Randenborgh, M. (1994) 'The Financial and Operating Performance of Newly Privatized Firms: An International Empirical Analysis', *The Journal of Finance*, 49(2), 403–52.

Megginson, W. L. and Netter, J. M. (2001) 'From State to Market: A Survey of Empirical Studies on Privatization', *Journal of Economic Literature*, 39(2), 321–89.

Melody, W. H. (2008) 'Private Equity Funds and Public Utilities: Where Incentives Collide' in G. Arts, W. Dicke and L. Hancher (eds.) *New Perspectives on Investment in Infrastructure*, Amsterdam: Amsterdam University Press, 271–85.

Miller, A. N. (1997) 'Ideological Motivations of Privatization in Great Britain versus Developing Countries', *Journal of International Affairs*, 50, 391–407.

Molyneux, R. and Thompson, D. (1987) 'Nationalised Industry Performance: Still Third-Rate?', *Fiscal Studies*, 8(1), 48–82.

Monk, A. H. B. (2010) 'Sovereignty in the Era of Global Capitalism: The Rise of Sovereign Wealth Funds and the Power of Finance', available at SSRN: http://ssrn.com/abstract=1587327.

Moore, J. (1986) 'Why Privatise?' in J. Kay, C. Mayer and D. Thompson (eds.) *Privatisation and Regulation: The UK Experience*, Oxford: Clarendon Press, 78–93.

Muellbauer, J. (1986) 'The Assessment: Productivity and Competitiveness in British Manufacturing', *Oxford Review of Economic Policy*, 2(3), 5–25.

Mussacchio, A. and Flores-Macias, F. (2009) 'The Return of State-Owned Enterprises: Should We Be Afraid?', *Harvard International Review*, March 2009 (online edition), available: http://hir.harvard.edu/index.php?page=article&id=1854 [accessed 23 January 2010].

NAMA (2010a) *The National Asset Management Agency: A Brief Guide*, Dublin: National Asset Management Agency.

NAMA (2010b) *Key Tranche 1 Data – 10 May 2010*, Dublin: National Asset Management Agency.

NAMA (2010c) *NAMA Business Plan – 30 June 2010*, Dublin: National Asset Management Agency.

*National Development Plan 2000–2006* (1999) Dublin: Stationery Office.

NCC (2009) *Annual Competitiveness Report 2009 Volume 1: Benchmarking Ireland's Performance*, Dublin: National Competitiveness Council (Forfás).

NCEO (2007) *Employee Ownership and Corporate Performance: A Comprehensive Review of the Evidence*, Oakland, CA: The National Center for Employee Ownership.

NESC (1986) *A Strategy for Development, 1986–1990*, Dublin: National Economic and Social Council.

Nunes, F. (2006) 'Geographical Gaps in the Portuguese Broadband Access. Rethinking the Role of Public Funding After Years of Trade Liberalisation', *Telecommunications Policy*, 30(8–9), 496–515.

O'Donnell, R. (2008) 'The Partnership State: Building the Ship at Sea' in M. Adshead, P. Kirby and M. Millar (eds.) *Contesting the State: Lessons From the Irish Case*, Manchester: Manchester University Press, 73–99.

OECD (2003) *Privatising State-owned Enterprises: An Overview of Policies and Practices in OECD Countries*, Paris: OECD.

OECD (2005) *Corporate Governance of State-Owned Enterprises: A Survey of OECD Countries*, Paris: OECD.

OECD (2008) 'Integrated Product Market Regulation Indicators', available: http://www.oecd.org/document/0,3343,en_2649_34323_35790244_1_1_1_1,00.html [accessed 8 May 2010].

OECD (2009a) *Privatization in the 21st Century: Recent Experiences of OECD Countries*, Paris: OECD.

OECD (2009b) *SOEs Operating Abroad: An Application of OECD Guidelines on Corporate Governance of State-Owned Enterprises to the Cross-Border Operations of SOEs*, Paris: OECD.

OECD (2010) *OECD Economic Outlook, No. 87 (Preliminary Edition)*, Paris: OECD.

O'Malley, E. (1989) *Industry and Economic Development: The Challenge for the Latecomer*, Dublin: Gill and Macmillan.

Palcic, D. and Reeves, E. (2005) 'An Economic Analysis of Privatisation in Ireland, 1991–2003', *Journal of The Statistical and Social Inquiry Society of Ireland*, XXXIV, 1–27.

Palcic, D. and Reeves, E. (2010a) 'Costly Business: Privatisation and Exchequer Finances in Ireland', *Administration*, 58(1), 29–53.

Palcic, D. and Reeves, E. (2010b) 'Organisational Status Change and Performance: The Case of Ireland's National Telecommunications Operator', *Telecommunications Policy*, 34(5–6), 299–308.

Parker, D. (1998) 'Privatisation in the European Union: An Overview' in D. Parker (ed.) *Privatisation in the European Union: Theory and Policy Perspectives*, London: Routledge, 10–48.

Parker, D. (1999) 'Privatization in the European Union: A Critical Assessment of its Development, Rationale and Consequences', *Economic and Industrial Democracy*, 20(1), 9–38.

Parker, D. (ed.) (2000) *Privatisation and Corporate Performance*, Cheltenham (UK): Edward Elgar.

Parker, D. (2003) 'Privatization in the European Union' in D. Parker and D. S. Saal (eds.) *International Handbook on Privatization*, Cheltenham, UK: Edward Elgar, 105–28.

Parker, D. (2009) *The Official History of Privatisation, Vol. I: The Formative Years 1970–1987*, London: Routledge.

Parris, H., Pestieau, P. and Saynor, P. (1987) *Public Enterprise in Western Europe*, London: Croom Helm.

Pendleton, A., Poutsma, E., Van Ommeren, J. and Brewster, C. (2003) 'The Incidence and Determinants of Employee Share Ownership and Profit Sharing in Europe' in T. Kato and J. Pliskin (eds.) *The Determinants of the Incidence and the Effects of Participatory Organizations, Advances in the Economic Analysis of Participatory and Labor Management, Vol. 7*, Greenwich: JAI Press, 141–72.

Pentzaropoulos, G. C. and Giokas, D. I. (2002) 'Comparing the Operational Efficiency of the Main European Telecommunications Organizations: A Quantitative Analysis', *Telecommunications Policy*, 26(11), 595–606.

Pestieau, P. (1989) 'Measuring the Performance of Public Enterprises: A Must in Times of Privatization', *Annals of Public and Cooperative Economics*, 60(3), 293–305.

Petrovic, A. and Tutsch, R. (2009) 'National Rescue Measures in Response to the Current Financial Crisis', *ECB Legal Working Paper Series*, No. 8, June 2009.

Poggi, A. and Florio, M. (2010) 'Energy Deprivation Dynamics and Regulatory Reforms in Europe: Evidence from Household Panel Data', *Energy Policy*, 38(1), 253–64.

Privatization Barometer (2005a) *The Privatization Barometer Newsletter, Issue N. 2*, Milan: Fondazione Eni Enrico Mattei.

Privatization Barometer (2005b) *The Privatization Barometer Newsletter, Issue N. 3*, Milan: Fondazione Eni Enrico Mattei.

Privatization Barometer (2007a) *The Privatization Barometer Newsletter, Issue N. 6*, Milan: Fondazione Eni Enrico Mattei.

Privatization Barometer (2007b) *The Privatization Barometer Report 2007*, Milan: Fondazione Eni Enrico Mattei.

Privatization Barometer (2008) *The Privatization Barometer Report 2008*, Milan: Fondazione Eni Enrico Mattei.

*Programme for Economic and Social Progress* (1991) Dublin: Stationery Office.

*Programme for National Recovery* (1987) Dublin: Stationery Office.

Rae, D. and van den Noord, P. (2006) 'Ireland's Housing Boom: What has Driven It and Have Prices Overshot?', *OECD Economics Department Working Papers*, No. 492.

Rees, R. (1988) 'Inefficiency, Public Enterprise and Privatization', *European Economic Review*, 32(2–3), 422–31.

Regling, K. and Watson, M. (2010) *A Preliminary Report on the Sources of Ireland's Banking Crisis*, Dublin: Government Publications Office.

Reinhart, C. M. and Rogoff, K. S. (2008) 'Banking Crises: An Equal Opportunity Menace', *NBER Working Paper*, No. 14587.

Reinhart, C. M. and Rogoff, K. S. (2009a) *This Time is Different: Eight Centuries of Financial Folly*, Princeton, NJ: Princeton University Press.

Reinhart, C. M. and Rogoff, K. S. (2009b) 'The Aftermath of Financial Crises', *American Economic Review*, 99(2), 466–72.

Roland, G. (ed.) (2008) *Privatization: Successes and Failures*, New York: Columbia University Press.

Saal, D. S. (2003) 'Restructuring, Regulation, and the Liberalization of Privatized Utilities in the UK' in D. Parker and D. S. Saal (eds.) *International Handbook on Privatization*, Cheltenham, UK: Edward Elgar, 560–82.

Sappington, D. E. M. and Stiglitz, J. E. (1987) 'Privatization, Information and Incentives', *Journal of Policy Analysis and Management*, 6(4), 567–82.

Saunders, P. and Harris, C. (1994) *Privatization and Popular Capitalism*, Philadelphia: Open University Press.

Schmidt, K. M. (1996) 'Incomplete Contracts and Privatization', *European Economic Review*, 40(3–5), 569–79.

Shaoul, J., Stafford, A. and Stapleton, P. (2007) 'Partnerships and the Role of Financial Advisors: Private Control Over Public Policy?', *Policy & Politics*, 35(3), 479–95.

Shapiro, C. and Willig, R. (1990) 'Economic Rationales for the Scope of Privatization' in E. Suleiman and J. Waterbury (eds.) *The Political Economy of Public Sector Reform and Privatization*, Boulder, CO: Westview Press, 55–87.

Shapiro, D. and Globerman, S. (2009) 'The International Activities and Impacts of State-Owned Enterprises', Western Washington University (mimeo).

Sheshinski, E. and López-Calva, L. F. (2003) 'Privatization and its Benefits: Theory and Evidence', *CESifo Economic Studies*, 49(3), 429–59.

Shirley, M. M. (1994) 'Privatization in Latin America: Lessons for Transitional Europe', *World Development*, 22(9), 1313–23.

Smith, N. J. (2005) *Showcasing Globalisation? The Political Economy of the Irish Republic*, Manchester: Manchester University Press.

Somers, M. (1992) 'The Management of Ireland's National Debt', *Journal of The Statistical and Social Inquiry Society of Ireland*, XXVI(IV), 133–51.

Starr, P. (1988) 'The Meaning of Privatization', *Yale Law and Policy Review*, 6, 6–41.

Stiglitz, J. E. (1991) 'The Economic Role of the State: Efficiency and Effectiveness' in T. P. Hardiman and M. Mulreany (eds.) *Efficiency and Effectiveness in the Public Domain*, Dublin: IPA.

Stiglitz, J. E. (2008) 'Foreword' in G. Roland (ed.) *Privatization: Successes and Failures*, New York: Columbia University Press, ix–xix.

Sweeney, P. (1990) *The Politics of Public Enterprise and Privatisation*, Dublin: Tomar.

Sweeney, P. (1991) 'The Employment Effects of the Commercialisation of Irish Public Enterprise', *Labour Market Review*, 2(1), 16–25.

Sweeney, P. (1998) *The Celtic Tiger: Ireland's Economic Miracle Explained*, Dublin: Oak Tree Press.

Sweeney, P. (1999) *The Celtic Tiger: Ireland's Continuing Economic Miracle*, 2nd ed., Dublin: Oak Tree Press.

Sweeney, P. (2004) *Selling Out?: Privatisation in Ireland*, Dublin: TASC/New Island.

Teague, P. (1995) 'Pay Determination in the Republic of Ireland: Towards Social Corporatism?', *British Journal of Industrial Relations*, 33(2), 253–73.

Telecom Éireann (1985–1999) *Annual Report & Accounts*, Dublin: Telecom Éireann.

Thynne, I. (1994) 'The Incorporated Company as an Instrument of Government: A Quest for a Comparative Understanding', *Governance*, 7(1), 59–82.

TSB (1992–2000) *Annual Report & Accounts*, Dublin: TSB Bank.

Vagliasindi, M. (2008) 'Governance Arrangements for State Owned Enterprises', *World Bank Policy Research Working Paper*, No. 4542.

van Ark, B., Inklaar, R. and McGuckin, R. H. (2003) 'ICT and Productivity in Europe and the United States: Where Do the Differences Come From?', *CESifo Economic Studies*, 49(3), 295–318.

van der Linde, M., Minne, V., Wooning, A. and van der Zee, F. (2000) *Evaluation of the Common Organisation of the Markets in the Sugar Sector*, Amsterdam: Netherlands Economic Institute.

Vickers, J. (1997) 'Privatization, Regulation and Competition: Some Implications for Ireland' in A. W. Gray (ed.) *International Perspectives on the Irish Economy*, Dublin: Indecon Economic Consultants.

Vickers, J. and Yarrow, G. (1988) *Privatization: An Economic Analysis*, Cambridge, MA: MIT Press.

Vickers, J. and Yarrow, G. (1991) 'Economic Perspectives on Privatization', *Journal of Economic Perspectives*, 5(2), 111–32.

Walsh, K. (1995) *Public Services and Market Mechanisms: Competition, Contracting and the New Public Management*, London: Macmillan.

Wettenhall, R. (1993) 'The Globalization of Public Enterprises', *International Review of Administrative Sciences*, 59(3), 387–408.

Wettenhall, R. and Thynne, I. (2002) 'Public Enterprise and Privatization in a New Century: Evolving Patters of Governance and Public Management', *Public Finance and Management*, 2(1), 1–29.

Whelan, K. (2009) 'Policy Lessons from Ireland's Latest Depression', *UCD Centre for Economic Research Working Paper Series*, No. WP09/14.

Willner, J. (2001) 'Ownership, Efficiency, and Political Interference', *European Journal of Political Economy*, 17(4), 723–48.

Yarrow, G. (1986) 'Privatization in Theory and Practice', *Economic Policy*, 1(2), 323–77.

Yarrow, G. (1999) 'A Theory of Privatization, or Why Bureaucrats are Still in Business', *World Development*, 27(1), 157–68.

Young, S. (1986) 'The Nature of Privatisation in Britain, 1979–85', *West European Politics*, 9, 235–52.

# Index